The Java Sourcebook

Ed Anuff

WILEY COMPUTER PUBLISHING

John Wiley & Sons, Inc.

New York • Chichester • Brisbane • Toronto • Singapore

Publisher: Katherine Schowalter
Editor: Tim Ryan
Managing Editor: Frank Grazioli
Text Design & Composition: Benchmark Productions, Inc.

Library of Congress Cataloging-in-Publication Data:
ISBN 0-471-14859-8

Printed in the United States of America

10 9 8 7 6 5 4 3 2 1

The Java Sourcebook

Ed Anuff

INTRODUCING JAVA

Thanks for picking up this book. If you're reading this, you're probably interested in learning more about Java, which could be argued is one of the most important things to come to the World Wide Web since its inception. By now, you're probably familiar with the Web and have used a Web browser like Mosaic or Netscape to pull information from anywhere in the world simply by pointing and clicking on hot links. Some links, instead of jumping you to other pages, cause more interesting things to happen, such as taking information you enter on-screen and using that to bring you a specific stock quote or a customized news page. The interactive nature of the Web differentiates it from other information systems.

The second unique aspect of the Web is that with virtually any computer, you can access the Web and view most of the Web pages you visit. What makes this possible is the Web's standard method of communication between Web servers and Web browsers called HTTP and a number of standard formats for information that most computers can display. This basic system has allowed many exciting Web pages to be built and enjoyed by thousands of Net surfers, but as the Web has started to grow, people have started to encounter this system's limitations. To understand why, you need to take a look at the elements that make up the Web itself.

Java and the Future of the WWW

The Web at its simplest consists of two programs, the browser (which runs on your computer) and the server (which usually runs on a remote system). Most browsers can do only a few basic things. A browser can either request information from the server or ask the server to run special programs called CGI scripts for it. Although it would be unfair to call a browser "dumb," most of the interactivity you experience while using the Web, beyond simply clicking on hot links, is the result of CGI scripts being run on remote Web servers that use the output of those scripts to decide what to show you or where to take you next.

For example, many pages have clickable graphics images, called image maps, that can be clicked to jump to another Web page or cause some other action to occur. When you click on the image map, the coordinates of where you clicked within the image are transferred to a CGI script running on the Web server. The CGI script looks at these coordinates and decides what page to send back to the browser in response. Considering that the Web server your browser is talking to may be half a world away, it's understandable that the Web might not be responsive enough to give you the type of real-time feedback you'd experience using a CD-ROM or other interactive applications. If your browser could handle more complex tasks itself without asking the server every time it needed something done, you could have truly dynamic, responsive, and complex interactivity as part of the Web.

After you've used the Web for a while, you notice that every page consists of certain basic types of media. The main thing you see is text, with some simple formatting. The second thing you'll see is graphics, primarily in the form of GIF or JPEG images. If you don't recognize these formats, don't worry; it's enough to know that they are special file formats, often used because they can be viewed on a number of platforms and can be compressed for quick downloading over the Net. Occasionally, you'll click on a link and a file will be downloaded to your computer; after that a separate application, called a helper application, will be launched that may play the downloaded file if it is a sound or a movie clip or may handle the file in some other special fashion. Helper applications are so named because they help the browser with file types it doesn't know how to handle. You'll quickly notice the difference between how elegantly the browser deals with files it does know how to handle (text, GIF files, etc.) and the ones for which it needs helper apps. The files the browser knows how to handle are *inline*, meaning their contents are displayed right on the Web page.

When you see a graphic on a Web page, it is really a graphic file that the browser recognizes and knows how to deal with and that is inlined on the page. Because the browser knows about these files, it can do cool things like starting to draw the file as it downloads rather than waiting until the whole file has loaded. Compare this to the clunky usage of helper applications, which need to have the whole file downloaded to your hard disk first and then the application to be launched. Depending on the configuration of your computer, a number of things might go wrong. You might not have the appropriate helper app, or there might not be enough memory to load. It is usually preferable to have a browser that supports a type of file than to have to use a helper app. Because of this preference, some of the more ambitious vendors of browser software (i.e., Netscape) have teamed up with the makers of some of the more popular helper applications to build the code for the helper apps directly into the browsers. A good example of this is Netscape's alliance with Adobe to built support for Adobe's Acrobat page description files into Netscape, rather than requiring Netscape users to have the Acrobat Reader configured as a helper application. The problem here is that every day someone comes up with a great new application that can be used as a helper app. The browser makers will be extremely busy if they create new versions of their products every time someone creates a new file format. The elegant solution—if it were possible—would be for the browser to automatically download the correct helper app when it encountered a file it didn't recognize; the ideal solution would dynamically integrate the helper into your browser after it had been downloaded.

Early in 1995, Sun announced a solution to these problems in the form of HotJava and made early versions of the software available on the Net. The name HotJava actually refers to the Web browser built using the Java language, although it is sometimes incorrectly used to describe any Web-related usage of Java. HotJava takes advantage of the properties of the Java language to enable use of Java applets within the browser. Applets are sometimes described as client-side scripting. This means that the script, rather than running on the remote server, runs on your (the client's) machine. Applets are also often referred to as executable content—essentially, content that knows the best way to present itself. If it's a music file, it knows how to play itself. If it's an animation, it knows how to draw itself and what to do if it is clicked. Client-side scripting and executable content are both good ways of thinking about applications of Java applets, but that's not the whole story. The range of things made possible by Java is expanding every day as more and more people create new and amazing applications using this extremely powerful, yet remarkably easy-to-use technology.

HotJava and Java Browsers

HotJava properly describes Sun's Web browser, which is written using the Java language and supports HotJava applets. When most people refer to HotJava, they actually mean Java applets, which are programs written in Java and included in HTML pages. The HotJava browser is similar to other popular browsers in the way it displays pages and allows you to navigate the Web. At the time of this writing, HotJava supports an earlier version of Sun's Java standard, but by the time you read this, a new version that supports the latest versions of Java applets as well as HTML 3 and the Netscape HTML extensions should be available.

Most of your experience with Java applets will come from using Netscape 2.0. Netscape licensed Java from Sun and incorporated support for Java applets in Netscape 2.0, which went into public beta in the Fall of 1995. Netscape intends to support Java across all the platforms on which the Netscape Navigator will run. Because Netscape owns the largest share of the browser market, its support for Java represents a significant endorsement of the technology.

In the next chapter, we will talk more about HotJava and Netscape and show you where you can find the latest versions of both.

Java, the Language

Java is a simple, object-oriented language that has many elements in common with C and C++, but has removed or streamlined the areas where many programmers have had difficulty or that have been the most frequent sources of bugs. Java also is a secure language, making it possible to restrict the access of Java programs to parts of the system, such as files and memory address, without limiting the language capabilities. This is one of the most important reasons why Java is so well suited for use on the Web.

Java has the benefits of an interpreted language and the performance of compiled code. Users of rapid application development and scripting languages such as Visual Basic, Delphi, Perl, HyperCard, or AppleScript will be able to start programming in Java in a very short time. Seasoned C and C++ programmers will find that they are able to translate their skills easily to this new language and that most of their code and algorithms are reusable as well. Java is well suited to Internet related tasks, and it is a solid, general-purpose language that Sun intends to use in a variety of applications. No doubt, through Sun's licensing efforts, Java will turn up in a variety of products.

Where to Go from Here

This book is organized into four parts. Part 1 covers how to get and install the Java Development Kit, run the HotJava browser and Netscape, and visit any Java-enhanced site on the Web. Part 2 covers the nuts and bolts of the Java language. Part 3 covers building applets in HotJava, line by line. Part 4 summarizes the reference material available in the SDK API packages, the standard libraries for handling I/O, graphics, and Net communications.

This book assumes that your goal is ultimately to be able to program your own Java applets. If you're new to Java and the Web, then you can focus on the chapters in Part 1. If you're interested in learning how to program in Java, then you'll want to read through Part 2. Experienced programmers will be able to skip many of the chapters in Part 2, but they may find that certain areas bear a closer look, especially objects, interfaces, packages, and threads. Part 3 is essential for understanding how to build applets, and both novice and experienced programmers will want to study the chapters in this part. Part 4 contains reference material that you'll need to have on hand when writing applets and trying to understand example code.

CONTENTS

PART 1

GETTING READY

FOR JAVA

To use this book, you will first need to obtain two different pieces of software. This first is the JDK, or Java Development Kit. This package contains all the software needed for writing, compiling, and testing Java applets and applications. The second piece of software is a Java-capable browser. At the time of this writing, two Java-capable browsers are available, with several more announced to be on the way. You'll need a Java-capable browser in order to test applets you've created as well as to try out interesting uses of Java applets that are on the Web. In this chapter, we'll take a look at obtaining these pieces of software and installing them on your computer.

Where to Get the JDK

The Java Developer's Kit can be found on the Java Web site or the Java ftp site; as a consequence, you'll need a Web browser or FTP program to download it. When using a browser to download the JDK, point the browser to the URL

```
http://java.sun.com
```

The Java home page should have a link to the Developer's Corner. If you follow that link, you will be taken to a page that has links to other pages on the site of interest to developers. One of these links should be to the Java Developer's Kit home page. From that page, you'll find instructions for downloading the appropriate version of the JDK for your platform.

Alternately, you can ftp to the Java ftp site by ftping to java.sun.com and going to the pub/directory, which contains the files for all the JDK releases. If you take this route, make sure you download the file using binary transfer mode.

If you have any problems, make sure you are following the downloading instructions on the Java Web site correctly. You might also want to try one of the Java mirror sites in the event that the Sun Java site is having difficulties.

HotJava or Netscape?

As we mentioned earlier, you'll need to get a Java-capable browser to try out Java applets. At the time of this writing, there are two browsers that support Java applets. The first is HotJava, Sun's Java browser. The HotJava browser has a number of nice features. It is entirely written in Java and, as such, represents one of the largest applications written in Java. Because the source code is included with the browser, HotJava is an excellent way of learning more about Java application design. The currently available version of HotJava, however, was written with a previous version (the alpha3 release) of Java, which is not compatible with the version in the JDK. Consequently, although HotJava it is interesting to try, it won't be as useful a tool for your Java development efforts. By the time you read this, Sun may have released a new version of HotJava; in that case, you would likely want to use that version for applet testing. Make sure you check the Sun Java Web site frequently to watch for new versions of HotJava and the JDK.

The other Java-capable browser is the one used by most people who are using the Web. Netscape 2.0, which went into public beta testing in the fourth quarter of 1995, supports the latest release of Java and the JDK. You can download Netscape 2.0 from the Netscape home page at:

```
http://home.netscape.com
```

The home page will have numerous links on it to the Netscape download page. When you are prompted for which version you want to download, make sure you select version 2.0. If a 2.0 beta version is the only version available, go ahead and download it, then monitor the Netscape download pages for the release of newer versions.

Once you've obtained a copy of Netscape 2.0, follow Netscape's instructions for installing it. Netscape on some platforms, especially the UNIX variants, requires that certain files be placed in special directories; it won't be able to run Java applets unless these requirements are met. If you have problems running Java applets within Netscape, check out the release notes for the version of Netscape that you are using at:

```
http://home.mcom.com/eng/mozilla/2.0/relnotes/
```

These URLs might change, so if you have problems bringing them up in your browser, go to the Netscape homepage and follow the appropriate links from there.

Installing Java under Sun Solaris

Take the gzipped JDK file (i.e., JDK-beta-solaris2-sparc.tar.Z) that you downloaded from the Sun Java site and place it in the directory where you want the Java files to be located. In our case, we installed them in /usr/local/. Then, uncompress the JDK file with the following command:

```
zcat JDK-beta-solaris2-sparc.tar.Z | tar xf -
```

The JDK files will be unpacked into a subdirectory named java/. After the files have been unpacked, you need to set your PATH to include the java/bin/ directory. This will depend on what shell you use and where you put the java directory. In our case, we edited this line in the .profile file in our home directory:

```
PATH=/usr/bin:/usr/ucb:/etc:.:/usr/local/java/bin
export PATH
```

If you have located the java directory in a different place on your file system, you should modify this accordingly. Refer to your Solaris documentation or consult your system administrator if you have any additional questions about how to set the PATH or have any difficulties doing so.

Installing Java
with Windows 95/NT

Take the .exe JDK file (i.e., JDK-beta-win32-x86.exe) that you downloaded from
the Sun Java site and place it in a directory where you want the Java files to be
located. In our case, we installed them in C:\. Then, uncompress and install the JDK
file by running the .exe file, either from the Windows Explorer or the MS-DOS
Prompt command line, like this:

```
C:\JDK-beta-win32-x86.exe
```

The JDK files will be unpacked into a subdirectory named java\. After the files have
been unpacked, you need to set your PATH to include the java\bin\ directory. In our
case, we edited this line in the AUTOEXEC.BAT file in C:\ directory:

```
PATH C:\WINDOWS;C:\WINDOWS\COMMAND;C:\DOS;"C:\java\bin"
```

If you have located the java directory in a different place or on a different drive, you
should modify this accordingly. Refer to your DOS documentation if you have any
additional questions about how to set the PATH or have any difficulties doing so.

Java on the Macintosh

At the time of writing, Java has not been released for the Macintosh although Sun
and several other vendors have announced that they will do so. The Sun release
should be out by the time you read this, so you should check the Sun Java Web site.
The details of downloading and installing the release will accompany the software
when it becomes available. Mac browsers may support Java playback before the
Mac JDK becomes available because Netscape is handling the porting of Java for
its releases independently of Sun's porting of the JDK kit. For example, the SGI version of Netscape can play back Java applets although part of the JDK for that platform is not available from Sun.

Several other companies have announced intentions of creating Java releases for the
Macintosh. Among these is MetroWerks, the developer of the popular CodeWarrior
integrated development environment. Given MetroWerks' track record with
CodeWarrior, we have every reason to believe that its Java support will be top
notch.

Java and Other Platforms

Although Sun intends to directly support only a select group of platforms, it has taken steps to ensure that Java will eventually be ported to every platform where there is interest to do so. Sun has made the source code to the JDK freely available for non-commercial use and has a fairly reasonable (as far as these things go) license fee for commercial use. By the way, this license fee doesn't apply to Java programs you write, check Sun's Web site for details.

Because the Java source code is readily available, a number of efforts have been undertaken to port Java to different platforms including Linux, Next, Irix, and Amiga. You can find out details about these efforts by subscribing to the java-porting mailing list. Information about this mailing list as well as others can be found on the Sun Java Web site at:

```
http://java.sun.com/mail.html
```

WEB BROWSING

AND JAVA

In this chapter we'll talk about some of the differences between ordinary Web browsers, native Java Web browsers, and Java-capable Web browsers and about Web surfing pages that feature Java content. We assume that you've used a Web browser before and are comfortable with URLs and the mechanics of finding something on the Web.

A Java-capable browser is a browser that supports Java applets. An applet is a small program that is automatically downloaded from a Web site and run within your Web browser in response to instructions to do so contained within the Web page you are viewing. The browser provides a display area for the applet in the browser window, which is displaying the Web page in the same way that the browser displays images on a page. The applet can use this display area however it sees fit, using the area to display buttons and other user interface controls or to display graphics and animation.

Java and Web Browsers

People often encounter some confusion about the terminology for Java support within Web browsers. Because HotJava was the first browser to support Java applets, the names HotJava and Java became synonymous, much to the chagrin of the people at Sun, who take great pains to point out that Java is a language and HotJava is an application written in Java. For a while this distinction was genuinely irrelevant because the only publicly available large application written in Java was the HotJava browser, and HotJava was, in turn, the only Web browser to support Java applets.

When Netscape released 2.0 of Netscape Navigator, it was the second browser to support Java and the first to do so that wasn't written in Java. Netscape is a Java-capable Web browser, as opposed to a native Java Web browser such as HotJava. There are definite boundaries between the C code in which the Netscape browser was written and the Java code of the applets that the browser runs. An applet in Netscape will be isolated from the code that makes up the browser and will be able to extend the browser's menus or override any other functionality of the browser.

This limitation contrasts with the way applets are run within HotJava, where the distinction between the applet code and the browser code is not clear-cut. Applets running in HotJava can have much more control over the browser's user interface environment, and the browser can be extended to support new media formats and protocols through the use of Java code.

These distinctions might indicate that Netscape is more secure than HotJava, but this is not necessarily the case. The Netscape browser is designed for secured financial transactions and similar considerations, and it generally errs on the side of heavier security than other browsers. Because applets are full-fledged objects within the HotJava application, they gain additional flexibility when running within a native Java browser, rather than talking to the browser through Java to C interfaces.

The Netscape model of Java support is important to understand because it is likely to become the predominant form of Java support in the short term. Several other browser vendors have announced support of Java applets, as have a number of vendors of other types of applications such as Web servers, multimedia authoring tools, and other software products. These applications are written in a language such as C, but they have the ability to load and execute Java applets and allow the applets to share the application's user interface.

Elements of a Java-Enhanced Page

Applets on a Web page are modeled on the way that images such as GIFs are displayed on a page. On most graphical browsers, when the HTML file that describes the Web page's contents indicates that an image should be placed on the page, the image is loaded from the Web server and displayed inline, meaning that the image is drawn inside the browser window, with the page text flowing around it, rather than in an external window.

In a Java-capable browser, the applet is also displayed inline on the Web page. As a consequence, with some applets, you might not be able to tell immediately whether an image on a Web page is an inlined GIF or a Java applet. Figure 2.1 demonstrates how an applet can be inlined on a Web page.

When an applet is placed on a Web page, it is given an area of the page as its display area. This display area belongs to the applet, and it is free to do with it as it wishes. Some applets will use this area to present animations; others will use it to display information from a database or to allow the user to select items from an order form. The number of ideas being implemented as Java applets grows every day.

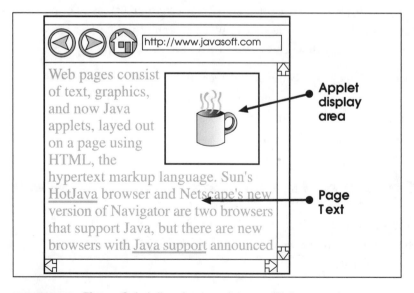

■■■■■■ **Figure 2.1** Inline Java applet on a Web page.

Browsers and Security

Different Java-capable browsers provide different levels of security when dealing with Java applets. Security in the context of Java applets means how much access will applets be allowed to have to local files, how much freedom the applet will be given to initiate network communications, and what permissions the applet will have for performing sensitive activities. There are two issues to security in Java. The first is the security restrictions imposed on Java code as it is run; and the second is the aspects of the language that prevent a programmer from circumventing those restrictions. Security in Java-capable browsers works because when the browser allows only a certain level of security to the applet, the language enforces that security by preventing the applet from accessing resources disallowed by the given security level.

When a browser lets you set the security level, it usually will let you choose what level of network access an applet will be allowed. The options usually are to disallow all network access to applets, to allow applets to communicate to the Web server from which they were downloaded, or to have unrestricted access to the Net, in which case they can initiate socket communications with any machine on the network. The browser may also provide configurable levels of class access. The applet will either be restricted from accessing all but a select group of classes or be allowed to access any public class in the system. When an applet has its class access restricted, it is able to use only those classes that are part of the JDK API.

If a browser does not allow you to configure the security level for applets, this usually means that the browser allows the applet to communicate only to the applet host and gives the applet only restricted access to local classes. Netscape is a good example of a browser that works this way.

Java Info and Interest on the Web

A number of Web sites feature Java content. There are several URLs that you should know about; the first is one we've seen already—http://java.sun.com. You should know about this URL:

```
http://www.gamelan.com/
```

The Gamelan Web site is run by EarthWeb, a provider of Internet services and development. According to EarthWeb, Gamelan is "an Internet directory and registry of Java-based programs and resources for developers and users of Sun's Java programming language." The Gamelan site contains the latest cool applets from developers around the world. You should know about this resource as well:

```
http://www.io.org/~mentor/J___Notes.html
```

Digital Espresso (formerly J*** Notes) is a weekly summary of posts from the Java mailing lists and newsgroups. This page is one of the best sources of information for developers on the Web, and it is required reading for anyone interested in Java development. Digital Espresso Web site is run by David Forster and Mentor Software Solutions, which provides custom software development and consulting services. Another list of Java resources can be found at:

```
http://www.acm.org/~ops/java.html
```

The W3VL/Java is a good, quick summary of Java resources and information on the Web.

```
http://www.yahoo.com/Computers/Languages/Java/
```

The Yahoo! entry for Java contains a number of links to Java-enhanced sites on the Web as well as useful information.

```
news:comp.lang.java
```

Although not qualifying as a Web site, the comp.lang.java USENET newsgroup is a high-traffic discussion of Java programming issues and has frequent postings by Sun Java engineers. The Java-Interest mailing list is cross-posted to the newsgroup as well. Like any other newsgroup, it does contain a lot of noise, but if you're serious about getting into Java development, it should be in your .newsrc file.

PART 2

3

UNDERSTANDING JAVA

J ava is a language developed by Sun with the intent to create a dynamic, object-oriented programming language suitable for use for the same types of development tasks as C and C++, but without the difficulties and sources of bugs common to those languages. Sun describes Java as a "simple, object-oriented, distributed, interpreted, robust, secure, architecture neutral, portable, high-performance, multi-threaded, and dynamic language." While that's quite a mouthful, it's also a good checklist of the key features of the language. In this chapter, we'll discuss what some of those terms mean, as well as why they are important to you.

This chapter and the rest of Part 2 will serve two purposes: stand as a reference for the language and to step through a number of small example applications that demonstrate how to use the various language constructs. The goal of this book is to get you comfortable enough with Java that you are able to start building Java applets. Part 2 is intended to make you competent in reading Java code and in structuring a Java application. As such, the content will contain a number of simple example applications, many of which will be less than 10 lines long, that demonstrate important aspects of the language. This way, when we get to Part 3 we can focus on how to tackle more complex Java applets, without having to deal with language details.

We assume that you have had some exposure to programming, although not necessarily in C or C++, and probably not with an object-oriented language. For more seasoned programmers, this chapter will guide you to where you should focus your efforts. Java was not created in a vacuum. It benefits from and is reflective of many of the languages that have come before it, particularly C and C++. Experienced programmers will find that they probably need only a cursory examination of Part 2 before they jump into Part 3 and start writing their own applets. The rest of us, though, need not worry; we will step through the language so that by the time you get to Part 3, you too will be ready to get started building Java applets.

Java as an Object-Oriented Language

Java is an object-oriented language. "Object-oriented" is a buzzword these days, used to describe languages, styles of programming, user interfaces, and just about anything else, however appropriately or inappropriately. From a conceptual point of view, object programming is often described by example in terms of how you model real-world objects (cars, people, houses, computers, etc.) by using software objects in an object-oriented language. For instance, if you were creating a program that dealt with different kinds of computers, you would write code that dealt with each different type of computer as a different kind of object. Obviously, existing languages can be used in this way; otherwise, nobody would have ever been able to write a complex program until object-oriented languages had been invented.

Java vs. Procedural Languages

Many procedural languages today provide some object-oriented functionality. At a fundamental level, though, procedural languages are designed first to provide you with a framework for issuing commands for the computer to execute (hence the term "procedural") and second to allow you to organize and manipulate data. Depending on the language, how intuitively a procedural language lets you do this can vary quite a bit. An object-based language like Java is designed first to allow you to define the objects that make up your program and the data they contain, and second to define the code that makes up the program. If you've programmed in a procedural language like C, you may remember that your early programs consisted mainly of simple variables and you accomplished most tasks by coding explicitly the steps you wish the computer to take. As your programming skills advanced, you probably started to write programs in which you defined your own data types and data structures. At this point, you may have started to design your program from an object-based perspective, first defining the data structure to organize the data used to define a window or button, for example, and then writing modular code to deal with the different types of data. This approach is often referred to as procedural programming in an object-oriented style. If you're now programming this way, you can appreciate that although you can gain many of the advantages of object-oriented programming by using this approach, the language doesn't do anything to help you explicitly in organizing your code this way.

Many programmers are now using C++ or languages like Object Pascal (i.e., Borland's Delphi), Perl 5.0, and Objective C. What these languages have in common is that they are hybrid languages, or procedural languages with object-oriented extensions. These languages make it possible for you to use objects within your programs, but they allow you—and in many cases require you—to use procedural code to accomplish certain tasks. When using one of these languages, for example C++, you will usually become very familiar with the procedural aspects of the language before you deal with the object-oriented parts of it. Just look at a typical book on C++ programming; you will probably read three-fourths of the book before you even encounter objects.

Java vs. Other Object-Oriented Languages

Experienced programmers of object-oriented languages will want to know if Java is a pure object-oriented language. One of the measures of the purity of an object-oriented language is whether all data in the language is represented in the form of objects. In a language like SmallTalk, which is generally considered a pure object-oriented language, every aspect of the language is object- or message-based and all data types, simple or complex, are object classes. Java implements the basic C simple data types, such as integers, characters, and floating point numbers, outside the object system, but deals with everything else as objects. We will see the implications of this when we talk about subclassing objects later in this chapter and find that we can't subclass the simple types. However, this language design enables Java to avoid many of the performance pitfalls found in a purely object-oriented language. In all other ways, however, Java is a pure object-oriented language. All program code and data reside within objects and classes.

Java as a Compiled Language

Most computer languages are either compiled or interpreted. When using a compiled language, you need to run a program called a compiler to translate the human-readable source files of your programs into a machine-readable object format. Compiled languages have the benefit of producing high-performance code that is tailored for execution on a specific type of processor or processor architecture, such as the Intel X86 family. Compiled applications, referred to as binary executables, can be run only on the type of computer they were compiled for since they consist of actual machine language instructions understood and executed by the microprocessor.

Interpreted languages, such as most scripting and shell languages, usually exist only as source code. When they are run, a program called an interpreter takes the source file and performs the actions indicated by the commands in the file. A program written in an interpreted language essentially consists of a series of instructions for the interpreter to perform. The interpreter is the only real application that is running. Among the benefits of interpreted languages is that programs written using them can be run easily on a variety of platforms because they exist only in source file form. They are also much easier to debug.

Java is both compiled and interpreted. After writing a Java program in a text editor, you save it as a source file. You then compile the Java source file to produce a type of binary object file called a class file. These files are not directly executable because they do not contain instructions directly understandable by the processor. Java programs are compiled to a byte-code format. This byte code represents machine language instructions for a virtual microprocessor, which doesn't exist as an actual chip inside your computer. This virtual microprocessor is called the Java Virtual Machine. The Java interpreter implements the Java Virtual Machine in software so that it can execute Java class binary files. This process is not unlike the way that emulator software allows you to run programs for one type of computer, such as an Intel PC, on another, such as the Macintosh. Because Java byte codes are very similar to the native machine code instructions that the computer understands, they can be executed with performance that approaches that of native compiled languages.

Because Java code is being run by an interpreter, Java programs will run unmodified on any platform to which the Java interpreter has been ported. That the language is interpreted means the interpreter can check the code for questionable activity before executing it. In this way, the interpreter can prevent a Java application from accessing sensitive areas of the system and memory, so that most virus-like code is headed off before it can cause trouble.

Java Object Basics

We've talked about objects quite a bit so far. Now let's get a little more specific about what an object is in Java. We will revisit objects in Chapter 7 (we'll take a closer look at them within the context of the language), but it is important to cover the major conceptual aspects of objects now.

Objects and Classes

When we talk about an object, we usually mean an *instance* of a *class*. To understand what we mean by that, we need first to define classes. A *class* is used to describe a type of object. For example, if you were writing a program that dealt with the different types of computers on a network, you might have a class called Macintosh. The class would define all the properties of a Macintosh computer (such as who its owner is, how large the hard drive is, and so on), as well as what messages the Macintosh can respond to (such as start the computer, shut down, send an e-mail to, etc.). The Macintosh class describes a hypothetical Macintosh; it is essentially the blueprint that tells the computer how to build a Macintosh object when it is instructed to do so. For example, Ed's Macintosh would be a Macintosh object created from the Macintosh class. An object created from a class is often referred to as an *instance* of the class, or it is said to have been *instantiated* from a class. If you've used other object-oriented programming languages, you may have seen terms like factories, object types, templates, or a variety of similar names used to describe classes.

Member Data

Member data refers to the data stored within an object or class. Member data is also sometimes referred to as properties or, if within an instantiated object, instance variables. You define which member variables are part of a class in the class definition, and new instances of these variables are created every time a new object is created from the class. This means that every instance of a class will have the same types of variables contained within it, but what's stored in those variables will be different from one object to another. An object that contains only member data can be thought of as being functionally very similar to a traditional C struct or Pascal RECORD data structure that has been dynamically allocated in memory.

Figure 3.1 is an example of a rectangle class and two different rectangle instances that depict using a graphical object notation. A number of different styles of graphical object notation are used for presenting a conceptual view of a class or object and its contents; if you're used to something different, don't let our choice of symbols deter you. We'll use this notation mainly in this chapter until we show you how the same thing is represented in code.

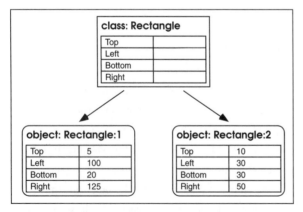

■■■■■■ **Figure 3.1** Rectangle class with two different rectangle instances depicted with a graphical object notation.

This illustration demonstrates a rectangle object class (denoted by the box at the top of the picture) and two instances (denoted by the two rounded-corner boxes at the bottom). You can see that the Rectangle class contains four member variables, named Top, Left, Bottom, and Right; although it specifies that these variables are present in any objects created from the Rectangle class, it doesn't define what value is stored in each variable (from a practical standpoint, in Java if the class doesn't specify the value to be stored in an instance variable, it will be set to zero). Each of the objects instantiated from the Rectangle class contains these variables, but the actual values stored in them in each instance are different. You might use this type of class in a drawing program to show several rectangles on-screen. Each rectangle would be represented in the program as an object.

There is one more thing that you need to know about member variables; they can be hidden from code in other objects or classes. For example, we could have included a fifth variable called Color and specified that it was hidden or private to the Rectangle object. This process is called *encapsulation*; we'll explain why you'd want to do this in the next section, and we'll cover it in detail in a later chapter.

Methods

In the previous section, we talked about how the data in an object-oriented program is contained within objects. In this section, we'll see how the code in an object-oriented program is also incorporated into your program's objects. In a traditional procedural language you deal with procedures and functions and, for the most part, where you put this code in your program is a matter of personal choice. In an object-oriented language, instead of procedures and functions, you have methods, and each method is associated with a particular class.

In the last section, we talked about how you might use your rectangle class in a drawing program. If you were going to do this, you'd probably want to have the object know how to paint itself on-screen and perhaps how to resize itself. You would do this by defining two methods for the Rectangle class: Paint and Resize. Figure 3.2 shows how we will depict this using our graphical object notation.

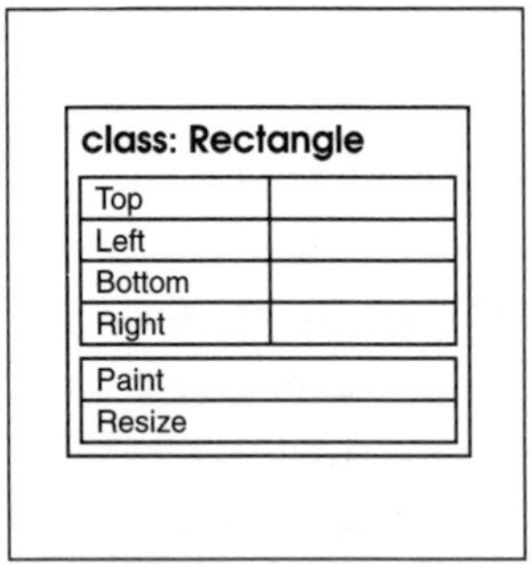

class: Rectangle	
Top	
Left	
Bottom	
Right	
Paint	
Resize	

■■■■■■■■ **Figure 3.2** Rectangle class with two methods: Paint and Resize.

Each object you created from this class would contain the Paint and Resize methods. Sometimes people get confused when seeing this for the first time; they take this to mean that the code contained in the Paint and Resize methods gets duplicated each time you create an instance of the class, just as new instance variables are created each time a new class is created. This is not the case; we'll get a better picture of what is happening in the rest of this section.

Calling a method is also referred to as sending a message to the object that contains the method. For example, calling the Paint method of a Rectangle object is referred to as sending a Paint message to that object. Methods are used in much the same manner as you would use a procedure or function in a language like C, with some important differences. First, when a method is invoked (yet another term for calling a method), any reference to a member variable in the methods code will actually deal with the instance variable contained in the object of which the method is a member. For example, in the previous section we defined two Rectangle objects. Let's take a look at a method (implemented as pseudo-code rather than actual Java code for illustrative purposes) that manipulates the instance variables of an object.

```
Rectangle.MoveLeft {
    set Left to the value of Left + 5
    set Right to the value of Right + 5
}
```

When this MoveLeft method is called for the Rectangle 1 object, Left is going to contain 100 and Right is going to contain 125. After this method is called, both

Left and Right will have had their contents increased by 5. If we were to call the same method but were to apply it instead to the Rectangle 2 object, Left and Right would instead refer to the instance variables contained in the Rectangle 2 object, the values 30 and 50.

Class Basics

Now that we've gone through the basics of objects, we need to look at some of the important aspects of classes and how they relate to how objects and classes are used within your programs. As we mentioned earlier in this chapter, when you set about writing a program in Java, you're going to do so by breaking up your task into objects that you can model in your program. This is done by defining a class for each type of object you're going to model. For example, we might choose to write a program dealing with computers. You might be inclined to create a different class for each type of computer—Macintosh, PC, SPARCstation, and so on. Before you do that, you should know about a new aspect of object-oriented design, *abstraction*. In the case of the Macintosh example, you would use abstraction by considering what properties all computers have in common and creating a class that contains those properties. You would then use this class as the *parent class* for your Macintosh class, PC class, and so on. We'll see exactly what we mean by a parent class in the next section. The process of identifying a general-purpose class that contains common properties and methods that you want to use as the parent class for a number of related classes is called *abstraction*.

Hierarchy and Inheritance

In all of our examples so far, we've used classes that are simple and stand on their own. One of the big benefits of object-oriented programming is that once a class is created, you can use it to define another class. For example, if we had first declared a general-purpose Computer class that contained properties like hard drive size, megabytes of memory, owner, and so on, we could use that Computer class as the super class or parent class of our Macintosh class. The Macintosh class would inherit the properties of the Computer class without our having to explicitly mention those properties in our specification of the Macintosh class. Any actual

Macintosh objects we created from the Macintosh class would contain the properties of the Macintosh class as well as those of its parent class, the Computer class. A class that is defined as having a parent class is called a *subclass* or *child class*, and the process of creating a subclass of a given parent class is called *subclassing* that parent class. Figure 3.3 illustrates this process.

What we see here is that the Macintosh class is a subclass of the Computer class; when we create an instance of the Macintosh class, we have a Macintosh object that contains all the properties and methods of the Macintosh class and Computer class. The ability to use the properties and methods of a parent class within a subclass and the objects created from it is called *inheritance,* and a subclass is said to inherit specific member data and methods from its parent class. In the above example, the Macintosh class has inherited the Memory, Drive, Display, and Owner properties (member data) from the Computer class, as well as the Start, Shutdown, and MoveMouse methods. You might also have noticed that the Macintosh class has defined its own MoveMouse method in addition to the MoveMouse method it inherits from the Computer class. When a subclass defines a method that replaces one it inherits from its parent class, it is said to have *overridden* the original method.

Another thing to know about subclassing is that you can keep creating subclasses. For example, if you wanted to create a subclass of Macintosh called PowerBook,

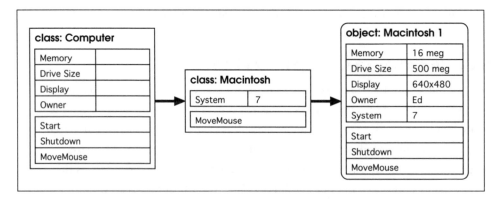

■■■■■■■ **Figure 3.3**

you could do so; the resulting subclass would inherit from both Macintosh and Computer. In our example of the drawing program, we would probably have created a basic geometry object, then created subclasses for lines, circles, and rectangles. We then would probably want to subclass the Circle class to create an Arc class, and we might subclass the Rectangle class to create a Square class. The process of creating subclasses is called *designing by difference*, and it is especially useful in Java, where you have a large library of prewritten classes that you subclass to create classes more appropriate to your needs. Designing by difference allows you to create a new class by simply defining the parts of it that are different from the parent class. In the case of the Macintosh class, the difference was that we needed to have a member variable that contained a System version value, and we needed to redefine the MoveMouse method to accommodate the way a Macintosh handles the mouse being moved as opposed to the way the parent Computer class accommodates it.

When a message is sent to an object to invoke a method, the object finds the most recent ancestor class that implements the method and invokes that method. For example, with the previous computer example, sending the Macintosh instance a MoveMouse message will invoke the MoveMouse method of the Macintosh class, rather than the MoveMouse method of the Computer class because the MoveMouse method of the Macintosh class is the most recent ancestor that implements that method. If, however, we were to send the Shutdown message to the Macintosh instance, the Shutdown method of the Computer class would be invoked. Because the Macintosh class does not implement a Shutdown method, the Computer class is the most recent ancestor class to implement the method and, consequently the Computer class's implementation of the method is the one that gets invoked.

We hope this review of the basics of objects will help you understand what they are all about. The goal here has been to get you thinking about programming from an object-centered perspective. In later chapters, we'll see how objects are implemented in Java and how they are used in Java programs.

Summarizing
Object-Oriented Terminology

In many places we will use different terms to describe the same process. You've already seen that calling a method in an object can be referred to as invoking the method or sending the object a message. Part of the goal of this book is to expose you to the concepts and terminology of object-oriented programming. This is done for a variety of reasons. Java is a new language, with relatively few reference sources available for learning its concepts. Consequently, if you choose to look into other references on object-oriented programming or try to apply concepts you've learned from other languages, you will need to be comfortable with the underlying ideas that each author or language expresses differently. This section lists the various ways of describing the same process in the language. The obvious question now is why mix terminology at all? Each description is essentially a metaphor, and in the process of describing how to accomplish a task, some metaphors might be more appropriate than others. This is illustrated by the "send a message" versus "call a method" terminology. When you discuss communication between objects as part of a system, it is useful to imagine these objects sending messages to each other. When you talk about methods as code constructs, or look at flow of control from a more programmatic approach, it is more appropriate to use terms like calling or invoking a method, which are more evocative of the calling of functions, as in C.

An Object's Variables

Instance variables

Member variables

Properties

An Object's Methods

Methods

Member functions

Calling an Object's Method

Calling a method

Sending a message

Invoking a method

Creating an Object

Instantiating an object

Allocating an object

Creating a new object

Creating an instance of a class

A Class Derived from Another

Subclass

Derived class

Child class

Descendant

A Class from Which Other Classes Are Derived

Base class

Parent class

Superclass

Ancestor

Deriving a New Class from an Existing Class

Subclassing a class

Creating a subclass

Creating a derived class

Deriving a class

BUILDING JAVA APPLICATIONS

In this chapter we will take a look at two of the tools that are part of the Java Development Kit, the Java compiler and the Java interpreter. We'll see how you can use these tools to build the simple Java applications that we use to learn the language in Part 2, and we will take a look at the fundamentals of Java programs.

Because Java is an object-based language, you write an application by creating one or more classes, which contain all the necessary code to implement your program. In later chapters we will look in detail at classes and objects, but right now you just need to understand two specific kinds of objects. These objects are called applets and applications, and, as you will see later, they are basically special kinds of objects that the HotJava browser and the Java interpreter know about and look for specific methods in.

In addition to introducing applications conceptually, we will also use two of the tools in the Java development environment, *javac*—the Java compiler—and *java*—the Java interpreter.

Applets vs. Applications

As we mentioned previously, a Java application is a class that the Java interpreter knows is going to have a specific method in it called main(), which it looks for when it tries to run the application. We assume that your primary interest is in building applets; before you can write an applet, it makes sense to understand Java applications in general. Note that most of our examples in Part 2 will be simple Java applications, rather than applets. As you learn the nuts and bolts of the language, dealing with small programs that can communicate via text output and keyboard input is easier. We will cover the user interface aspects of applets after you are more comfortable with the language.

A Java applet is a specific kind of application that is run from the HotJava browser. Rather than having a single main() method, a Java applet instead implements a set of methods that deal with the issues of how to initialize itself, when to draw itself, what to do when someone clicks on it, and so forth. The HotJava browser makes use of the dynamic capabilities of the Java language to pull applets over the Web and dynamically link to them. The applet is, for all intents and purposes, a part of the browser after it is downloaded. Applets will be covered in detail in Part 3; we will not only examine the structure of an applet, but also go through a number of examples of interesting things you can do with applets.

Compiling and Running a Java Program

In earlier sections we mentioned that Java is an interpreted language, but that instead of interpreting the source code of your program, it works with a byte-code representation of the program. Byte code is similar to the binary machine code produced by a typical compiler, except that instead of being executed by the CPU in your computer directly, byte code is executed by the Java virtual machine, which you think of as the equivalent of a microprocessor written in software. This concept may be familiar to users of the PowerMacintosh, which uses a similar method to run software written for older Macintoshes.

As you might expect, because byte code is similar to machine code, you need to use a compiler to translate your source file to the Java byte code format in the same way you would use a C compiler to translate a C source file to machine code. In Java, the compiler is called javac, and it must be run with any files you wish to compile. Once you've compiled a program to byte code, you run it with the java interpreter, which is appropriately called java. Although basic usage of the compiler and interpreter are described in this chapter, the details of their operation can be found in the documentation included with the JDK as well as on the Sun Java Web site by following the Documentation links to the Tools Documentation.

A Simple Java Application

The rest of this chapter will show you how to enter a java application, compile it, and run it. You should learn the process of building a Java application, not every detail of the language. Notice that platform-specific instructions are given for most of the steps in the process. The creators of Java worked hard to make Java a cross-platform language. Even though the actual Java code and files are compatible across platforms, the steps you take to build the files will be slightly different on each platform due to differences in file systems. The remainder of Part 2 will assume that you have mastered the steps of building a Java application and will present information in a platform-independent form. Examples in this chapter will be for Windows 95/NT, Macintosh, and Solaris operating systems. If you use a different system that is capable of running Java, you will want to follow the instructions that came with the Java release for that platform. For most UNIX implementations, the steps will be similar to those for Solaris.

Creating the Source File

To create a Java application, you must first create a source file that contains the code for the classes that make up your application. For our first example, we will write a simple, single-class example that writes out the string "Hello from Java!"; this is our version of the traditional HelloWorld application.

Depending on the platform you're using, you will have a variety of text editors or word processors available that you can use to create your Java source file. Every system has a simple text editor that gives you the basic capability to enter and edit text. On Windows, it is called Write; on the Macintosh, it is Simple Text; on Solaris it is TextEdit. Any of these applications will work for the small applications we'll go through here; however, you may want to find a more robust text editor as you work on longer and more challenging applications. If you have a text editor that came with a development environment, such as Visual C++, you may find that it is more suited to writing code. A variety of excellent text editors are available on the Internet as well for most platforms.

For the following example, create an empty directory in which to put your Java application. For these examples, you can name the directory anything you want, but we recommend you name it classes; we will refer to it by that name throughout Part 2.

Launch your text editor and enter in the following lines of code. Don't worry about their meaning now, but try to pay close attention to the spelling. Any typos will result in compilation errors in the next step when we compile the file.

```
// HelloJavaApp.java
class HelloJavaApp {
    public static void main (String args[]) {
        System.out.println("Hello from Java!");
    }
}
```

When you're done entering the code, save the file under the name HelloJavaApp.java in the classes directory. The above code defines a class named HelloJavaApp, which contains a single method called main(). When HelloJavaApp is run, the Java interpreter will send a main message to the HelloJavaApp class, which will cause the code in the main() method to be executed. Most real-world Java applications would contain additional methods, but all applications must contain the main() method.

Compiling the Application

Before you can run this class, you need to compile it by running the Java compiler, called javac. The process of running the compiler differs slightly, depending on which platform you're using. We'll cover the Windows and Solaris platforms separately.

Windows   For Windows 95 and NT users, you'll need to open a DOS shell window. Make sure you are in the directory you are using to store your Java classes, then enter the following command:

```
javac HelloJavaApp.java
```

After a short time, the command should complete. If everything goes correctly, that should be all you need to do to compile the class. If something goes wrong, you'll receive one of the following error messages indicating one of the following problems:

```
Bad command or file name
```

This message probably means that you mistyped the command; try entering it again, this time more carefully.

```
Invalid expression statement
```

This message means that you mistyped something in the HelloJavaApp source code, in which case you'll probably get an error message to this effect. If so, you should double check that, fix any typos you see, resave the source file, and try the command again.

```
Bad command or file name
error: Can't read: HelloJavaApp.java
```

The final problems you might encounter are that either the javac compiler command or the HelloJavaApp.java file might not be found. If the command is not found, you may want to check the installation instructions again, specifically the part dealing with paths, and make sure you entered in the word javac correctly. If the HelloJavaApp.java file is not found, then you want to make sure you are in the correct directory. Type

```
dir
```

and make sure that the HelloJavaApp.java file is in the list of files in the directory.

Solaris   For Solaris users, you'll need to open a shell tool or command tool window. Make sure you are in the directory you are using to store your Java classes by typing

```
ls
```

Make sure that HelloJavaApp.java is in the list of files displayed. If so, enter the following command:

```
javac HelloJavaApp.java
```

After a short time, the command should complete. If everything goes correctly, that should be all you need to do to compile the class. If something goes wrong, you'll receive one of the following error messages indicating one of the following problems:

```
/bin/sh: javac: not found
```

This message probably means that you mistyped the command; try entering it again, this time more carefully.

```
Invalid expression statement
```

This message means that you mistyped something in the HelloJavaApp source code, in which case you'll probably get an error message to this effect. If so, you should double check that, fix any typos you see, resave the source file, and try the command again.

```
/bin/sh: javac: not found
file HelloJavaApp.java not found
```

The final problems you might encounter are that either the javac compiler command or the HelloJavaApp.java file might not be found. If the command is not found, you may want to check the installation instructions again, specifically the part dealing with paths, and make sure you entered in the word javac correctly. If the HelloJavaApp.java file is not found, then you want to make sure you are in the correct directory. Type

```
ls
```

and make sure that the HelloJavaApp.java file is in the list of files in the directory.

Running the Application

Once you've compiled your source file, look in the classes directory; you will now see two files:

```
HelloJavaApp.class
HelloJavaApp.java
```

HelloJavaApp.java is the file you created in the text editor, and HelloJavaApp.class is the class file that the javac compiler created. HelloJavaApp.class contains a special type of platform-independent code called byte code, which the java interpreter executes when it runs your program.

To run the program, type:

```
java HelloJavaApp
```

This code tells the java interpreter to load the HelloJavaApp class and run the main method. Notice how we omitted the .class from HelloJavaApp.java when we ran the java interpreter. The interpreter knows to add .class when looking for a class file.

At this point, if everything goes right, we should see the following output:

```
Hello from Java!
```

Congratulations, you've written your first Java application. If you didn't get this output, backtrack and make sure that there weren't any error messages that you missed or forgot to correct. Make sure you are able to build the HelloJavaApp application and run it before you proceed to the next chapter. We'll revisit HelloJavaApp at the end of the next chapter, after we've introduced you to objects in a little more depth; at that point, our focus will be on what the actual lines of code mean, and we will assume that you're able to build and run the files yourself.

Other Build Techniques

The Java compiler and interpreter can be used as tool applications that can be either driven from Make scripts or invoked from other applications. On UNIX platforms, such as Solaris, you can create a Makefile for use with Java and build your Java programs using the Make command. To learn more about this, refer to the main page for the Make command for details on how to create a Makefile. Here's an example of a simple Makefile that can be used to build Java programs:

```
#Makefile
#Example makefile for compiling Java programs


#List the public classes used in the program
```

```
CLASSES-Class1 Class2 Class3

#Make rules

all: classes

OBJ=${CLASSES:%=%.class}

classes: $(OBJ)

$.class: %.java
    javac $<
```

Windows users who have Microsoft's Visual C++ installed can configure it so that it launches the JDK tools. This is a relatively straightforward process.

The Visual C++ IDE can be set up to invoke the JDK compiler, interpreter, and appletviewer. You will not be able to use the JDK debugger from Visual C++ because the Visual C++ console window is read-only and the Java debugger tool requires keyboard.

To configure VC++, choose the Customize menu item from the Tools menu. You will be presented with a dialog box that lists the tools available from the Tools menu. Use the Add button to add java.exe, javac.exe, and appletviewer.exe. Figures 4.1–4.3 show how the tools should be configured. Make sure that your settings match theirs.

```
Javac:
    Menu Text:            Javac
    Command:             c:\java\bin\javac.EXE
    Arguments:           -verbose $File
    Initial Directory:
```

■■■■■■ **Figure 4.1** Java compiler configuration.

Java:

Menu Text:	Java
Command:	c:\java\bin\javac.EXE
Arguments:	
Initial Directory:	

████████ **Figure 4.2** Java interpreter configuration.

AppletViewer:

Menu Text:	AppletViewer
Command:	c:\java\bin\appletviewer.EXE
Arguments:	$FileName
Initial Directory:	$FileDir

████████ **Figure 4.3** AppletViewer configuration.

When the tools are configured, you can use the Javac, Java, and AppletViewer menu commands to compile and test your Java programs and applets. Here's how this works. With the Java source file the frontmost window, select the Javac command from the Tools menu. The output from the compiler will appear in the Output window. If the program compiled without error, you can run the application or applet. If the program is an application, choose the Java menu item from the Tools menu. You will be prompted for a class name. Enter the name of the Java class that contains the main() method you wish to execute. This name should not have a .java or .class extension at the end. The Java interpreter will run the class, and the output of the program will appear in the Output window. If the program is an applet, open the .html file that invokes the applet and make the .html file's window the frontmost window. Then, select the AppletViewer menu item from the Tools menu. The AppletViewer will be launched with the .html file, and it will open the file and display its applet. Any output text from the appletviewer or the applet will appear in the VC++ Output window.

Many programmers find this technique to be an easy way to compile and run applets under Windows 95. Although we don't recommend purchasing Visual C++ solely to compile Java programs, it's worthwhile to try this technique if you already have Visual C++.

CHAPTER 5

JAVA BASICS

In this chapter we will introduce the nuts and bolts of the Java language. We will describe how basic lines of code in Java or statements are constructed out of *expressions* and how they're organized into *blocks*. We'll also show you how *comments* fit into this.

After that, we'll look at how Java deals with data, first by covering how values are represented in your code as *literals*, described using *types*, named using *identifiers*, and stored in *variables*.

The final sections of the chapter will cover the basics of expressions and operators.

Code Basics

Statements, Expressions, and Blocks

Programs in Java consist of a series of *statements* that are organized into *blocks*. Statements can broken up into *expressions* which consist of data and *operators*. In

Chapter 4 we demonstrated a simple application called HelloJavaApp, which printed out the string "Hello from Java!". This was accomplished by the following statement:

```
System.out.println("Hello from Java!");
```

The important thing to notice is the semicolon (;) at the end of the statement. The semicolon tells the Java interpreter that the statement is complete and to execute it before moving on the next line. Performing the instructions contained in a statement is referred to as *executing* the statement. The process of the Java interpreter executing statements is called the *flow of execution*; when all the statements in a program have been executed and the program finishes, execution is said to be complete.

Most statements will contain one or more expressions. An *expression* is a series of values and operators (e.g., +, –, >) that, when evaluated, return a *value*. Some examples of simple expressions are:

```
a / b
2 + 2
i = i + 1
```

These examples are all valid expressions. However, in order for them to be used within a valid Java program, they must exist within statements. Adding a semicolon at the end of the expression causes it to become an expression statement; for example, this code is now an expression statement:

```
i = i + 1;
```

It is a common mistake to omit the semicolon, which causes the compiler to think that the next line of code is part of your statement and a syntax error to result.

The other element of Java program organization we need to cover is the *compound statement* or *block*. We will cover blocks again later, but now you need to understand that they are used to organize a collection of statements. You saw an example of a block in HelloJavaApp earlier:

```
{
    System.out.println("Hello World!");
}
```

Blocks are defined by enclosing them within braces ({ }). A block can be used anywhere you can use a statement. The block does not need a semicolon after the trailing brace.

Comments

Comments are text included in the source code of your program that are ignored by the compiler but used to provide information to the reader or the programmer about some aspect of the code. We will use comments extensively in our example programs to detail what each line of code does. In your own programs, you may not want to comment to the same degree. Although we will attempt to use examples and code that represent good coding style, you will likely want to refer to a text that covers, among other things, proper commenting strategy. My personal favorite is *Code Complete* by Steve McConnel (Microsoft Press 1993).

Comments are indicated either by surrounding the text with /* and */ or by preceding the text with a double slash //. The double slash causes the text that follows it, the end of the line, to be treated as comments. The next line will be treated as normal code unless it too starts with a double slash.

Some examples of valid comments are as follows:

```
/* Comment example # 1*/

/* A multiline
   comment example
*/


// A single-line comment
```

Any code to the left of the comment is valid; for example:

```
a = a + 1 // The code gets executed, this text is ignored
```

Any code within a comment is ignored. This is especially important to note in a multiline comment:

```
/* A multiline comment
   a = a + 1;
   The above statement will never be executed.
*/
```

Data Basics

Literals

A *literal* is the basic explicit representation of a data type within your code. Any time you use a number, Boolean, character, or string in a statement or expression and intend for the value to be used as written rather than as the result of an expression, you are using a literal.

Let's take a look at a few examples of literals used in simple expression statements:

```
a = 2;                   // 2 is an integer literal
s = "A String Literal";  // The quoted text is a literal
```

Different types of literals have special rules about their use. In this section, we'll cover each type of literal in Java and its rules.

Numbers

Numerical values in Java can be integer, floating point, and character values.

Integers   *Integer literals* are whole numbers that can be represented in decimal, hexadecimal, or octal formats. An integer literal is assumed to be 32 bits if it is in the range of -32768 to 32768. If it is outside that range or has an L or l appended to the end of its value, it is considered a long integer and is assumed to be 64 bits. This distinction will be more relevant when we get to integer *types*, which are used to describe the containers or *variables* in which integer values can be stored.

The following are examples of integer literals used in simple expression statements:

```
a = 2;     // 2 is an integer literal
b = 5L;    // 5 is a long integer literal
```

Hex values can be used by preceding a value with a leading 0x or 0X. Octal values can be used by preceding a value with a leading 0.

The following are examples of integer literals used in simple expression statements:

```
a = 0xA;   // 0xA is a hex literal for hex value A (10)
b = 055;   // octal 55 = ???
```

Floating Point Numbers   A floating point number is any number with a decimal point. Here is an example of a floating point literal used in a simple expression statement:

```
a = 2.0;    // 2.0 is a floating point literal
```

You can use exponential values by appending a trailing e (or E) and the exponent value, as in this example:

```
b = 2.0E4;
```

Characters   Characters are 16-bit integer values, represented as a single character enclosed in single quotes. Characters are represented as Unicode values so that international software is easier to create. Some characters must be represented as escape sequences to be used as character literals. Table 5.1 shows these characters and how to represent them as escape codes.

Boolean Literals

Boolean literals are represented as being either true or false. The following are examples of Boolean literals used in simple expression statements:

```
a = true;    // true is a Boolean literal
b = false;   // false is a Boolean literal
```

■■■■■■■ **Table 5.1** Escape Codes

Escape Code	Character
\b	backspace
\f	formfeed
\n	newline
\r	carriage return
\t	horizontal tab
\v	vertical tab
\\	backslash
\?	question mark
\'	single quote
\"	double quote
\000	octal number
\xhh	hex number

■■■■■■■

Strings

Literal strings are zero or more characters enclosed within quotation marks. For example, in the expression statement

```
a = "Hello World";
```

"Hello World" is a text literal. Although a string contains a series of characters, it is not accessible as a character array as it is in languages such as C. However, any character or escape code that would be valid within a character literal is valid within a string literal.

Here are some more examples of strings used in expression statements:

```
a = "";                       \\ Empty string
b = "Hello World\n";          \\ Note the \n newline
c = "He said \"Hello World\"";  \\ Note the \" double quotes
```

A common mistake is to use single quotes with string literals and double quotes with character literals. In most cases, such as using a string literal enclosed in single quotes, the compiler will halt with an error if the string has more than one character or if you are using the character in a string in a situation which requires a string *type*. In some cases, however, you may be able to inadvertently confuse the two and have a program compile but perform unexpectedly. Java, as opposed to more "free-wheeling" languages such as C, will catch most cases where you try to do this; however, visually double checking your code to make sure that you are using literals as you intended is a good practice. Here's an interesting example, though, of a case of a legal operation that produces unexpected results:

```
System.out.println("Hello" + '!');
```

The error in this example is that the programmer intended the exclamation point to be a string literal instead of a character literal. Because he enclosed it in single quotes instead of double quotes, the compiler decided that it was a character literal and converted it to its Unicode integer value of 33. The output of the example would be

```
Hello33
```

instead of the intended

```
Hello!
```

The corrected usage would be:

```
System.out.println("Hello" + "!");
```

As we progress through the next sections, and as we talk more about strings in general, you will see how language constructs such as types work to prevent most cases of these errors.

Basic Types

Types are used to describe the contents of variables as well as the values returned by expressions. Types are primarily used in the declarations of variables. We will discuss variables in depth later in this chapter, but we will introduce the concept here.

The following is a simple variable declaration statement that creates a single integer variable:

```
int i;
```

This statement tells the compiler that i is a variable of type integer. Literal values, as described in the previous section, can be assigned to their corresponding types:

```
i = 20;
```

For the purposes of our examples in this section, we'll combine the declaration and assignment into a single statement:

```
int i = 20;
```

Java has two kinds of types: *fundamental* (or *simple*) types and *derived* (or *composite*) types. This section will discuss the basic simple types that Java provides.

Numbers

Java provides you with four kinds of integer types and two kind of floating point types. These types differ in their sizes, meaning that each type is capable of defining a different range of values.

The four integer types are:

```
byte    8 bits    -128..127
short   16 bits   -32768..32767
int     32 bits   -2147483648..2147483647
long    64 bits   -4294967296..4294967295
```

The two floating point types are:

```
float     32 bit
double    64 bit
```

Here are some example declaration statements for the various numeric types:

```
byte b = 100;
short sh = 32000;
int i = 50000;
long l = 3000000000;
float f = 2.5;
double dl = 6.5e10;
```

Characters

Character types are defined 16-bit unsigned Unicode values. Strictly speaking, a character is a numeric type, equivalent to a short (i.e., a 16-bit) integer value. Here's an example that declares a character variable:

```
char theChar = 'a';
```

Because characters are numeric values, it is possible to assign a numeric literal to a character typed variable and a character literal to an integer variable:

```
char theChar = 48;
integer theValue = 'a';
```

Booleans

Boolean types can have a value of true or false and are represented by the Boolean keyword:

```
Boolean
```

Here's an example of a Boolean declaration:

```
Boolean isDone = false;
```

Identifiers

Identifiers are sequences of letters and digits used whenever you need to name a variable, method, class, or any other element in Java that requires a name. The following characters are considered valid in identifier names: uppercase and lowercase a through z, the underscore character (_), the dollar sign ($), and, except for the first character, the digits 0 through 9. Identifiers are case sensitive, meaning that two identifiers that differ only by case are considered different identifiers.

Java reserves certain identifiers for use as keywords and forbids their use otherwise. These are:

abstract	for	protected
boolean	future	public
break	generic	rest
byte	goto	return
case	if	short
cast	implements	static
catch	import	super
char	inner	switch
class	instanceof	synchronized
const	int	this
continue	interface	throw
default	long	throws
do	native	transient
double	new	try
else	null	var
extends	operator	void
final	outer	volatile
finally	package	while
float	private	

Here are some examples of variable declaration statements containing valid identifiers:

```
int i;
double a_long_variable_name;
Boolean $paid;
char letter_U_and_the_number_2;
```

The following are variable declaration statements using illegal identifiers:

```
int 2i;          // identifier starts with a number
char val%;       // % not a legal character in an identifier
double switch;   // switch is a keyword
```

Simple Variables

We talked about variables briefly in the previous section on types. We will go into them in more depth here. Variables serve as containers for the data you use in your programs. To use a variable, you need to know two things about it: its name and its type. We introduced you to the rules of naming variables in the previous section on identifiers, and we talked about types earlier in this chapter as well. We will now see how that information is applied when dealing with variables.

Declaring Variables

Before a variable can be used in a program, it must first be declared. Declaring a variable means giving the variable a name and describing what kind of data can be put in it. As we discussed earlier, names in Java are called *identifiers*, and data is described using *types*. The declaration statement uses this information using the following syntax:

```
type identifier;
```

For example, to declare an integer variable called shoes, you would use the following declaration statement:

```
int shoes;
```

Any of the types we've discussed can be used as variables. Here are some more examples:

```
byte age;
short price;
int colors;
long milliseconds;
float inches;
double miles;
Boolean has_been_filed;
char first_initial;
```

When naming variables, it is usually a good idea to be as descriptive as possible, unless the variable is being used temporarily. For example, when we cover loops in the next chapter, we will often declare a variable with a single letter name, usually i, to keep count of the number of times we have gone through a loop.

Assignments

The first thing you'll want to do with a variable (*literally* the first thing, as the next section points out) is to put a value into it. The step of putting a value into a variable is called *assignment*. The following are some examples of assignment statements:

```
number_of_cars = 1;
myName = "Ed";
billPaid = false;
```

To assign a value to a variable, the value must be compatible with the variable's type. In some cases it is possible for the interpreter to translate values automatically from one type to another through a process called *type casting*, which we will discuss in more detail in the next section. Usually, though, storing a value of the wrong type into a variable is an error. For example, attempting to store a string directly into an integer variable would result in an error (although we will show you the correct way of converting a string to a number in later chapters).

Type Casts When you attempt to store a value of one type in a variable of another type, the compiler performs type checking to see if this assignment is allowable. The compiler will allow you to assign a numerical value of one type into another and will perform a type conversion or *type cast*; this simply means that the value is converted from the original type to the type of the variable to which the value is being assigned. For example, assigning a float value of 1.5 to an int variable will result in the float value being converted to an int value of 1 and then being stored in the int variable. However, the compiler will assume that you were not aware that this conversion might be the result of your assignment, and it will warn you with the message that a "possible loss of precision" will occur and to "use an explicit cast" to perform the operation. In general, using an explicit cast is good practice—it spares you from a slew of warning messages from the compiler. Here's the syntax for an explicit type cast:

```
type variable_a = (type) variable_b;
```

For example, the following code shows an assignment of an int to a byte using an explicit type cast:

```
int a = 5;
byte b = (byte)a;
```

In this example, we cast the value of variable a, which is an int value, to a byte. This can still result in a loss of precision (or, in this case, a potential overflow), but the explicit cast tells the compiler you know what you're doing and to spare you the warning.

Casts are possible between compatible types, which essentially means that you can cast values between the numerical types (including char), but you can't cast Boolean values or string literals. In later chapters, you will see how you can also cast between object class types, but until then, you'll see us using type casts only on numerical values.

Initializing and Initializers

Before a variable can be used, it must be initialized. That means that a value must be put into a variable before you can do anything with the variable. For example, the following lines of code declare a variable and then attempt to add 1 to it:

```
int i;

i = i + 1;    // illegal - i has not yet been initialized
```

In the above code, for the expression i + 1 to be correctly evaluated, there needs to be a value in i. In some languages, uninitialized variables will contain either 0 or an unknown value. The Java compiler keeps track of whether a variable has been previously initialized before it allows you to use it in an expression, and it will halt with a compiler error if it sees that you have done this. The exception to this that you will see later is with member variables that are initialized to 0.

To fix the above lines of code, you could add an assignment statement in between the variable declaration and the i = i + 1 statement, like this:

```
int i;

i = 0;

i = i + 1;    // illegal - i has not yet been initialized
```

The more efficient method is to use an initializer. An *initializer* is an optional assignment as part of the declaration statement. For example, the following line declares integer variable i and assigns it an initial value of 1:

```
int i = 1;
```

This is a more convenient way of ensuring that a variable is initialized before you try to use it.

Scope and Blocks

When you declare a variable, you declare it for use within a specific area of code within your program. When the flow of execution leaves that area of code, the contents of the variable disappear (specifically, a process called *garbage collection* frees the memory used by the variable). The area of the code where the variable is usable is called its *scope*.

Here's an example that should make this more clear:

```
{
// Block A

int x = 1;
System.out.println(x);    // a is declared in this block

    {
        // Block B
        // This is a nested block -
        // it has access to variables declared
        // within it as well as to variables declared
        // in the blocks within which it is nested -
        // in this case any variables in block A

        System.out.println(x);    // OK

        int y =2;
        System.out.println(y);    // OK

        // After we leave this block, y will no longer
        // be declared, and it will be an error to
        // refer to it
    }

System.out.println(y);
// BAD - y is not declared in this block

}
```

As you can see in the above example, once a variable is declared within a block, it is usable within any blocks nested within that block. However, it is not usable in any blocks "above" it.

Expressions and Operators

We will now take a closer look at expressions. We've talked a little bit about where expressions fit in within statements, and we've seen some examples of their use; now we will take a look at how an expression is constructed and at the basic kinds of expressions.

An *expression* is anything that returns a value. A typical expression consists of two values or operands separated by an operator, but, in fact, the value itself could be considered an expression. You'll see examples of this in the form of Boolean variables in the next chapter when we introduce the if statement.

Let's look at an example expression again:

```
a = a + 1;
```

This expression statement actually contains two expressions:

```
a + 1
a = (the value of a + 1)
```

The first expression consists of the value of variable a and the number 1 separated by the + operator. The second expression consists of variable a and the value of a+1 separated by the assignment operator. The compiler knows that the expression a+1 needs to be evaluated before it can be assigned through a set of rules called *precedence*, which we'll talk about soon.

Operator Syntax

As demonstrated above, operators take one or more values and create a new value, through calculation, comparison, or some other method. A number of operators are available to you when you are programming in Java. This section will cover the basic rules of using these operators.

There are two types of operators in Java, *binary* and *unary*. Binary operators are probably more familiar to you as they are more commonly used both in programming and in real-world math. A *binary operator* is defined as an operator that uses two values in the form:

```
value1 operator value2
```

For example, the following are all examples of binary operators:

```
a + 2
x / y
2 * c
```

The second type of operator is called a *unary* operator. A *unary operator* is a type of operator that uses only a single value. Some examples of unary operators are:

```
a++
-b
!done
```

We'll explain what these operators actually mean in the next few sections.

Precedence   An important aspect of using operators is understanding *precedence*. You may remember from grade school math the concept of order of operations. For mathematical operators, Java uses the basic rules of order of operations, also called *mathematical precedence*. Precedence can be overridden by using parentheses to specify explicitly the order of evaluation.

Figure 5.1 shows the order of precedence for Java operators. Note that some of the operators listed here are introduced in later chapters.

Mathematical Operators

Java provides a full set of operators for mathematical calculations. Unlike some other languages, Java can use the same operators on both integer and floating point values. Java provides a set of 11 binary operators, the first five of which you probably are familiar with and which are usable on both integer and floating point numerical types. The basic binary mathematical operators are listed in Table 5.2.

Table 5.3 shows the set of unary operators that can be used on numerical values in Java.

The unary minus operator changes the sign of the value it precedes. It is mathematically equivalent to multiplying a value by -1. For example, the following expressions are functionally equivalent:

```
-(-1)
-1 * -1
```

```
.        ()      []
!        ~       ++      --      instanceof
*        /       %
+        -
<<       >>      >>>
<        <=      >       >=
==       !=
&
^
|
&&
||
?:
=        +=      -=      *=      /=      %=      &=      ^=      |=      <<=     >>=
```

■■■■■■ **Figure 5.1** Order of operator precedence in Java. Operators are ranked top to bottom, highest to lowest precedence; operators on the same line have equal precedence.

■■■■■■ **Table 5.2** Binary Mathematical Operators

binary operator	meaning
+	addition
-	subtraction
*	multiplication
/	division
%	modulus

■■■■■■

■■■■■■ **Table 5.3** Unary Mathematical Operators

unary operator	meaning
-	unary negation
++	increment
--	decrement

■■■■■■

The unary increment and decrement operators are basically shorthand ways of incrementing or decrementing the value of a variable and storing the resultant value back into the same variable. For example, the following two statements are functionally equivalent:

```
a++;
a = a + 1;
```

Integers   In addition to being able to use the mathematical operators listed above, Java provides several bitwise operators that can be used only with integer values. These are shown in Table 5.4.

Floating Point Values   Floating point values can also make use of the full range of mathematical operators with a few caveats. The principal issues of floating point math are what happens when floating point calculations produce special values such as NaN and Inf. NaN stands for "Not A Number" and is a special value that indicates a value has been produced that is essentially unusable. Any mathematical operation performed on an NaN or an operation in which one of the values is NaN will result in a value of NaN. Inf represents infinity and can be positive or negative (-Inf). An infinite value is larger than any numerical value of the same sign, and all valid numbers fall within the range:

```
-Inf < all finite values < Inf
```

■■■■■■■■ **Table 5.4** Bitwise Operators Used with Integer Values

operator	meaning
UNARY OPERATORS	
~	bitwise complement
BINARY OPERATORS	
&	bitwise AND
|	bitwise OR
^	bitwise XOR
<<	left shift
>>	sign-propagating right-shift
>>>	zero-fill right-shift

■■■■■■■■

Here are a few examples of how special values can be created from mathematical operations:

```
a = -1/0;      // a = -Inf
b = 1/0;       // b = Inf
c = Inf/Inf;   // c = NaN
```

Comparisons, Tests, and Booleans

Most programs need to make decisions based on the results of calculations or comparisons. For example, you might have a program that prints out a message once a day at 6:00 A.M. To do this, you would likely have a program that repeatedly checked the value of the current hour until it equaled 6:00 A.M. When this condition is met, the program would perform a certain task (such as ringing a wake-up alarm), then keep checking the value of the current hour until it was again equal to 6:00 A.M. Tests like these are implemented as expressions that return a Boolean value of true or false. The following sections will demonstrate the operators that return this type of Boolean result.

Equality and Inequality   Table 5.5 shows the basic tests that you are likely to use, those of equality and inequality.

Here are some examples:

```
Boolean test1 = 2 == (1 + 1);    // true
Boolean test2 = 2 != (2 + 1);    // true
Boolean test3 = 'A' == 'A';      // true
Boolean wakeUp = hour == 6;      // true if hour equals 6
```

The first example expression (2 == (1 + 1)) evaluates to true. The addition of 1 + 1 is performed first, and then the equality comparison is performed. The second example expression (2 != (2 + 1)) compares 2 against 2 + 1; since the two values

■■■■■ **Table 5.5** Basic Equality and Inequality Tests

operator	meaning
==	equals
!=	is not equal

are unequal it returns a value of false. The third example expression ('A' == 'A') compares the Unicode values of two character literals and finds that they are equal, resulting in a Boolean value of true. The last expression is an example of how you might implement our alarm clock example as a Boolean expression. In this case the variable hour is compared to the value 6, and the result is stored in the variable wakeUp. Later on, we'll see how you would use this value to determine what subsequent code in your program gets performed.

A common mistake that C programmers will recognize, one that afflicts Java programs as well, occurs because of the similarity of the assignment operator (=) and the equality operator (==). Let's take a moment to highlight the similarities and differences between Java and C. In C, because numbers can be used as Boolean types, the following code would compile, even though the results would not be what the programmer expected:

```
int a = 5;
if (a = 4) a++;
```

We'll look at the if construct in the next chapter, but simply put, it performs a statement if a Boolean expression evaluates to true. In the case of this code example, the programmer intended for the statement a++ to be performed if a is equal to 4. The problem is that the programmer incorrectly expressed this as (a = 4) instead of (a == 4). Because C allows an integer to be used in the place of a Boolean result, the compiler allows this to compile. At run time, (a = 4) is evaluated as an assignment expression which results in a value of 4, which C then takes to mean true because it considers non-zero values to be equal to true. As a result, the statement a++ is performed. We can see how a simple typing error could result in two bugs in a single line of code—first, the variable is set to 4 in the botched equality test; second, the test always evaluates to true and performs the a++ statement.

Java heads off this type of problem at compile time by implementing Booleans as a distinct type and then using what is called "strict" type checking; this means that you can't use values of one type in situations expecting values of another type. Java won't prevent you from making this kind of mistake in the source code, but the compiler will catch the error when the value 4 is attempted to be used as a Boolean value in the if construct. When porting code from C to Java, you must be aware of this and scrutinize your usage of Boolean values.

Ordering   Ordering refers to comparing one value against another and determining if one value is greater than or less than another. Table 5.6 shows the four operators for performing ordering comparisons in Java.

Here are some simple examples:

```
Boolean test1 = 'a' < 'b';      // true
Boolean test2 = 2 <= (1 + 1);   // true
Boolean test3 = 4 > (2 + 2);    // false
Boolean test4 = 4 >= (2 + 2);   // true
```

Logical Operations   A logical operator allows you to group together one or more Boolean expressions and return a result based on the values to which these expressions evaluate. Table 5.7 shows the six operators for performing logical operations in Java.

■■■■■■ **Table 5.6** Operators for Ordering Comparisons

operator	meaning
<	less than
<=	less than or equal
>	greater than
>=	greater than or equal

■■■■■■

■■■■■■ **Table 5.7** Operators for Logical Operations

operator	meaning
!	Boolean negation (NOT)
binary logical operators	
&	Boolean AND
|	Boolean OR
^	Boolean XOR
&&	short-circuit AND
||	short-circuit OR

■■■■■■

The ! unary operator is referred to as the *negation* or *not* operator. This operator returns a result that is the opposite of the given Boolean value. For example, !(false) is the same as true. Usually, you will use this with an expression such as !(a < 5), which will return true only if it is not less than 5.

The & binary operator is referred to as the *and* operator. It takes two Boolean values and returns true only if both values are true. For example, the expression ((a > 3) & (a < 7)) evaluates to true if the variable a is between 3 and 7.

The | binary operator is referred to as the *or* operator. It takes two Boolean values and returns true if either or both of the two values is true. For example, the expression ((a < 5) | (a > 10)) evaluates to true if the variable a is either less than 5 or greater than 10.

The ^ binary operator is referred to as the *xor* operator. It returns true if either of the two values is true, but it returns false if they are both true.

&& and || are the short-circuit versions of & and |. Normally, when evaluating an expression, all the elements of the expression are evaluated before the final value is delivered. For example, in the expression ((a > 3) & (a < 7)), both (a > 3) and (a < 7) are evaluated and then the two Boolean value results are evaluated using the & operator. In the case of the value of the variable a being less than or equal to 3, (a > 3) evaluates to false. At this point, because one of the values used by the & operator is false, and because & requires both the values to be true in order to return true, we know that the whole expression is going to return false. This means that (a < 7) is still evaluated even though we know what the final outcome will be. In some cases, it is useful to discontinue evaluation of the expression once one of the values evaluates to false. You would do this by using && instead of &, or || instead if |. Using these operators causes evaluation of the expression to cease once the outcome of the final expression has been determined. You'll see practical examples of the use of short-circuit operators in later chapters once we introduce methods and objects, where you want the evaluation of the expression to discontinue because evaluating it under certain conditions would cause a program error. In this case, you would use something like:

```
if ((Boolean expression A) && (Boolean expression B that fails if A is false)) {
    statements to perform;
}
```

At the beginning of this chapter we stated that a program is a collection of expressions and statements that are executed in a sequential order. Now that we've seen how expressions and statements are constructed in Java, we're ready to move on to the next chapter, where we'll see how the flow of execution is controlled within a Java program. The language basics that we reviewed in this chapter will be used throughout the book as we build and demonstrate more complex programs.

CHAPTER 6

FLOW OF CONTROL

As we mentioned at the beginning of Chapter 5, a Java program runs by executing a series of statements. The process of performing one statement after another is called the *flow of execution* or *flow of control*. Normally, this flow consists simply of going to the next statement in the program after the current statement has been performed, and when the last line of the program has been performed, completing the program. This was demonstrated in our HelloJavaApp program. Let's take a look at a similar program, which instead of printing out a single line, prints out three lines, one after another:

```
class FlowOfControlApp {
    public static void main (String args[]) {
        System.out.println("A,");
        System.out.println("B,");
        System.out.println("and C.");
    }
}
```

You'll notice that for this example, we've included a full program listing. You may want to try out some of the example programs listed in this chapter. If so, type in the example program as listed and save it using the name of the class with .java appended to the end. For the above example, you would use the name FlowOfControlApp.java as the source file name. After saving the source file, compile and run it, following the instructions for building and running Java applications from Chapter 4. Most of the examples listed in this chapter are similar to the FlowOfControlApp listed above but with a few changes in each example to illustrate a particular point.

If you run the FlowOfControlApp program, you'll get the following output:

```
A,
B,
and C.
```

You can see that, as expected, the three System.out.println statements executed one after another. This chapter will show you how you can change this flow based on criteria you set in your program.

If..Else

The most common statement you will use for changing the flow of control in your programs is the if statement. There are a few variations on how you can use this statement, but essentially it is used to control whether a statement or block gets executed based on the value of an expression.

if

The basic form of an if statement is as follows

```
if (test-expression) statement;
```

If the test expression evaluates to true, then the statement gets executed. For example:

```
if (3 < 2) System.out.println("This will never be printed");
```

In the above example, the test expression (3 < 2) is clearly false, and as a consequence, the statement that follows it will not be executed. We could use something like this:

```
int count = 5;
if (count > 0) System.out.println("This will be printed");
```

In this case, the test expression (count > 0) will evaluate as true, and as a consequence, the statement System.out.println("This will be printed") will be executed.

Sometimes executing more than one statement if the test expression is true is desirable. This is a case where using a compound statement or block comes in handy. As we mentioned in Chapter 5, we can use a compound statement anywhere we would use a single statement. Here's an example:

```
class IfApp {
    public static void main (String args[]) {

        int count = 5;
        if (count > 0) {
            System.out.println("This will be printed");
            System.out.println("and so will this");
            System.out.println("as will this.");
        }
    }
}
```

else

Many times, you'll want to have a different statement or set of statements executed if the test expression is false than if it is true. To do this you use the else statement. The general form of this statement is:

```
if (test-expression) true-statement else false-statement;
```

Here's an example:

```
class IfElseApp {
    public static void main (String args[]) {

        int count = 32;
        if (count == 0)
            System.out.println("This will not be printed");
        else
            System.out.println("This will be printed");
    }
}
```

In this example, the test expression is false, so the statement following else is executed.

?:

A special form of the if..else statement is referred to as the *conditional expression* or *ternary operator*. The conditional expression is used when you want to assign one of two values based on an expression evaluating as true or false. The form of this is:

```
test-expression ? true-value : false-value
```

In this example this expression is used to determine the lesser of two values:

```java
class TernaryApp {
    public static void main (String args[]) {

        short value1 = 10;
        short value2 = 5;
        short theLesser;

        theLesser = (value1 < value2) ? value1 : value2;
        System.out.println(theLesser);
    }
}
```

Note that this is functionally equivalent to:

```java
class Ternary2App {
    public static void main (String args[]) {

        short value1 = 10;
        short value2 = 5;
        short theLesser;

        if (value1 < value2)
            theLesser = value1;
        else
            theLesser = value2;
        System.out.println(theLesser);
```

```
        }

    }
```

In general, you should use the more readable if statement except in situations in which you can be sure that the code will still be readable and understandable.

Switch

The switch statement is used to jump to a specific statement or block based on the value of an expression matching a specific integer value. Let's look at the basic form of the statement first, and then we'll discuss what the elements of it mean.

```
switch (case-expression) {
    case literal-value: statements
    case literal-value: statements
    default: statements
}
```

The case expression will evaluate to an integer value (which means that it could also be a character value, from our discussion of characters in Chapter 5), which will be matched against one or more possible literal values in an attempt to find a match. If the match is found, the statements associated with it will be executed. If not, and a default case is specified, the statements associated with default will be executed. Let's take a look at a simple use of case:

```
class SwitchApp {
    public static void main (String args[]) {

        int whichOne = 5;
        switch (whichOne ) {
           case 1:
              System.out.println("This will not be printed");
              break;
           case 5:
              System.out.println("This will be printed");
              break;
           default:
```

```
                System.out.println("Just in case");
                break;

        }

    }

}
```

In the above example, we set the value of the variable whichOne to 5 and then use a switch statement to test its value. As you can see, the first case compares the value to 1, and as a consequence it is not executed. The second case compares the value to 5, and in this case, is matched. As a consequence, the System.out.println("This will be printed") statement is executed. Now, notice that the next line contains the single statement break. A break statement indicates that it is time to exit the switch statement and continue with the program.

As mentioned before, you can also use a switch statement with character values. Here's an example where we wait for a key to be hit on the keyboard and then test to see if it is "y" or "n":

```
class SwitchApp2 {
    public static void main (String args[]) {

        System.out.println("Please enter Y/N");
        char c = (char)System.in.read();
        switch (c) {
            case 'y': case 'Y':
                System.out.println("Yes");
                break;
            case 'n': case 'N':
                System.out.println("No");
                break;
            default:
                System.out.println("Wrong answer.");
                break;

        }

    }

}
```

There are two important things to notice in this example. The first is that we used a character instead of a number. We can do this because a character is the same as a 16-bit integer. The second thing to notice is that we used multiple case comparisons in the same case statement:

```
case 'y': case 'Y':
    System.out.println("Yes");
    break;
```

This approach allows us to associate a statement to be executed with one or more comparisons, which can be useful in situations where you want to check on uppercase and lowercase characters or where a series of different values needs to cause the same actions to take place. By the way, if you were to try the above example, you would find the program would prompt you to enter Y or N and then would not do anything unless you followed your response by hitting the return key. This situation occurs because when you use System.in for input, the incoming characters are buffered, which means that they are stored in memory until the return key is pressed. Although we will use System.in in some of our examples, you will find you seldom use System.in when writing applets, as input is usually handled through different mechanisms.

Loops

Loops, which are sometimes referred to as *iterators*, are used when you want to have certain parts of your code repeated over and over until a condition is met or until the code has been executed a certain number of times. Loops are one of the most important tools you will use in your programs, so we will demonstrate here how loops are implemented in Java. Java provides three basic kinds of loops: while loops, do loops, and for loops.

while

The first type of loop that Java provides is called a while loop. A while loop checks to see if a condition is true and, if so, executes a statement or set of statements. After executing those statements, the condition is again checked. If it is still true, it executes the statements over again, continuing in the same fashion until the condition is finally false.

The basic form of the while loop is:

```
while (test-expression) loop-statements;
```

Here's an example that builds on the one we used for switch:

```
class WhileApp {
    public static void main (String args[]) {


        System.out.println("Please enter your number:");
        char c = (char)System.in.read();
        while (c <> '6') {
                System.out.println("Try again.");
                System.out.println("Please enter your number:");
                c = (char)System.in.read();
        }
        System.out.println("Correct.");
    }

}
```

This example will prompt you to enter a number. If you type any number other than 6, you'll be asked to try again. The character in the variable c is compared to 6 in the while statement:

```
while (c <> '6') {
```

This comparison is being made in the expression (c <> '6'). This expression evaluates to true if c is not 6. If the expression is true, the statements in the block following it are executed, then the condition is tried again.

do..while

We saw in the while loop above that the statements contained in the while loop get executed only if the test expression evaluates as true. Sometimes having the test condition take place at the end of the loop is desirable. The do..while loop is used in this case. The general form of the do..while loop is as follows:

```
do
    loop-statements
while (test-expression);
```

The statements in the do..while loop are always executed at least once and are executed again only if the loop condition evaluates to true. Here's an example similar
to the previous one, but this time it uses a do..while loop:

```
class DoWhileApp {
    public static void main (String args[]) {

        System.out.println("Please enter your number:");
        char c;
        do {
            System.out.println("Please enter your number:");
            c = (char)System.in.read();
        } while (c <> '6');
        System.out.println("Correct.");

    }

}
```

for

One of the more powerful types of loops is the for loop. The for loop is mainly
intended to be used to loop through a range of values, although it can be used in a
variety of different situations. The basic form of the for loop is:

```
for (initialization; test-expression; increment)
    loop-statements
```

To understand this better, compare a for loop to the while loop. A for loop is identical to:

```
{
    initialization;
    while (test-expression) {
        loop-statements
        increment;
    }
}
```

Let's look at some examples of how you can use for loops. The following example counts from 1 to 10:

```
class ForLoopApp {

    public static void main (String args[]) {


        int i;
        for (i = 1; i <= 5; i++) {

            System.out.println(i);

        }

    }

}
```

In this example, the variable i is initialized to 1, and the expression i <= 5 is evaluated, which checks to see if i is less than or equal to 5. If the expression evaluates as true, which it would in the first pass through the loop, then the statement System.out.println is executed. The expression i++, which increments i by 1, is then executed. The i <= 5 expression is then evaluated again, and the process continues until i is incremented to 6, at which time the test expression evaluates to false and the loop ends.

The output of the above example would look like this

```
1
2
3
4
5
```

Let's take a look at how you would use the same example to count down from 5 to 1:

```
class ForLoopApp2 {

    public static void main (String args[]) {


        for (int i = 5; i >= 1; i--) {

            System.out.println(i);

        }

    }

}
```

The main difference from the previous example is that we changed the incremen-tor expression from i++ to i--, as well as initializing i to 5 and changing the test expression to check for i being greater than or equal to 1. An important thing to notice about this example is that we changed where we declared the variable i from outside the loop to the initialization expression in the for statement. This defines the variable within the scope of the loop, which is good if your intent is to create a temporary variable for use within the loop; this can be a bad thing, though, if you want to use the value outside the loop because once you leave the loop, the variable disappears. If you're still unclear on this, take a look again at the description of the scope of a variable in relationship to blocks and compound statements in Chapter 5.

break

We saw break used in our discussion of the switch statement earlier. The break statement is also usable within most forms of loops to allow you to exit from a loop before the test condition is met. Let's take a look at another example of while loops where we use the break command to exit the loop:

```java
class WhileBreakApp {
    public static void main (String args[]) {

        int i = 1;
        while (true) {
            System.out.println(i);
            i++;
            if (i == 5)
                break;
        }
        System.out.println("Done.");
    }
}
```

The first thing you'll notice is that we use the literal Boolean value true as our test condition:

```java
while (true) {
```

This means that the loop will never exit in the normal fashion because the test expression will never be false. This is often referred to as an *infinite loop*, something you usually try to avoid. In this case, however, we're going to use it to illustrate how to exit a loop with the break command. In the above example, we initialize the variable i to 1 and then enter the while loop. Each pass through the loop we increment the i variable by 1 and then test its value with the following statement:

```
if (i == 5)
   break;
```

This is your basic if statement in which we test the value of i to see if it is equal to 5. If so, we execute the break statement and exit the loop, continuing execution with the line:

```
System.out.println("Done.");
```

continue

Continue is used to start execution from the top of a loop without having to execute the remaining statements in the loop. It can be useful when you want to skip certain statements in complicated loop code. Here's an example based on the for loop example we used earlier:

```
class ForLoopContinueApp {
   public static void main (String args[]) {

      int i;
      for (i = 1; i <= 5; i++) {
         if (i==3) continue;
         System.out.println(i);
      }
   }
}
```

In this loop, when i equals 3, the continue statement is executed, which causes the loop to skip executing the remainder of the loop. This means that the program's output will look like this:

```
1
2
4
5
```

Notice that 3 was skipped. You may have noticed that this example could have just as easily been done with an if statement, along the lines of the following:

```
for (i = 1; i <= 5; i++) {
    if (i!=3) {
        System.out.println(i);
    }
```

This is just another case where you can accomplish the same thing through several different methods. Actually, in some of the more complex examples in Part 3, you'll see where the choice of how to build a loop can make a big difference in code readability.

Labels

A *label* is an identifier that you use to name a particular statement so that you can cause the flow of control to jump to it by executing a break or continue statement. This is an important area where Java differs from C: Java has no goto statement, so if you are used to using labels in conjunction with gotos, you should pay particular attention here.

Where you can use a label depends on whether you intend to use it with a break statement or a continue statement. With a break statement, the label can be any enclosing statement, while a continue statement must use the label of an enclosing loop. Let's take a look at what we mean by this. The following example uses break to exit a statement block (which can be used anywhere you can use a statement):

```
int i = 0;
test: {
    if (i == 0) break test;
    System.out.println(1 / i);
    ...
}
System.out.println("Done.");
```

In this example, we use the label test to name the block defined within the two brackets. The line:

```
if (i == 0) break test;
```

checks to see if the variable i is equal to 0 and, if so, exits the test statement block. The flow of execution jumps to the next statement outside the block and continues with the line:

```
System.out.println("Done.");
```

If the enclosing statement block is a loop, the break statement can be used to break out of a nested loop. We see an example of this in the following code fragment:

```
loop1: for (int rows = 0; i < 100; i++) {
    loop2: for (int cols = 0; j < 100; j++) {
        if ((char)System.in.read() == 'q') break loop1;
        ...
    }
}
System.out.println("Done.");
```

This code fragment is part of a program that reads character input into a table of values until the table is full or the 'q' character is read. If the 'q' character is read, the break statement is executed with the loop1 label, which causes both loops to be exited and execution to continue with the line:

```
System.out.println("Done.");
```

Labels can also be used with the continue statement. In this case, the label must be applied to a loop statement. As you'll recall from our introduction of the continue statement, it causes flow of control to jump to the next iteration of the enclosing loop. In the case of nested loops, like the one we saw in the last example, you may find the need to use the continue statement with a label in order to jump to the next iteration of an outer loop. Let's use the code fragment from the previous example with a small change to show how the continue statement works:

```
loop1: for (int rows = 0; i < 100; i++) {
    loop2: for (int cols = 0; j < 100; j++) {
        if ((char)System.in.read() == 'x') continue loop1;
        if ((char)System.in.read() == 'q') break loop1;
```

```
        . . .
     }
  }
  System.out.println("Done.");
```

In this example, we want to stop reading columns in a given row and skip to the next row if we encounter the 'x' character. We do this by using the continue statement with the label loop1, which causes the flow of control to jump to the next iteration of the outer loop. If we had not explicitly used the outer loop's label with the continue statement, that statement would have instead caused the inner loop to jump to the next iteration.

OBJECTS

AND CLASSES

In Chapter 3 we covered objects from a conceptual standpoint. In this chapter, we will deal with objects in more concrete detail.

Let's quickly review the basics of object-oriented programming, starting with its differences from traditional languages. In a traditional language such as C, you create a program by determining the task you want your program to accomplish and then figuring out the steps or *procedures* that are needed to accomplish that task. The code you write is essentially the result of breaking those steps down until you are describing them as actual lines of code. Code is organized into *functions*, and in general, you create a new function every time you find that a particular series of instructions needs to be used more than once or from various places in your program. For many types of programs, procedural programming is adequate. However, many applications, especially interactive ones, become very cumbersome to program solely through procedural means.

In an object-oriented language, you create a program by first determining what objects the program will use to accomplish its goal or what types of real-world objects will be simulated in your code. For each kind of object, you determine what data the object needs to contain, and what *messages* the object should respond to. For example, if you were creating a drawing program, you might organize your program around geometric objects such as lines, circles, and rectangles. A line object would want to contain data that described its location on the screen, and it might want to respond to messages that indicated that it had been click on or resized.

Now, let's review the basic terminology of objects. An object is a combination of code (functions) and data (variables) joined together into a single entity. An object's functions are referred to as *methods* or *member functions* and its data is referred to as *member data* or *properties*. Calling a specific method in an object is described as sending the object a message.

A *class* is essentially a description of how to make an object. Every object has a class which is used to determine how to create the object, what variables the object will contain, and what messages the object will respond to. To make creating new classes faster and simpler, a new class can be a *subclass* of an existing class. A subclass is able to use the variables and methods of its parent class; this is called *inheritance*. A parent class can, in turn, be a subclass of another class. Classes inherit methods and variables up the *chain of inheritance*, which means that if class B is a subclass of class A, and class C is a subclass of class B, then class C inherits from both class A and class B.

An object is created or *instantiated* from a class. The object is also referred to as an *instance* of the class. When an object is created, memory is allocated for the object's data. This data exists in the form of variables inside the object, and these variables are called *instance variables*. When a message is sent to an object, the object is called the target of the message, and the method that gets executed or *invoked* in response to the message is able to access the instance variables belonging to the target object.

For the most part, all of the memory allocated in a Java program is in the form of objects instantiated from classes. When an object is created, it is assigned a *reference*. This reference is a special type of value that you use whenever you want to perform any sort of action on the object. You typically store this object reference in a variable, so that you can use the object again later in your program. When an object is no longer in use (i.e., no references to the object are stored in any variables anywhere in your program), the object is automatically disposed of and the memory it used is freed for use by other objects. The process of automatically freeing unused objects is referred to as *garbage collection*, which is an important aspect of the language in that it frees you from having to deal with the types of memory management issues that plague a typical C or C++ program.

In this chapter, we will go into classes and objects in depth. In many cases, we face a chicken-and-egg situation in trying to introduce certain features of classes or objects, considering that some of these features (like instance variables) are defined in the class, but are used only once the object has been created. This is one of the reasons why we introduced these ideas from a conceptual standpoint in Chapter 3 and quickly summarized them in the preceding paragraphs. In spite of this, and despite our best intentions, you might find it necessary to go over this chapter a second time in order to understand the concepts.

Using Classes

With all the talk of objects and object-oriented programming, it's sometimes easy to forget that to program anything in Java, you've got to start first with classes. You've seen classes in use in the various implementations of our small sample:

```
class SimpleApp {

    public static void main (String args[]) {

        System.out.println("Hello");

    }
}
```

In the above example,. we've got a class named SimpleApp with a single method called main(). A Java application is simply a class that contains a main() method. When the Java interpreter is told to run a specific class such as SimpleApp, it sends a main message to the class. At this point, you may have a few questions:

- Is a message sent to the class and not to an object?
- What do the various keywords such as class, public, static, and void mean?

By the time we finish this chapter, you will understand what just about everything in the above example means (with a few exceptions; we won't cover arrays and strings until later).

Class Definition

The class definition is the program code that defines all the specific details of a class that are needed to use it in a program. The minimum requirement for a class is that it has a name. For example, the following would be a valid although mostly useless class definition:

```
class Nothing {

}
```

This definition defines a class named Nothing, with the rest of the class definition empty. Let's take a look at the basic form of a class definition:

```
class classname [extends classname] [implements interface] {
    [variable declaration;]
    [method declaration;]
}
```

Let's fill in the details and create a simple class that contains a single variable and two methods:

```
class Lamp {
    boolean power_on;

    void SetState(boolean on_state) {
        power_on = on_state;
    }

    void PrintState() {
        if (power_on) {
            System.out.println("Lamp is on");
        }
        else {
            System.out.println("Lamp is off");
```

```
        }
    }
}
```

This class is named lamp and will create objects that contain a single instance variable power_on and respond to two messages: SetState and PrintState. As we mentioned earlier, in order to respond to a message, we need first to have a method defined. In the above example, we have defined two methods called SetState() and PrintState(). When objects created from this class are sent the SetState or PrintState messages, the code contained in those methods will be executed. Also, each object of the Lamp class will contain a variable named power_on, which in our code we use to indicate whether a Lamp object is turned on or off. Now let's take a closer look at methods and variables.

Methods

We saw in the last example that methods are used to *bind* code with objects. You may be accustomed to creating functions when writing a program using a traditional language. In an object-oriented language, you instead create methods, and in keeping with the philosophy of object-oriented programming, you place these methods within the objects whose data you intend to use the methods to manipulate. For example, in the Lamp class, we put the method to turn on the lamp in the lamp class alongside the variable that contained the state of the lamp.

Let's take a look at the basic form of a method:

```
[Modifiers] return-type method-name (parameter-list) {
    [statements;]
}
```

We'll skip the modifiers part for now. The return-type specifies what type of value will be returned. This can be any of the simple data types we've talked about so far, as well as class types. The method name is an identifier that must follow the rules of naming that we talked about in Chapter 4. The parameter list is always enclosed in parentheses and must be present even if it is empty. The parameter list contains the type and variable name of all the values we want to be able to pass to the method. The rest of the method is the actual code of the method. Let's take a look at the method from the previous example:

```
void SetState(boolean on_state) {
    power_on = on_state;
}
```

What we're looking at here is a fairly basic, although not uncommon, type of method definition. We see that the method has a return type of void. This means that the method does not return a value. As noted in earlier chapters, Java uses the C function syntax for defining methods, so this may look familiar to you. In other languages, such as Visual Basic or Pascal, you need to make distinctions between subroutines and functions depending on whether they return a value. Java, like C, uses the same syntax whether or not a method (function) returns a value. If we had used the type int instead of void, the method would be expected to return a value of type int when it completed executing.

The method name in our example is SetState; this is the name we would use to invoke this method in a method call. Following the method name is the parameter list. In the case of this example, we have a single parameter, a boolean value that is passed to the method in the variable named on_state. Recalling our discussion of scope in Chapter 6, we can say that this variable is local to the scope of the SetState method. This means that this variable exists only within this method. Its value is loaded when the method is called. We'll talk about calling methods in the next section.

Inside the method declaration is the code that gets executed when the method is invoked. In this case, we have a single line where the variable power_on is assigned the value contained in the variable on_state. Again, recalling our discussion of variables in Chapter 6, you may be wondering where the variable power_on came from, since it is not declared in this method. power_on is an instance variable defined in the class declaration. This variable exists in every object created from the Lamp class. You can access this variable from any method within the Lamp class. In terms of scope, this means that your member variables are local to the scope of the Lamp class.

An important aspect of Java is that Java requires all variables to be initialized before you use them. In the case of instance variables, initialization is done automatically. However, the local variables that you use in your methods must be initialized before they are used. Simply put, you must put a value into a variable before you can use it in an expression that needs to use the variable's contents. This is part of the design philosophy of Java, whose intent is to eliminate the most common sources of bugs in programs. Forgetting to set the value of a variable before you use it is a frequent source of errors in languages like C. The following example demonstrates a method declaration that would result in a compiler error if you tried to compile it:

```java
void BadVariableExample () {
    int some_variable;
    System.out.println(some_variable + 1);
}
```

In this example, we try to print out the value of some_variable + 1 before first putting a value into some_variable. You could fix this method by simply assigning a value to some_variable before trying to use it, like this:

```java
void GoodVariableExample () {
    int some_variable;
    some_variable = 5;
    System.out.println(some_variable + 1);
}
```

Most of the time, you'll just declare and initialize the variable in one line, like this:

```java
void GoodVariableExample () {
    int some_variable = 5;
    System.out.println(some_variable + 1);
}
```

Overloaded Methods

Java supports overloaded methods. An *overloaded method* is a method that you can call with different sets of parameter lists. This let's you create several different versions of your method to make calling it from various places in your program

easier, or in the case of library code, more versatile than different types of programs. We will cover overloaded methods in a little more detail because they're an
important concept that you'll need to understand before we can properly discuss
constructors in the next section. Keep in mind that the Java API classes (*packages*)
use overloaded methods.

Let's take a look at an example where you have created a progress bar object that
shows the progress of a lengthy operation in the form of a thermometer-style
progress bar. We won't get into the actual details of how this object would draw
itself right now; instead we'll concentrate on how you would build such an object
so that you could use it from different programs. Your object would look something like this:

```
class ProgressBar {
    float percent_done;

    void SetProgress(float new_percent_done) {
        percent_done = new_percent_done;
    }
}
```

Just to make sure you've been following the considerable amount of new material
we've introduced so far, let's do a quick recap. The above code defines a class called
ProgressBar. It has one instance variable called percent_done, and (so far) one
method called SetProgress. The SetProgress method is called with a value of type
float, which it holds in the parameter list variable new_percent_done. When the
SetProgress method is called, it takes the value that has been passed to in new_
percent_done and stores it in percent_done. We hope you've followed this far. If
you're still a little puzzled, take a few minutes to review some of the earlier
sections, then look at the listing again.

Let's assume that in a real program you would use a more complicated version of
this object, which updated the on-screen progress bar each time you sent the
SetProgress message to the object with a new float value indicating the percentage
done. Let's further assume that a value of 0 would mean that nothing had yet been
done, and that a value of 1 would indicate that the operation was complete. In

some other part of your program you might have the following line of code where you called the SetProgress method:

```
float done_value;
done_ratio = items_processed / total_items;
myProgressBar.SetProgress(done_ratio);
```

In this fragment, we've got a variable called items_ processed that contains the number of items that have been processed in some lengthy operation. The variable total_items contains the total number of items to be processed. To use these values to call SetProgress, we need to create a ratio of the values and store it in a temporary variable. If you notice that you needed to do this same thing before calling SetProgress in several places in your code, it probably indicates that overloading the SetProgress method would be useful. Let's take a look at how this might be done:

```
class ProgressBar {
    float percent_done;

    void SetProgress(float new_percent_done) {
        percent_done = new_percent_done;
    }

    void SetProgress(int items_done, int items_total) {
        percent_done = items_done / items_total;
    }
}
```

In this version of the ProgressBar class, you can see that we've added a second SetProgress method, which takes two parameters instead of one like the original. You'll also notice that the original method still exists. This means that in your programs, you'll be able to call SetProgress with either set of parameters, and Java will determine which version of the method to call by looking at which method's parameter list most closely matches the actual parameters passed. Now that SetProgress has been overloaded, both lines of code would be valid:

```
myProgressBar.SetProgress(done_ratio);

myProgressBar.SetProgress(items_processed, total_items);
```

Notice that we said that Java will determine which version of the method to call by looking at which method's parameter list *most closely matches* the actual parameters passed. This might have set you thinking what was meant by that and how Java determines what "most closely matches" means. In the above example, we call SetProgress with the variables items_processed and total_items. The SetProgress method is defined as accepting two values of type int. It would still be possible to call that version of the SetProgress method if you passed two values of type char, or even of type float. In this case, Java will automatically cast the values to the appropriate type before calling the method. Now, what if we had added a third overloaded version of SetProgress that looked like the following:

```
void SetProgress(long items_done, long items_total) {
    percent_done = items_done / items_total;
}
```

If we were to call SetProgress with two values of type float, this method would be called instead of the SetProgress method, defined as being called with two values of type int. In this case you might wonder how Java decides to cast the float values to long values and calls this SetProgress method instead of casting them to int values and calling the previous SetProgress method. The answer is that Java assigns a cost to each type of value conversion, and it chooses the version of the method that involves the least conversion cost to call. The cost of converting from one type of value to another is illustrated in Table 7.1.

Table 7.1 Cost of Converting from One Type of Value to Another

From:	To:						
	byte	short	char	int	long	float	double
byte	0	1	2	3	4	6	7
short	10	0	10	1	2	4	5
char	11	10	0	1	2	4	5
int	12	11	11	0	1	5	4
long	12	11	11	10	0	6	5
float	15	14	13	12	11	0	1
double	16	15	14	13	12	10	0

In cases where the conversion cost is greater than 10, precision is lost; the compiler will alert you to this fact. In the case of our previous example, calling the method with two float values would result in the choice of a conversion cost of converting a float to long of 11 or a float to int of 12. Because 11 is less than 12, the compiler is going to choose to convert the float to a long integer. Because the cost is greater than 10, precision will be lost, and the compiler will warn you of this fact.

Member Variables

We saw a simple case of using variables within classes in the last example. In your programs, in addition to using classes for the types of objects we've talked about, you will also use classes to create container objects that do not contain any code. Let's take a look at a class that shows how you might have multiple variables in a class without defining any methods:

```
class DateObject {
    int Day;
    int Month;
    int Year;
}
```

This example class contains three integer variables for the day, month, and year needed to specify a particular date. Every time you needed to have a variable that contained a date, you could declare it as type DateObject and create a DateObject object to store the values. This would be more convenient, especially if you needed to store a number of dates throughout your program. By the way, for readers who may have skipped ahead or have any familiarity with the Java utility classes, don't confuse this DateObject class with the Date class that comes with java.util. This is just an example that we're going to use to illustrate some points.

Most times when you use classes, you will have both methods and variables within the class. Variables in classes are accessible by all the methods in the class. One way of looking at this is to extend the concept of scope that we introduced in Chapter 3. All the member variables and methods are within the scope of the class, which means that the code within a method can "see" the member variables, but can't see the variables inside other methods, and cannot automatically see the variables in other objects. Let's take a look at what this means in the following example:

```
class Test {
    int a;

    void method_1 (int b) {
        int c;

        // from here we can see variables a, b, and c
        a = 1;    // legal - a belongs to class Test
        c = 5;    // legal - c is local to method_1
        b = 10;   // ok - b is local to method,
                  // but its unusual to write
                  // to parameter list variables

        // from inside method_1 we cannot see variables d and e
    }

    void method_2 (int d) {
        int e;
        // from here we can see variables a, d, and e
        a = 1;    // legal - a belongs to class Test
        e = 5;    // legal - c is local to method_2
        d = 10;   // ok - but unusual to write
                  // to parameter list variable

        // from inside method_2 we cannot see variables b and c
    }
}
```

In the last section, we pointed out that variables in Java must be initialized before they are used. We haven't followed this rule with member variables, and we should take a moment to point out why. When an object is instantiated, all the member variables are initialized to 0 or null. However, you can still use initializers to automatically initialize a variable to a specific value when the object is created. For example:

```
class DateObject {
    int Day = 14;
    int Month = 4;
    int Year = 68;
}
```

Using Final Variables as Constants

Sometimes you want to refer to a value by name, but you don't want to change the value in your code. Obviously, you could just avoid writing any code that changes the variable's contents; however, the language gives you a way to make sure that if you make a mistake and inadvertently try to change the value, the compiler will warn you of it. This is achieved by using the *final* keyword. The final keyword is used in a number of other areas of the language, but right now we'll talk about how it applies to member variables.

To specify that a variable is final, you precede the variable type with the final keyword, as in the following example, where we create a constant final variable to hold the maximum value for months:

```
class DateObject {
    int Day = 14;
    int Month = 4;
    int Year = 68;
    final int Max_Month = 12;        // cant be changed
}
```

A benefit of using final variables is that the compiler is able to optimize the byte code it creates so that it will run faster than if you were using a non-final variable.

Constructors

Initializers are one of the tools that you'll use to ensure that a newly created object has been properly set up. The other is *constructors*. A constructor is a function that gets called when an object is created; it is used to perform any further initialization code that you need executed.

Constructors are defined as methods that have the same name as their class. It's important to note that a constructor method has no return value. Here is an example of the DateObject class with a constructor method:

```
class DateObject {
    int Day = 1;
    int Month = 1;
    int Year = 1900;

    DateObject() {
        Year = 1995;
    }
}
```

In this example, we introduced a constructor method that would get called when a DateObject object was created. In this example, the constructor simply sets the Year variable to 1995. You may have noticed that the constructor doesn't have a parameter list. A constructor that takes no parameters is called the *default constructor* because it is called if an object is created without any parameters. A default constructor is automatically created by the Java compiler if you don't explicitly create one.

In the section earlier in this chapter on methods, we discussed method overloading. Constructors can be overloaded in the same way, and in many cases it is desirable to have several versions of a constructor available when you create an object. (This will make more sense later in this chapter when we show you how to create an object.) When you create a new object from a class, you can specify a number of parameters to be passed to the constructor. If you don't specify any parameters, the default constructor is called. If you do specify parameters, the appropriate constructor method will be used. Here's another example using the DateObject class that let's you create a DateObject object using either the default constructor, in which case it initializes the date to 1995, or by passing values for the day, month, and year:

```
class DateObject {
    int Day = 1;
    int Month = 1;
```

```
    int Year = 1900;

    DateObject() {
       Year = 1995;
    }

    DateObject(int new_month, int new_day, int new_year) {
       Day = new_day;
       Month = new_month;
       Year = new_year;
    }
 }
```

Static Methods and Variables

In the previous sections we've seen how methods and variables work. We will now introduce static methods and variables, which are different from normal methods and variables in that they are part of the class rather than the object created from the class. In all the examples we've seen so far, an object had to be created for the methods or member variables to be used. Static variables and methods can be used at almost any time, as we'll see in this section.

Static variables are used when you want to have a variable common to all instances of an object. One of the most common examples of this is having a variable that keeps count of how many objects of a class have been created. The following example demonstrates this and shows both static and normal variables used in a class:

```
 class SpaceAlien {
    boolean alive;
    static int alien_count = 0;

    void SpaceAlien () {
       alive = true;
       alien_count++;
    }
```

```
void Blast() {
    if (alive) {
        alive = false;
        alien_count−;
    }
}
}
```

The SpaceAlien class is an example of the type of class you might use if you were creating a video game. Every time an object is instantiated from this class, the constructor is called. As you can see, the SpaceAlien constructor performs two actions. The first is to set the instance variable alive to true. The second is to increment the value of the static variable alien_count. This example illustrates the difference between static variables and instance variables. The variable alive is an instance variable, so there is a copy of it in every instance of the SpaceAlien class; when you assign a value to it, only the copy that is part of the current instance is modified. The alien_count variable is a static variable, which means that there is only one copy of it shared by all the instances of the SpaceAlien class. In this example, because every time a SpaceAlien object is created we increment the value of alien_count, at all times the value of alien_count will contain the total number of SpaceAlien objects that have been created.

Use static methods when you want to have methods that can be called without having to instantiate an object. There are several reasons you might want to do this. One of the most common reasons is to have a method that creates an object of the target class and returns it. We'll see some examples of this later in the chapter. You will also use static methods if you have "global" functions that should be associated with a specific class. Static methods are defined the same way that normal methods are defined, except that they are preceded with the keyword static; the code inside the method cannot access any non-static member variables. In the next example, we show how you can use static methods to provide utilities methods to the rest of your program:

```
class MathStuff {
    static int SquareIt(int x) {
        return x * x;
```

```
        }
    }
    static int HalfIt(int x) {
        return x / 2;
        }
    }
}


class SomeClass {
    void SomeMethod() {
        int i = MathStuff.SquareIt(4);
        int j = MathStuff.HalfIt(i);
        System.out.println(j);
    }
}
```

In this example, we have two methods that we want to use in a number of places in our program. Because these methods do not need any data other than what they are passed as parameters, instantiating the object that contains them is unnecessary. If these methods were useful to several classes, copying them into each of the classes would be wasteful. One way to make these methods available is to make them static methods in a "utility" class. Because these are static methods, we can call the methods directly, without having to instantiate the object first. When we call a static method, we have the option of calling the method using the form:

```
    class_name.static_method_name(parameters);
```

We use this form when we call SquareIt() and HalfIt() from the SomeMethod() method.

A variation of static methods is static initialization code, which is code that gets executed when a class is loaded. This is useful when you want to create constant data that is useful to all the instances and subclasses of a class. Here's an example where we use some static initialization code to fill in a name table:

```
    class Users {
        static String user_list[] = new String[5];
```

```
    static {
        user_list[0] = "Ed";
        user_list[1] = "Joe";
        user_list[2] = "Brett";
        user_list[3] = "Scott";
        user_list[4] = "Oliver";
    }
}
```

In this example, we fill an array of strings using static initialization code. We won't cover arrays until later chapters, but since static initialization code is often used to fill static array elements, it makes sense to show them here.

Most static initialization code is used to initialize variables, but there is no actual requirement that it be used this way. For example, you might want, for debugging purposes, to have something printed out when a class is loaded into the system. You could do this like so:

```
class Users {
    static String user_list[] = new String[5];
    static {
        user_list[0] = "Ed";
        user_list[1] = "Joe";
        user_list[2] = "Brett";
        user_list[3] = "Scott";
        user_list[4] = "Oliver";
        System.out.println("Users loaded and initialized.");
    }
}
```

This is actually an interesting thing to do because it let's us see exactly when a class gets loaded into the system. This will become more important later when we see how classes can be loaded over a network or the Internet. If we had another class that used the Users class, we would see that the class was not actually loaded (and the static initialization code executed) until an object was instantiated from the Users class, or a static variable or method was accessed or invoked.

Working with Objects

We've talked about the various issues in defining classes in order to create objects, but until now, you may not have had a very clear picture of what happened to these objects once they were created. In this section, we're going to fill in the blanks for these details, and you're going to see why we introduced classes first, even though, in a few cases, some of the concepts introduced have been difficult to explain without talking about how objects are created. That said, let's get started with how to create objects.

Creating Objects

An object in Java is essentially a block of memory that contains space to store all the instance variables contained in an object (as well as some other data that Java uses internally). Creating an object is also referred to as *allocating* or *instantiating* it, and it is the only way to allocate memory in Java (outside of local variables or static class variables).

Objects are instantiated by using the new operator. The new operator creates an object of the specified type and calls the appropriate constructor for the parameters passed in the parameter list. It then returns an *object reference* to the newly created object. We'll talk more about object references in the next section; it is enough to know at the moment that a reference is a special kind of value that can be assigned, compared, and otherwise used as long as you don't try to perform any operations on it. Java uses object references to refer to specific objects. In other languages, object references usually exist as *memory addresses* or *pointers*, but because Java doesn't allow pointer or direct memory manipulation, object references in Java can't be manipulated using techniques like *pointer arithmetic* that you might be accustomed to using in languages like C.

Let's take a look at allocating an object from one of the classes we talked about in the previous section:

```
DateObject theDate;
theDate = new DateObject();
```

In the above example we first declare a variable to hold the object reference that is going to be returned by new. In most cases you're going to want to keep a reference to the newly created object, so your code will be some variation of this. The action takes place when we call new in the next line. Notice that we provide a class name and parameter list when we call new. In this case, the class is DataObject, and the parameter list is empty. As you might have surmised, this is going to allocate an object of type DateObject and call the default DateObject constructor method. If we had passed parameters in the parameter list, like this:

```
DateObject theDate;

theDate = new DateObject(4, 14, 68);
```

the constructor method whose parameters most closely matched the passed parameters, using the rules of overloaded methods, would be called instead of the default constructor.

Object References

Once we've allocated an object and have stored the returned object reference, we can use the object reference in a variety of ways. Object references are used to access variables and methods in other objects. For example, assume you've allocated a DateObject and stored it into the object reference variable theDate, as demonstrated in the previous example. Now suppose you wanted to access one of the instance variables contained in that object from a method in a different object. To do this, you would need to use the object reference and the object accessor operator (.) to access the variable. Let's look at an example:

```
DateObject theDate;

theDate = new DateObject(4, 14, 1968);

theDate.Year = 1995;
```

In this example, we store the value 1995 into the instance variable of the DateObject object referred to by theDate. Methods are called in the same way. Let's take a look at an example that uses the Lamp class shown earlier in this chapter:

```
Lamp theLamp;

theLamp = new Lamp();

theLamp.SetState(true);

theLamp.PrintState();
```

In this example, we send the SetState message to the object referenced by theLamp, then follow that by sending the PrintState message.

this

Java provides you with a special read-only variable (i.e., a variable whose value you can't change) that contains a reference to the current object appropriately named this. You can use the this variable to get a reference to the current object in order to pass it to a method in another object. Let's take a look at an example where we would do this, which will also show off some of the other features we've learned about:

```java
class LightBulb {
  Lamp myLamp;

  LightBulb (Lamp theLamp) {
    myLamp = theLamp;
  }

  void PrintState() {
    if (myLamp.power_on) {
      System.out.println("Lamp is on");
    }
    else {
      System.out.println("Lamp is off");
    }
  }
}


class Lamp {
  boolean power_on;
  LightBulb myLightBulb;

  Lamp() {
    myLightBulb = new LightBulb(this);
  }

  void SetState(boolean on_state) {
```

```
        power_on = on_state;
    }

}
```

In this example, we create a LightBulb object in the Lamp constructor and pass a reference to the Lamp object to the LightBulb object's constructor method using the this variable. In this way, the LightBulb object can refer back to the Lamp object that created it as needed. In this example, we use this technique so that the LightBulb object can tell whether the Lamp object is on or off. Most serious Java programs will consist of a number of interlocking objects that are tied together by passing object references to each other in much the same way.

Another important use of the this variable is to differentiate between the usage of local variables and instance variables of the same name. For example, in a constructor, you may have parameters with the same name as the class's instance variables (remember, parameter variables and local variables):

```
class Lamp {
    boolean power_on;
    LightBulb myLightBulb;

    Lamp() {
        myLightBulb = new LightBulb(this);
    }

    Lamp(boolean power_on) {
        this.power_on = power_on;
        myLightBulb = new LightBulb(this);
    }

    void SetState(boolean on_state) {
        power_on = on_state;
    }

}
```

In the above code fragment, we see an example of using the this variable in this way. This example is essentially the same as the previous example, with the addition of the overloaded second version of the constructor. We decided that it would be nice to be able to create a new Lamp object and pass a value to the constructor to be used as the initial value of the power_on variable. Because the parameter variable is essentially used to hold the value being passed, and is used nowhere else in the method, we might decide that we don't want to come up with a new (and potentially not as clear) name for the parameter variable. In this case, we used the same name as the instance variable for the parameter variable. We now have a problem because local variables of the same name as instance variables take precedence, so that any assignments or access of the variable will refer to the local variable (in this case, the parameter variable), instead of the instance variable. To do this, we again make use of the this variable to explicitly indicate that we are talking about the instance variable named power_on and not the local parameter list variable named power_on:

```
Lamp(boolean power_on) {
    this.power_on = power_on;
    myLightBulb = new LightBulb(this);
}
```

null

For the most part, the value that gets stored in the object reference is not known to your program. You assign the value to variables and pass it to other methods, but you don't really use it like other values. The exception to this occurs when you use the null object reference value. You can assign null to any variable that can contain an object reference, and some methods return null to indicate that they were not able to allocate a specific object. You can also test an object reference to see if it is equal to null. If it is null, then the reference is invalid (i.e., refers it to an object that doesn't exist). If it is not null, then it is valid, and you can use it. Here is a code fragment which shows the typical test of an object reference:

```
if (myLightBulb != null) {
    System.out.println("Lightbulb exists");
}
```

Operators and Object References

As we've seen already, object references are values that can be used in comparison expressions. You will use three operators with object references, as listed in Table 7.2.

■■■■■■■■■ **Table 7.2** Operators for Object Reference

operator	meaning
==	equals
!=	is not equal
instanceof	is instance of class

We've seen the equality (==) and inequality (!=) operators used in previous examples. They can be used to determine whether two object references refer to the same object or whether an object reference does not refer to any object, in which case the reference equals null.

The third operator that can be used with object references is the instanceof operator. This operator allows you to determine whether the object referred to by an object reference was instantiated from a given class or one of its subclasses. For example, the following code uses the instanceof operator to test whether it is safe to send a message to an object if we don't know the class of a message that will only be understood by objects instantiated from a specific class or one of its subclasses:

```
if (someObject instanceof Lamp) {
    ((Lamp)someObject).SetState(true);
}
```

In this example, we've got in the variable someObject a reference to an object whose class we don't know. You'll see how you can get into this situation when we explore inheritance in the next section. To understand this example, you'll need to know that not only is it not uncommon, but also often desirable, to deal with objects without knowing much about the specific class from which they have been instantiated. In the above example, we can imagine that the code is part of some program that deals with a number of objects of different types, perhaps cataloging and sorting them. At some point in the program, it becomes necessary to take a closer look at an object and do something that is applicable only to its particular class. In the case of the Lamp object, we want to turn it on using the SetState() method. To prevent attempting to send the SetState message to an object that doesn't respond to that message, we first check the class of the object using the instanceof operator. If the test returns true, then we know that it is safe to proceed. The next line uses a technique called casting to treat the object reference stored in someObject as a reference to an object of class Lamp. You'll learn more about casting later in this chapter.

Understanding Inheritance

One of the most important benefits of object-oriented programming is the concept of *inheritance*. Inheritance allows you to solve a problem by first focusing on generalities, that is, by determining what aspects the different objects you're working with have in common, and then going back and working on the specifics of how these objects are different from one another. This involves designing classes that are either *base classes*, which represent the generalized model or abstraction of the type of objects you are dealing with, or *derived classes*, which represent specialized objects constructed by customizing the base class for a specific purpose.

From a conceptual standpoint, this means that once a class has been defined, a second class can be defined by stating that the new class is based on the first class, then proceeding to describe the differences in the methods and variables. In practice, you use this technique by developing base classes for the broad classifications of the types of objects you need to deal with (i.e., a vehicle class) and then creating a new class derived from the base class by describing the differences (i.e., a bicycle class based on the vehicle class inherits its ability to move and adds the fact that it has two wheels; the automobile class is also based on the vehicle class but has four wheels).

When using inheritance in your programs, you will probably spend only half your time dealing with these textbook object design situations. Inheritance is also the way you make use of classes that exist within class libraries or, using Java's terminology, *packages*. In these cases, a class you wish to use might already exist (for example, a button class), but it doesn't perform exactly the way you want. In this case, you would create a subclass of the provided class that incorporates the changes you need to make. This saves you the time of writing a class from scratch by allowing you to focus on making the (often small) change in functionality you need and inheriting the rest of the original class "as is."

Strictly speaking, all classes in Java are subclasses in that they are automatically created as subclasses of the *root class* Object if they are not declared as a subclass of some other object. At some point, every object in Java inherits from Object. You'll want to refer to the Java API reference regarding the significance of this for the methods and variables that your objects will automatically inherit.

Subclassing

Subclassing is the process by which you actually derive one class from another. The new class can be called a *subclass*, *child class*, or *derived class* of the original class—all the terms are synonymous. To understand the syntax of creating a new class as a subclass, let's revisit the general form of a class definition:

```
class classname [extends classname] [implements interface] {
    variable declaration;
    method declaration;
}
```

You'll notice that we boldfaced the part of the class definition where we define the class on which the new class is based. Let's look at a very simple example that shows how this works:

```
class Feline {
    boolean hungry = true;
    void speak() {
    }
    void call() {
        System.out.println("Here kitty, kitty, kitty...");
        if (hungry) speak();
    }
}

class HouseCat extends Feline {
    void speak() {
        System.out.println("Meow!");
```

```
        }
    }

    class Lion extends Feline {
        void speak() {
            System.out.println("Roar!!!");
        }
    }
```

In this example, we have a base class (Feline) and two subclasses (HouseCat and Lion). We first created a base class that contains a boolean variable called hungry and two methods called speak() and call(). The speak() method is the method that will be called by all the subclasses of Feline when they receive a speak message, unless the subclass chooses to implement its own version of speak. That's exactly what we do in the two subclasses to have HouseCat objects respond to the speak message differently (Meow!) from Lion objects (Roar!!!). We also define a call() method, which you will notice is present only in the Feline class. If I send a call message to a HouseCat object, because we didn't define a different call() method in the HouseCat class, the call() method in the Feline class is instead invoked. If we had chosen to, we could have accessed the contents of the hungry variable in the subclasses without having to do anything differently than if we were to access it in the base class. To the subclass, all the variables and method from the parent class look no different than if they were part of the subclass itself. That's inheritance and subclassing in a nutshell.

Final Classes

Sometimes you will want to prevent a class from being further subclassed—for code management reasons (perhaps you feel that a class shouldn't be subclassed for QA or security reasons) or simply because you have determined that a particular class will never be subclassed. You want the Java compiler to take advantage of the optimizations that it can apply to classes when it knows that a class won't be subclassed.

A class that can't be subclassed is called a final class; to define a class as final, you use the final keyword, which you might remember from the section on variables in

Chapter 3. The keyword is used as a modifier in the class definition; for example, if we wanted to make the HouseCat class a final class we would precede the class definition with the modifier keyword final:

```
final class HouseCat extends Feline {

    ...
```

If you then tried to compile a program that contained a subclass of HouseCat, the compiler would flag it as an error and not allow it.

Base Classes and Object References

In the last section we talked about how subclassing can be used to create a hierarchy of classes that are all descended from a common base class. In the last example we used, we had a simple class hierarchy with a Feline base class and two subclasses, HouseCat and Lion, descended from it. We talked a bit about which methods in these classes would be invoked in response to methods being sent to objects of a specific class. We will now expand somewhat on that topic.

By defining HouseCat as a subclass of Feline, we are saying that objects of type HouseCat are also types of Felines. This means that any message we can send to a Feline object can also be sent to a HouseCat object. If we follow this line of thought a little further, it implies that an object reference to a HouseCat object could be assigned to an object reference variable of type Feline. Let's look at what this means from a code standpoint:

```
Feline theCat;
theCat = new HouseCat();
theCat.speak();
```

The variable theCat is declared as holding a reference to an object of type Feline. In the next line, however, we assign an object of type HouseCat to the variable. We can do this because HouseCat is a subclass of Feline and is consequently a *compatible class*. In the next line where we invoke the speak() method of the object reference by theCat, it is the speak() method of the HouseCat class that gets invoked. If you were writing a program that dealt with a number of HouseCat and Lion objects, you would not have to know in advance to which object you were sending

messages. As long as you communicated with the object using methods present in
the parent class, you could be sure that the object would know how to respond to
the message you sent it.

The ability for an object to respond to the set of messages defined in superclasses of
the object's class with methods implemented in the object class is called *polymorphism*. The subclass "speaks the language" defined by the super (parent) classes,
but responds to messages using its own code, which may be very different from the
code defined in the superclasses. To make use of the power of polymorphism in
your objects, you will typically only use the specific subclass (like HouseCat in the
previous example) when creating an object. When talking to the object, you will
usually use the superclass (Feline in the previous example) as the type of the variable holding the object's reference value. This way, you are able to talk to the
object using the methods defined in the superclass without having to know that the
functionality of those methods has been changed in subclasses. Let's take a look at
another example:

```
class CatWorld {
    Feline cat_list[] = new Feline[3];

    void set_up_cat_list() {
            cat_list[0] = new HouseCat();
            cat_list[1] = new Lion();
            cat_list[2] = new HouseCat ();
        }
    }


    void speak_all() {
        for (int i = 0; i < cat_list.length, i++) {
            Feline theCat = cat_list[i];
            theCat.speak();
        }
    }
}
```

In this example, we give you another preview of arrays to show a typical use of polymorphism. First, we allocate an array that can hold three objects of type Feline. In the method set_up_cat_list(), we allocate two objects of type HouseCat and one object of type Lion and store them in the cat_list array. In the speak_all() method, we are able to cycle through the array and send the speak() message to each object. Because all the objects in this array are created from subclasses of Feline, they all know how to respond to this message. These subclasses, as we have seen, can either implement the code themselves to respond to the message or pass the message up the chain of inheritance until the superclass responds.

Because all objects are subclasses of the Object class, you can use the reference variables of the Object type to hold references to any Object in Java. This is important because Object has a number of important methods in it, such as clone(), which creates a duplicate of the object, and toString(), which returns a string representation of the object (you typically override this method in your classes, so that your object can return an appropriate string representation).

Casting between Class Types

In the previous section, we saw that we can assign subclass to a variable that is declared as holding a reference to the superclass. It is also possible to accomplish the reverse: assigning a reference of the type of the superclass to a reference variable of the type of the subclass. Let's take a look at a code fragment that should make this clearer:

```
HouseCat theCat;              // Declare theCat as type HouseCat
theCat = new HouseCat();   // theCat now contains a reference
                              // a new HouseCat object
Feline theFeline;             // Declare theFeline as type Feline
theFeline = thaCat;           // theFeline now refers to the same
                              // object as theCat
HouseCat aCat;                // Declare aCat as type HouseCat
aCat = (HouseCat)theFeline;   // We can cast theFeline to aCat
                              // because theFeline is a reference
                              // to a HouseCat object
```

In this example, only one object is actually created. The HouseCat object is created and a reference to it is stored in the variable theCat. The reference is then copied into the variable theFeline. As we saw in the last section, when we assign a reference to a variable of the type of the parent class, we can deal only with the methods and variables that are present in the superclass. As a consequence, you might need to convert the reference back to the type of the subclass. To do this, you need to cast the object reference using the syntax:

```
classname new_ref = (classname)old_ref;
```

Keep in mind that you cannot cast a reference to a subclass type. For example, the following cast would compile but would result in a run-time error:

```
HouseCat theCat = (HouseCat)new Feline();
```

This won't work because we are attempting to cast an object of the Feline base class to the HouseCat subclass type. Because the subclass could have methods and variables not present in the base class, the compiler must disallow the cast.

Overriding Methods

As we've observed in the previous sections, one of the main reasons why you would subclass one object from another is to create several different objects that you would refer to through the same object reference but that would respond in different ways to the same message. You would accomplish this by *overriding* methods in the subclasses. We've seen several examples of how you do this so far; in this section, we'll take a closer look at how methods are overridden and some of the issues involved.

A method is overridden when you implement a version of it in a subclass that has the exact same name, return type, and parameters as the original method in the parent class. We saw this in the Feline example:

```
class Feline {
...
    void speak() {
   }
...
}
```

```
class HouseCat extends Feline {

    void speak() {

        System.out.println("Meow!");

    }

}
```

In this case, the speak() method is overridden in the HouseCat class, which means that method calls to the speak method of a HouseCat object will be handled by the overriding method. If we hadn't overridden speak(), then method calls would fall through to the parent class.

The Super Variable and Overridden Methods

In previous sections, we saw how Java provides us with a special reference variable named this that contains a reference to the current object whose method is being executed. Java provides a similar variable called super that allows you to call methods and access variables from the immediate parent class. You will use this variable in a couple of different ways in your programs, but its main use is to invoke the original version of an overridden method.

Let's take a look at the two main uses of the super variable, which are using it to call the parent version of an overridden method and the parent version of an overridden constructor. First of all, let's look at a simple version of an overridden method that makes use of the super variable:

```
class HouseCat extends Feline {

    void speak() {

        System.out.println("Meow!");

    }

}


class MagicCat extends HouseCat {

    boolean people_present;

    void speak() {

        if (people_present)
```

```
            super.speak();
        else
            System.out.println("Hello!");
    }

  }
```

In this example, we've decided that we want to create a subclass of HouseCat to
represent a special type of cat that can talk when no one is around. When anyone is
present, the cat behaves like any other cat. We accomplish this by creating a subclass of HouseCat called MagicCat, and we override the speak() method. This
speak() method checks the value of the people_present variable and, depending on
its value, calls the parent class's speak method or continues with execution of the
method. You can see how the super variable is used in this case:

```
    void speak() {
        if (people_present)
            super.speak();
        else
            System.out.println("Hello!");
    }
```

The second main use of the super variable occurs within the class's constructor
method. In this case, you would use something like the following:

```
  class class_A {
      int value;

      class_A() {
          System.out.println("class_A default constructor");
      }

      class_A(int a) {
          value = a;
      }
  }

  class class_B extends class_A {
```

```
class_B(int a) {
    super(a);
    System.out.println("class_B constructed!");
}
}
```

In this example, we show how we use the super variable to specify which constructor in the parent class (class_A) is called when the subclass is instantiated. As you recall from our previous discussion of constructors, when a subclass is instantiated, no matter which constructor in the subclass is used, the default constructor for the superclass is called first. What we have done here is indicate that instead of using the default constructor, we want to use the overridden version of the constructor in the superclass. Let's take a closer look at the constuctor in class_B:

```
class class_B extends class_A {
    class_B(int a) {
        super(a);
        System.out.println("class_B constructed!");
    }
```

The statement super(a) indicates which version of the parent constructor to invoke. If you choose to use this technique in your code, you must have this statement as the first statement in your method. If you've used other object-oriented languages, you may be used to executing some code prior to calling the constructor in a parent class. In Java, the constructor in the parent class must be executed prior to executing code in the subclass's constructor.

There is one last thing to know about the super variable: Although it behaves in most ways like other object reference variables, it is handled specially by the language. You should avoid assigning its value to another variable because the results will not be what you expect. The easiest way to deal with this is simply to avoid statements like the following, where the value of super is assigned to another variable:

```
class_A theSupe = super; // OK - but not advised
```

If you do this, you would expect that these two statements would then be equivalent:

```
super.someMethod();
theSupe.someMethod();
```

The problem is that the first statement will invoke the method from the parent class, while the second statement will invoke the method of the subclass, even though you would think that it would also invoke the method from the parent class. The solution is not to store the value of the super variable into another variable, because in most cases where you think to do this, you'll find that you can probably accomplish your goal instead by using the value of the this variable.

Final Methods

In some cases, you will want to indicate that a method can't be overridden. Just as you can prevent a class from being subclassed by declaring it as final, you can also declare a method as final as well. In most languages, methods are assumed to be final unless otherwise specified. C++ is one example; if you want to override a method in C++, you must define it as a virtual function. Java takes the opposite approach in that it assumes that you will want to override methods unless you explicitly mark them as final. You might declare a method as final if you want to prevent its functionality from being changed through subclassing for security reasons. Declaring a method as final allows the compiler to perform certain optimizations in your code that will result in faster programs. If you have a fairly small method that is never subclassed, you might want to declare it as a final method.

The following method is an example of a final method:

```
final boolean GetLampState() {
    return power_on;
}
```

Note the use of the final keyword, which indicates the method is final.

Abstract Methods and Classes

Just as you can specify that a method can never be subclassed by marking it as final, you can indicate that a method must always be subclassed by using the abstract keyword in your method definition. When a class contains one or more abstract methods, the class must be declared an abstract class and cannot be instantiated. As a consequence, you will often use abstract classes to create base classes that are intended to be used to construct other classes. This is mostly used if you are creating general-purpose classes that other people will use and if you want the compiler to enforce the fact that key functionality must be implemented by the user of the class, rather than just using the provided class. In our earlier example of the Cat class hierarchy, we had a Feline base class that was essentially an abstract base class, meaning that it was used as a parent class and objects were never instantiated directly from it. This class would be a good candidate to be an abstract class. Let's look at it again:

```
class Feline {
    boolean hungry = true;
    void speak() {
    }
    void call() {
        System.out.println("Here kitty, kitty, kitty...");
        if (hungry) speak();
    }
}
```

If we were to turn the speak method into an abstract method, the whole class would need to become an abstract class. Let's take a look at how this would be done:

```
abstract class Feline {
    boolean hungry = true;
    abstract void speak();
    void call() {
        if (hungry) speak();
    }
}
```

The abstract keyword is applied as a modifier to the Feline class definition. The abstract keyword is also used as a modifier in the speak() method declaration, and the method contains no implementation code. The declaration simply ends with a semicolon (;). The presence of the abstract method makes the Feline class an abstract class, which means that the following line would be illegal because it tries to instantiate the class:

```
Feline theCat = new Feline(); // compiler error! Feline is
                             // an abstract class
```

Inheritance and Data

We've seen in a number of examples now how a class can access variables in its parent class. When you use a variable in an object, the variable is searched for up the inheritance tree. Variables are first searched for in the current class, then up the chain of inheritance.

It is also possible to define the same variable in super and subclasses but it usually makes more sense to declare the variable once in the parent class and then inherit it rather than declaring it in the subclasses. In general, you will want to override methods, not variables.

If you do choose to override a variable, you need to be aware of what this means to your programs. For example, let's look at a code fragment where we define a parent class and a subclass and override the variable declaration in the subclass:

```
class class_A {
    int value = 5;
}

class class_B extends class_A {
    int value = 10;

    void print_values() {
        System.out.println(super.value);
        System.out.println(value);
    }
}
```

If we invoke the print_values() method of an object instantiated from class_B, we will get the following output:

```
5
10
```

The first line of the output (5) is the result of printing out the value variable of the superclass (class_A), and the second line of the output (10) is the result of printing out the value variable of the subclass (class_B). The default behavior for a method is, when accessing a variable that is declared both in the superclass and subclass, to use the variable that is declared in the same class as the method. Here's another example of this:

```
class class_A {
    int value = 5;

    void print_the_value() {
        System.out.println(value);
    }
}

class class_B extends class_A {
    int value = 10;

    void print_the_value() {
        System.out.println(value);
    }

    void print_values() {
        super.print_the_value();
        print_the_value();
    }
}
```

For this example, we reworked the code from the last example to show the relationship between methods, variables, and inheritance. The first thing you'll notice is that we've added a new method in both the superclasses and subclasses called print_the_value(). This method is the same in both classes. We see a difference, however, when we invoke the method print_values() in an object created from class_B. Notice that the first statement in this method invokes the print_the_value() method of the superclass by calling it using the super variable (which we discussed at length earlier). This results in the print_the_value() method in class_A being invoked and printing out the value variable of class_A. The second line invokes the print_the_value() method of class_B, and this results in printing out the value variable of class_B.

We hope this section has given you a picture of the issues you need to be sensitive to when overriding variables. At the start of the section, we recommended that you override methods, not variables, and that when adding a variable to a class, you add it to the appropriate base class and let the subclasses access it through inheritance rather than declaring the variable within every class.

Encapsulation

In the examples we've looked at so far, all the variables and methods have been completely accessible by any other objects in your program. This has not been a problem because we are working with simple objects with straightforward methods and data. As you build more complex objects, it will not be uncommon to have a large number of variables and methods in a single class. In these cases, only some of those variables will ever need to be modified from outside the object, and only a select group of methods will need to be used from other objects. To manage complexity in your classes, object-oriented programming provides a feature called *encapsulation*, which allows you to prevent the methods and variables of an object from being seen from other parts of the program.

Let's take a look at an example of how what starts out as a simple class can get more complex and how you can use encapsulation to reduce that complexity. We'll use a class for representing a line as our example:

```
class Line {
    int startpoint_x;
    int startpoint_y;
    int endpoint_x;
    int endpoint_y;
}
```

So far we've simply defined a class to hold the coordinates of the start and end points of a line. If you were going to use objects from this class, you could just assign values directly to the instance variables. This is one of those cases, though, where you need to use a little foresight when defining a class. Let's say that it became necessary to keep track of the midpoint of the line. You might just add two more variables to contain the coordinate of the midpoint:

```
class Line {
    int startpoint_x;
    int startpoint_y;
    int endpoint_x;
    int endpoint_y;
    int midpoint_x;
    int midpoint_y;
}
```

Although this will give you a place to store the midpoint values, you now have a new problem: How do you make sure that the midpoint is always correct? In our original version of the class, we set the start and end points by direct assignment. You can see that this approach will not work now that we need to keep the midpoint updated. The solution is to create a set of *accessor* methods and a *utility* method to update the midpoint's value. The class will now look like this:

```
class Line {
    int startpoint_x;
    int startpoint_y;
    int endpoint_x;
    int endpoint_y;
    int midpoint_x;
    int midpoint_y;

    void SetStartPoint(int x, int y) {
        startpoint_x = x;
        startpoint_y = y;
        CalcMidPoint();
    }

    void SetEndPoint(int x, int y) {
        endpoint_x = x;
```

```
        endpoint_y = y;
        CalcMidPoint();
    }

    void CalcMidPoint() {
        midpoint_x = startpoint_x + (endpoint_x - startpoint_x)/2;
        midpoint_y = startpoint_y + (endpoint_y - startpoint_y)/2;
    }
}
```

Setting the start or end point is now done by calling SetStartPoint and SetEndPoint. We referred to these as *accessor* methods because essentially all they do is access the instance variables of the Line object. In addition, we have a third method that you would never call directly, called CalcMidPoint. This method is called by SetStartPoint and SetEndPoint to update the midpoint. This class still has a problem—you can still directly change the values of the variables. In the simpler Line class, this wasn't a problem, but now if you were to modify the start point directly, for example, the midpoint would not be set correctly. If we were using the values of these variables to draw a line, that the midpoint was out of sync could result in a visible bug—when you try to draw something at the midpoint of the line it will be drawn out of alignment. You can solve this by using the private keyword to hide the variables from users of the object. Here the Line class is rewritten to use the private keyword:

```
class Line {
    private int startpoint_x;
    private int startpoint_y;
    private int endpoint_x;
    private int endpoint_y;
    private int midpoint_x;
    private int midpoint_y;

    void SetStartPoint(int x, int y) {
        startpoint_x = x;
        startpoint_y = y;
```

```
        CalcMidPoint();
    }

    void SetEndPoint(int x, int y) {
        endpoint_x = x;
        endpoint_y = y;
        CalcMidPoint();
    }

    private void CalcMidPoint() {
        midpoint_x = startpoint_x + (endpoint_x - startpoint_x)/2;
        midpoint_y = startpoint_y + (endpoint_y - startpoint_y)/2;
    }
}
```

In this version of the class, we have made all the variables private and required you to use the SetStartPoint and SetEndPoint methods to set their values. The private variables cannot be used from outside the object so we can be sure that they are set to the values we expect at all times. For good measure, we set the CalcMidPoint method to be private as well. Although being able to call CalcMidPoint from outside the object isn't harmful, we made it private to demonstrate that methods can also be declared as private. Now that we've seen the basics of encapsulation, we'll take a closer look at the keywords used to implement encapsulation in your classes.

Public..Private..Protected

The mechanism by which you control how people can see variables and objects is the use of the public, private, and protected *access modifier* keywords. These keywords can be applied to classes, variables, or methods. Limiting the ability for other objects and classes to access certain variables and methods and use certain classes is sometimes referred to as *controlling the visibility* of those classes, methods, and variables.

public

Methods and variables marked as public can be used from any other method in your program. To indicate a method or variable is public, precede it with the public keyword. For example, let's take a look at one of our classes from a previous example in which we've added a public variable and method:

```
class Line {
    ...
    public int object_color;

    public void PrintStartPoint() {
        System.out.println(startpoint_x);
        System.out.println(startpoint_y);
    }
```

In this case, we've added a public variable called object_color, and a public method called PrintStartPoint(). Because they are defined as public, any method that can access the Line class will be able to access the object_color variable and the PrintStartPoint() method.

In many of our previous examples, we haven't marked variables and methods as public, yet they were still accessible by other classes in the programs. If you do not precede a method or variable with an access modifier, it defaults to a limited version of public accessibility, where it is usable by other classes in the same package, but not by classes in other packages. Packages are a way to organize classes together; we will explore them in depth in Chapter 9. As you create more complex Java applications, you will find that you will use packages to make your code more manageable. If you find that the compiler prevents you from accessing a method or variable from a class in another package, check to make sure that the method or class is marked as public.

The public modifier can be applied to classes as well as methods and variables. It serves to make a class available to other classes in other packages. The current implementation of the Java compiler imposes a couple of rules about public classes that you must follow to compile your classes. These rules are not actually part of the language, but they concern the limitation in the way the compiler currently works. These rules may disappear or be relaxed in future versions of the compiler. The rule you will encounter most often is the requirement that there be only one public class per source file and that this class must have the same name as the source file (i.e., public class Test would have to reside in a source file called Test.java). The second rule you need to know applies when you are creating Java applets; There must be at least one public class in your applet that is a subclass of Java.Applet. For most applets, this means that you will have one Java source file that contains a public Applet subclass of the same name as the source file. The requirements for building applets will be discussed in depth in Part 3 of this book.

private

Variables and methods marked private can be used only from inside their class. We saw this in the Line class when we made the instance variables private. A private method or variable is not visible to methods in any other class, including subclasses. Declaring a method as private has the same effect as declaring it final: It prevents the method from being subclassed. Also, a subclass cannot override a non-private method and make the new method private.

Private cannot be applied to classes. In previous (alpha) versions of the Java compiler/interpreter, the private method was used to indicate that a class could be used only within its package. The current compiler will flag you with an error if you try to do this. If you are attempting to compile old Java code that you find on the Internet or in older magazine articles, you may find that the code won't compile because of the presence of private classes.

Variables and methods marked protected can be used only from inside their class or in subclasses of that class. Most of the time you will use protected instead of private because you will want the methods or variables to still be usable by subclasses. A subclass can still override a protected method or variable.

The protected modifier cannot be applied to classes.

INTERFACES

In Chapter 7, you learned about classes and inheritance. Java provides a secondary inheritance path in the form of *interfaces*. If you're familiar with the term interface from other programming languages, try not to get confused with Java's use of the term. Interfaces in Java are, for the most part, unique to the language, although, as we will see in the next section, they play a role similar to that of *multiple inheritance* in other object-oriented languages.

Interfaces and Multiple Inheritance

Languages that support multiple inheritance give you the ability to create a subclass from more than one superclass. Multiple inheritance is useful when you wish to create a class that inherits methods and properties from several distinct and, for the most part, unrelated classes. For example, in a computer game, you might create a class for representing on-screen opponents that inherits from a graphical object superclass such as a bitmap or sprite class in order to inherit the methods needed to draw the object on-screen. You would also want your class to inherit from a game character superclass so that you could abstract all the logic governing the character's behavior to that class. Your opponent class would be said to be a subclass of both your sprite class and your character class.

This type of simple example is often used to demonstrate the strength of multiple inheritance, but in practice, when you attempt to inherit from classes that are parts of complex class hierarchies, you will often experience many of the pitfalls of complex multiple inheritance that cause many experienced programmers to shy away from using this technique. Because of this, Java eliminates the kind of free-form multiple inheritance that you find in languages like C++; instead Java provides interfaces. Although a Java class cannot be a subclass of more than one other class, it can *implement* more than one interface. As we'll soon see, this can be as powerful a tool as multiple inheritance without being as complicated to use.

Working with Interfaces

An interface is essentially a special kind of class. Like classes, interfaces contain methods and variables. Unlike classes, interfaces are always completely *abstract*. Although methods are defined in a class, the code to implement the method is not; although variables are present in a class, they are *static* and *final*, which means that their values can never be changed so that you can use the variables in interfaces only as *constants*. While classes can inherit from only one superclass, they are able to inherit from as many interfaces as you see fit.

Using interfaces requires you to construct an interface definition, which is similar to the class definitions you learned to create in Chapter 7. Unlike most classes you create, interfaces exist for the main purpose of being used in subclasses. Let's take a look at the general form of an interface definition:

```
interface interface-name [extends interface-name] {
    [variable declaration;]
    [method declaration;]
}
```

You can see that this is very similar to the class definition syntax. You may want to take a moment and look at class definitions again just to compare the two. The first difference you will see is that we use the interface keyword instead of the class keyword. The second thing to notice is that interfaces can extend other interfaces. We'll talk about what this means later in the chapter. Let's take a look at a very simple example of using an interface so that we can get a feel for how the syntax is used:

```
interface Drawable {
    void drawMe(int x, int y);
}


class SpaceAlien implements Drawable {
    ...
    public void drawMe(int x, int y) {
        // Code for drawing the space alien
    }
    ...
}


class HouseCat extends Feline implements Drawable {
    ...
    public void drawMe(int x, int y) {
        // Code for drawing the house cat
    }
    ...
}
```

In this example, the interface Drawable is declared and contains a single method called drawMe(). The drawMe() method is an abstract method (although we don't use the abstract keyword in the interface declaration). This means that the code for the method is not included in the interface and that the method declaration simply ends with a semicolon (;). The class that implements an interface is responsible for including the code for that interface's methods. We see this in the case of the two classes that implement the Drawable interface. We borrowed two classes from the last chapter to use in our example. SpaceAlien, our videogame character, was a base class, which means that it did not inherit from any other classes. Our HouseCat class inherited from the base class Feline. In this example, we've taken both classes and defined them as implementing the Drawable interface. In addition to the methods and variables they contained before, they must now include a drawMe() method.

Using Interfaces as Class Types

By implementing the Drawable method in these classes, we are telling the compiler that it will always find a drawMe() method in them or their subclasses. This allows us to take advantage of the second important feature of interfaces—the ability to use interfaces as classes when using object references. Interfaces allow us to tie together a number of dissimilar classes and have them respond to the same messages. In the example we're working with, we are able to invoke a drawMe() method in both the HouseCat and SpaceAlien classes. Let's take a look at how this would be done using the following code fragment as an example:

```
HouseCat theCat = new HouseCat();
SpaceAlien theAlien = new SpaceAlien();

Drawable theDrawableObject;

theDrawableObject = theCat;
theDrawableObject.drawMe(10, 10);

theDrawableObject = theAlien;
theDrawableObject.drawMe(10, 10);
```

In this example we first create an instance of each class using the new operator and assigning the object references to the new objects to the variables theCat and theAlien. We then do something new in the next line. The variable theDrawableObject is declared as a reference to an instance (object) of Drawable, which, as we've seen, isn't a class but an interface. This means that the object that theDrawableObject refers to must implement the Drawable interface, which in turn means that the object must contain all the methods declared in that interface. In this case, it means that they must implement the drawMe() method. We see that in the next couple of lines of the example. First, we assign our reference to the HouseCat object that we had stored in theCat to theDrawableObject. When we call the drawMe() method of theDrawableObject, it is the drawMe() method of

HouseCat that is called. We then do the same thing with the variable theAlien. After assigning our reference to theAlien to theDrawableObject, we are able to call the drawMe( ) method of theAlien by invoking it through the reference stored in theDrawableObject.

Because interfaces can be used as class types, you might wonder how the instanceof operator applies to interfaces. As you might expect, you can use the instanceof operator to determine whether a given object is instantiated from a class that implements (or one of whose parent classes implement) a given interface. Here's an example where we do just that:

```
Object theObject = new SpaceAlien();
if (theObject instanceof Drawable) {
    ((Drawable)theObject).drawMe(10, 10);
}
```

This might be reminiscent of the example we used to introduce the instanceof operator. In this case, however, we are using the interface instead of a class in the test, then casting the object using that interface based on the results of the test. We hope this further illustrates the similarities between classes and interfaces.

Let's review what we've learned about interfaces so far. By declaring that a class implements an interface, that class (or one of its subclasses) must contain the code for all the methods contained in the interface. Interfaces contain no code of their own, only the abstract method declarations. Any number of dissimilar classes can implement an interface. Once they do this, you can send the same messages to them and expect that they will be able to respond to them. To talk to the objects created from these different classes as if they were objects of the same class, you need to refer to the objects as types of the interface rather than types of their respective classes. One way to do this is by using an object reference variable that is declared as the type of the interface. You can think of this as using the interface as an alternate common superclass of your objects.

In a later chapter, we will introduce container classes such as arrays and vectors, which are essentially collections of object references. One of the benefits of using interfaces is that if you store a number of objects that implement the same interface in something like an array, you can loop through every object in the array and call an interface method to perform some action. Although we will explain arrays later, let's take a look at a simple example here to illustrate the benefits of interfaces:

```
Drawable[] theDrawList = new Drawable[3];


theDrawList[0] = new HouseCat();
theDrawList[1] = new SpaceAlien();
theDrawList[2] = new HouseCat();


for (int i = 0; i < theDrawList.length; i++ ) {
    theDrawList[i].drawMe(x, y);
}
```

Because both HouseCat and SpaceAlien implement Drawable, we are able to store reference to instances of them in the array theDrawList, which we have declared as holding 3 references to objects that implement Drawable.

One last thought before we take a closer look at the elements of interfaces. In our examples, we could have simply had HouseCat and SpaceAlien share a common ancestor class, perhaps called DrawableCharacter, which would have contained the drawMe( ) method; by virtue of the fact that these classes are both subclasses of the ancestor class, they would both respond to the drawMe message. Choosing to use interfaces or common ancestors is one decision you will have to make on a case-by-case basis. In some cases, this will be decided for you if you are using interfaces provided in Java's package libraries. As with any other language, Java helps your programs without using every feature of the language indiscriminately, but where they make sense. Interfaces are a key case in point; many programs will never need to use interfaces.

Using Interface Methods

Now that we've seen how interfaces are defined and used, let's take a closer look at interface methods and the issues involved in their use. We said that interfaces contain only the method declaration but not the method body—the code that makes up the method. Interface methods are like abstract methods in a regular class. When a class implements an interface, the class needs to contain the code for the methods contained in the interface. In our examples in the last section, the SpaceAlien and HouseCat classes both needed to contain drawMe( ) methods. If a class implements an interface but doesn't implement one or more of the interface's methods, the whole class becomes an abstract class and cannot be instantiated. To instantiate a subclass of the abstract class, you would need to implement the remaining unimplemented methods of the interface. Let's take a look at a brief example of this:

```
interface my_interface {
    void interface_method_a ();
    void interface_method_b ();
}


class my_base_class implements my_interface {
    public void interface_method_a () {
        // code for interface_method_a
    }
    // oh no! no code for interface_method_b
}
class my_sub_class extends my_base_class {
    public void interface_method_b () {
        // code for interface_method_b
    }
}
```

In this example, we have defined an interface, called my_interface, and two classes, called my_base_class and my_sub_class. The interface contains two methods, aptly titled interface_method_a( ) and interface_method_b( ). The class my_base_class implements my_interface and contains the code for interface_method_a( ). However, it does not contain the code for interface_method_b( ), which is also part of the my_interface interface. This means that the class my_base_class becomes an abstract class and cannot be instantiated. We create a subclass of my_base_class called my_sub_class and implement interface_method_b( ), which means that all the methods from my_interface have been implemented. As a consequence, my_sub_class can be instantiated. If you try to compile a Java program and get an error that says you are trying to instantiate an abstract class, check to make sure that if you are using an interface you have not forgotten to implement all the interface's methods.

Accessing Interface Variables

Although we haven't seen an example of this so far, variables can appear in interfaces. When interfaces contain variables, they are used as constants that the implementing classes can share; they are considered final and static, although these keywords don't need to be present. What does need to be present, however, is an initializer that gives the variable its constant value. For example, suppose we had wanted our implementing classes all to use the same constant values for the bounds of the area on the screen where they were being drawn. We could do this by declaring these as variables in the interface, as shown here:

```
interface Drawable {
    int draw_area_top = 10;
    int draw_area_left = 10;
    int draw_area_bottom = 100;
    int draw_area_right = 200;

    void drawMe(int x, int y);
}
```

These values will now be available to any class that implements Drawable. The values can be used in any method, as part of any variable declaration, or anywhere else where you could use a final variable. Here's an example where we use this with the SpaceAlien class:

```
class SpaceAlien implements Drawable {
    int position_x = draw_area_left;
    int position_y = draw_area_top;
    ...
    public void drawMe(int x, int y) {
      ...
      if (x < draw_area_left) {
        position_x = draw_area_left;
      }
```

```
        ...
        // Code for drawing the space alien
    }
        ...
    }
```

"Subclassing" Interfaces

Like classes, interfaces also have a chain of inheritance. An interface can be subclassed from other interfaces. Interfaces are subclassed from other interfaces using the extend keyword, which goes to further demonstrate the similarities between interfaces and classes. For example, suppose we wanted to put all our constant values into one interface, so that we could use them in classes that didn't actually need to implement the draw method, and we wanted them to be available to classes that implemented the Drawable interface. We could do this with the following interface declaration:

```
interface Draw_Constants {
    int draw_area_top = 10;
    int draw_area_left = 10;
    int draw_area_bottom = 100;
    int draw_area_right = 200;
}

interface Drawable extends Draw_Constants {
    void drawMe(int x, int y);
}
```

A class that just needed access to the constants would implement Draw_Constants, while a class that needed access to the constants and needed to do drawing would implement Drawable.

Sometimes combining several interfaces together into a single interface is helpful. If we take a look at the last example again, we might decide that it's more elegant to redesign Drawable so that it was derived from two other interfaces: Draw_Constants, which would be unchanged from our last example, and

Draw_Methods, which would contain the methods for handling drawing. We could write this like so:

```
interface Draw_Constants {
    int draw_area_top = 10;
    int draw_area_left = 10;
    int draw_area_bottom = 100;
    int draw_area_right = 200;
}
interface Draw_Methods {
    void drawMe(int x, int y);
}


interface Drawable extends Draw_Constants, Draw_Methods {
}
```

Now we have a single interface (Drawable) to implement for classes that need to handle drawing (and, we can assume, need access to the Draw_Constant values). Classes that need only the constants would need only to implement the Draw_Constants interface.

PACKAGES

Understanding Packages

As we've seen in previous chapters, one of the main advantages of object-oriented programming is its ability to reuse code by subclassing existing classes, so that you need to program only the differences between your class and the one you've subclassed. Even though this is an extremely powerful capability, if you were limited to working with and subclassing from classes you had created, you wouldn't see the real benefits of object-oriented programming until you were an experienced developer with a personal library of classes. Even if you have built a collection of classes, you still face the task of using that code from a variety of programs without physically copying the classes into each of your programs, then keeping the code up to date in each program that used these classes. The solution to these problems is the use of *class libraries*, or what Java refers to as *packages*.

Packages are collections of classes, usually grouped according to functionality. By organizing your classes into packages, reusing these packages in other programs you might write becomes easier. All the functionality that Java gives you in the form of system classes for working with data, graphics, etc., is provided to you in packages that you import into your program. As a consequence, you will spend quite a bit of time poring over the Java API Package references.

At this point addressing the use of class libraries from a philosophical issue, rather than a technical one, is appropriate. Most programmers learned to program in procedural languages; although code reuse is common in procedural programs, it is not as intrinsic to productivity as it is with object-oriented programming. In fact, programmers sometimes show a general distrust of code written by others when evaluating code libraries for use with their programs. Many programmers carry this perspective with them when they approach object-oriented programming, and they ignore the robust class libraries that come with most modern object-oriented development environments. They instead choose to build their own class libraries from scratch.

Actually, for most applications you will need to use (at minimum) two different sets of classes, one for the internal representations of your program's data, one for the external presentation, aspects such as user interface elements like buttons, menus, and windows. It's usually a safe assumption that you are going to have to build the classes used for handling your application's data yourself. After all, this is what makes one application different from another. But the user interface code can usually be developed more rapidly by making use of an existing class library that handles the management of windows and other presentational elements, allowing you to subclass supplied user interface and system classes when you need to implement program-specific functionality. Even so, with most object-oriented languages and environments, you can use your own class libraries for managing these aspects of your program as well.

With Java, you have some flexibility in using or ignoring the language supplied classes, but not much, especially if you intend to write HotJava applets. We'll cover some of the classes in the Java API in the remainder of Part 2 and Part 3, but remember that since Java contains an extensive collection of these classes, we'll only scratch the surface of the available classes.

Using Packages

Most of the time, your primary dealings with packages involve the packages provided with the Java release. If you are writing applets for use with HotJava, you will end up using packages from the browser packages, and all Java programs will probably need to make use of Java utility classes. Making use of packages from the Java release is relatively easy, as we'll see in the next few examples. Making use of your own packages or packages you install is a little more complex; and we'll talk more about that, as well as how to create your own packages, later in the chapter.

When we talk about using packages, we really mean using classes and interfaces from packages. From here on, we'll simplify things by talking about using classes rather than using classes and interfaces. The same steps are followed for using either classes or interfaces, so we'll lump the two together for the sake of brevity. There are two ways to make use of classes stored in a package. The first way is to use the *fully qualified class name* of the class that you want to use. You create the fully qualified class name by taking the package name of the class and appending the class name at the end. For example, in the package java.util, there is a class called Date. Here's a code fragment that shows how you could instantiate an object from Date by using the full class name:

```
java.util.Date theDate = new java.util.Date();
System.out.println(theDate);
```

By preceding the class name with the package name, the compiler knows where to find the Date class. In cases where you need to get a class from a package only once, or you don't need to access any of the other classes of a package, this is probably the fastest and easiest way to get to the specific class.

In many cases, you will want to pull a class into your program for use in a number of places in the program, or you will want to pull in all the classes from a package. Java provides the import keyword to allow you to import specific classes or entire packages. The import keyword is used as follows:

```
import packagename.classname;
```

In the previous example if we used the import command to import the Date class, we could have rewritten the example like this:

```
import java.util.Date;
Date theDate = new Date();
System.out.println(theDate);
```

By importing the class, we no longer have to use its fully qualified class name to use it. In the above example, after import the class Date becomes usable from anywhere in the program. It's also possible to import every class in a package rather than a specific class. To do this, use the import statement like this:

```
import packagename.*;
```

For example, if we wished to import every class in java.util, we would use:

```
import java.util.*;
```

java.lang

Java automatically imports the classes from java.lang for you. This means that you can use any of the classes from java.lang, such as Thread or System, without having first to import them. An example of this is the System.out.println() call that we've used in some of our previous examples. Let's deconstruct that statement to get a better understanding of using a package class and to review some features of Java classes.

First, System refers to the class System in the package java.lang. The variable out in the class System is a static variable, which means that the variable exists without having to create an instance of the System class. In fact, the System class cannot be instantiated; it serves as a repository for static variables and methods. System.out is a static variable that contains a reference to a PrintStream object. All we need to know about the PrintStream class is that it has a println() method that can be used to send text to the standard output. Because to understand this is essential to mastering Java, we'll summarize this one more time. The statement *System.out.println("test");* causes the following steps to be taken:

1. Find the class System. Because of the automatic import of java.lang, the compiler knows where it is without being told.

2. Find the static variable out in the System class. Because we're looking for the variable in a class instead of an object, System.out must be a static variable.

3. Send the println message to the object referred to by System.out. In this case, System.out contains a reference to the PrintStream class, which contains the println() method that writes the string "test" to the screen.

Using Classes and Interfaces from the Java Packages

The Java Development Kit contains over 15 packages that you can use to obtain classes for use in your programs. However, most of your development will use only a specific subset of those called the Applet API. Applets that are written using the Applet API are guaranteed to run on any Java-capable browser such as Netscape. Even if you are writing full-fledged Java applications rather than applets, it is wise to restrict your usage of the Java packages to these core packages. These packages contain the classes that Sun is committed to porting and keeping current over a variety of packages. In the case of Java applets, the security features of the browser will restrict you to using these packages, but with a stand-alone Java application, you are free to use any packages you wish. However, if you use one of the Sun-specific packages to implement a piece of functionality that you can't figure out how to implement with the Applet API packages, you will create a non-portable Java application that will not work when you try to run it on a Macintosh or Windows computer. Table 9.1 shows the classes that belong to each Applet API.

▰▰▰▰ **Table 9.1** Applet APIs and Their Classes

Applet API	Class
java.applet	Base applet classes
java.awt	Another Window Toolkit (AWT) user interface classes
java.awt.image	AWT image-handling classes
java.awt.peer	AWT classes for interfacing to native user interface
java.io	I/O support (streams, files, etc.)
java.lang	Language support classes—automatically imported
java.net	Networking support classes (URLs, sockets)
java.util	Language utilities (vectors, hash tables, etc.)

We will discuss some of these classes in upcoming chapters and provide an abridged class reference in Part 4. You can also find more information about these packages on the Sun Java Web site at http://java.sun.com.

Organizing Your Project into Packages

Up until now we've talked about how you get classes from the system packages. As your programs get more complex and you develop classes that you wish to share with different programs, you will want to construct your own packages. You will be able to keep your programs uncluttered with the source for your utility classes, and you can easily share these classes among different programs. An added bonus is that if you are building HotJava applets, you can speed loading of a Web page that has several HotJava applets on it if these applets all use classes from the same package. Java is smart enough to load the package classes the first time and not have to reload them for the other applets.

Compiling with Packages

Compiling your program to make use of your own packages can be slightly more difficult than using the standard packages. The Java compiler automatically knows where to look for the Java packages. However, if you want the compiler to use your packages, you need to tell the compiler where to find them. Depending on where you want to keep your packages, this task can be relatively easy or moderately complex.

In Chapter 4 we talked about the steps necessary to compile a Java application. In later chapters we learned that Java applications are simply types of Java classes. When the Java compiler is compiling a class and finds that it needs to import a class from another package, its normal behavior is to look in one of two places on your local hard drive for the package classes. When the compiler encounters a package name, it looks in a list of directories stored in an environment variable called the CLASSPATH. The actual details of how this works are a little different from platform to platform, so we're going to discuss this from an operating-system-independent perspective for now. The CLASSPATH usually contains the directory where the class being compiled is stored as well as a directory in the Java release called classes, which contains the classes for the system packages. This means that the default behavior is to use the system classes and your custom classes, as long as these classes can be found in these locations.

When looking for a package class, the compiler uses the package name of the class to find a directory with the same name as the package in one of the directories in the CLASSPATH. If it finds the package directory, it look inside it for the .class file of the class it needs to load. In some cases, you will see a name like java.lang.Math. In cases like this, there is a directory called lang inside a directory called java. The package name java.lang tells the compiler to find the java directory inside one of the directories in the CLASSPATH, and once the java directory has been found, to look inside it for another directory called lang. The lang directory will contain the class Math. If you were to look at the .java file of the Math class, you would see that it defines itself as being part of the java.lang package, not the lang package.

Although it is possible to add more directories to the CLASSPATH, this often is not a good idea, especially if you are creating HotJava applets. If you use a modified CLASSPATH to compile your classes, you will likely need one to run them as well. If you are building stand-alone Java applications, this might be acceptable, but for HotJava applets, you will want to have your package directories in the same directory as your applet class.

Creating Packages

Now that we have a better understanding of how packages are used, let's take a look at the steps for creating a package. In this case we will create a simple single class package and see how to import and use it in another class. First, let's take a look at the listing of our example package class:

```java
package MyPackage;

public class MyClass {
    public void test() {
        System.out.println("test");
    }
}
```

This listing would be saved as a file called MyClass.java, which would be located in a directory named MyPackage. You need to look at two important things in this listing. The first is the line *package MyPackage;* in the first line of the listing. This indicates that the classes in the listing are part of the MyPackage package. For source files that are part of a package, the package declaration must be present at the beginning of the file, before any other statement, although it can be preceded by comments or empty lines.

To recap, if your source file is part of a package, it needs to contain a package declaration at the beginning of the file, and the package declaration has the following form:

```
package packagename;
```

When the source file is compiled, Java will create a classname.class file (sometimes called a .class file for short) for each class in the source file, and unless directed otherwise, will store the file in the same directory as the source file. As we've seen in some of our examples, a source file can contain more than one class or interface. The .class files must be located in a directory that has the same name as the package, and this directory should be a subdirectory of the directory where classes that will import the package are located.

Now let's finish the example by looking at a simple program that will import the class MyClass from the package MyPackage:

```
import MyPackage.MyClass;

class PackageTestApp {
    public static void main (String args[]) {
        MyClass theClass = new MyClass();
        theClass.test();
    }
}
```

This listing would be saved in a file called PackageTestApp.java, and would be saved in the directory of which MyPackage was a subdirectory. Our file directory tree might look like this:

```
classes
    PackageTestApp.java
    PackageTestApp.class
    MyPackage
        MyClass.java
        MyClass.class
```

The .class files are created by the Java compiler from the .java source files. In this
example, we ran the compiler twice: first to compile the java files in the package
(MyClass.java), then to compile the application that uses the package
(PackageTestApp.java). If we had any other files in the package, we might have
used the command javac *.java (this will be platform-specific). Once the package
files have been compiled, you can compile the classes that import them. In this case,
we would compile PackageTestApp.java. When the compiler hits the import
MyPackage.MyClass line in PackageTestApp.java it sees the class MyClass.class in
the MyPackage directory exactly where it expects it to be, and proceeds with the
compilation.

Although the compiler checks the file MyClass.class for information it needs for the
compilation process, it does not actually include the code from MyClass.class when
it creates PackageTestApp.class. When the PackageTestApp program is run, Java
looks for the file PackageTestApp.class and loads that using something called the
class loader. As soon as it does this, it sees that it needs the compiled class stored in
MyClass.class and loads it as well. However, a lot of things might have happened
to MyClass.class between the time when PackageTestApp.class was compiled and
the time it was run. If MyClass.class has been moved, renamed, or deleted, you're
in trouble, and Java will let you know this. But if the class is still present and contains the same methods or variables that the calling class needs, in this case
PackageTestApp.class, Java will still be able to deal with it. This is referred to as
dynamic binding—it is one of the reasons why Java is called a "dynamic" language.

10

MANAGING DATA
WITH OBJECTS

We saw in Chapter 4 that Java provides the familiar set of C simple data types (integers, floats, etc.). We didn't cover composite data types such as arrays, strings, or any of the other data structures that are common in all but the most simple of programs. These types of data are handled as classes in Java's API classes; now that we've covered the foundations of classes in Java, we can discuss these features in depth.

Data Utility Classes

Java provides a variety of classes for handling things like strings and hashtables that normally you would need to code yourself. In some cases (when using arrays and, to some extent, strings), the compiler will automatically generate code to instantiate objects or call methods behind the scenes without your having to deal with this. You'll see this primarily with array objects. In other cases, you'll need to use classes from Java's java.lang package, which is automatically imported into your programs. We'll talk about these classes in detail in the next section.

As we discussed in Chapter 3, Java is very close to being a "pure" object-oriented language. Its main point of departure is that it provides a set of simple types such as int, float, and char, which exist outside the class system. In a "pure" object-oriented language, all types are classes. The Java simple types are not classes, which means that they cannot be subclassed or used as the target of messages. This limitation has a disadvantage in that extending their functionality or, when using them, having available the methods that all Java objects inherit from the Java root class Object is not possible. Java's simple types can be used in a highly optimized fashion, though giving Java performance capabilities that are lacking in many interpreted languages. Because C-based code and algorithms are very similar to C's basic types they can be ported very easily to Java.

To deal with the occasional need to use simple data types as classes, Java provides a set of class-based versions of the simple data types in the package java.lang. These classes are intended, for the most part, not to be used as replacements for the simple types, but to supplement them. The term "wrapper" class is used in some of the Java documentation to refer to these classes: The original simple data type is "wrapped" by a class that provides a set of methods for dealing with the most common tasks you will need to perform with the type as well as an instance variable to contain the value of the simple type. These classes also often contain a number of static methods, which can be used without actually having to instantiate the classes. In addition, in cases where you need actual object-based representations of data stored in simple types, the "wrapper" classes are designed so that their constructor methods will accept the simple type value as a parameter, allowing you easily to create, for example, an Integer object from an int variable. "Wrapper" classes make available in an object-oriented manner the type of functionality that you would otherwise spend quite a bit of time writing yourself to convert numbers to strings, sort arrays, and conduct other common programming tasks. Investing the time to learn about the methods contained in wrapper classes will pay off with increased programming productivity.

A Quick Look at java.lang and java.util

In Chapter 9 we talked about packages and mentioned that Java automatically imports java.lang for us; java.lang contains a number of important classes, including the wrapper. A second, almost as important, package, called java.util, contains the Vector and Hashtable classes we will talk about later in this chapter. Let's take a look at classes in java.lang that are relevant to this chapter's focus on class-based or composite data.

The main classes we will look at in this section are the wrapper classes. Table 10.1 shows the simple data type and its corresponding class type.

These classes each have a number of unique methods for dealing with these types of data. In addition, they also share certain common methods, such as the method toString(), which will return a string representation of the data stored in the class. Each class can also be instantiated by calling its constructor with the simple data type value as a parameter. For example, to create an Integer object that contains a value of 5 you could use the following line:

```
Integer theInt = new Integer(5);
```

The other classes can be instantiated in the same way. Most of these classes also provide several other overloaded versions of their constructors as well. You will

▰▰▰▰ **Table 10.1** Simple Data Types and Their Corresponding java.lang Class Types

Simple Type	java.lang Class
boolean ⟶	Boolean
char ⟶	Character
double ⟶	Double
float ⟶	Float
int ⟶	Integer
long ⟶	Long

need to refer to the Java API reference in Appendices for complete listings of the methods available to use in each of these classes.

Arrays

Most languages can store data in arrays—Java is no exception. An array is a data type used to store a collection of other types of data. Arrays contain a fixed number of elements, referred to as the array's *size*. The size of the array is fixed when the array is created. If you need to create arrays with variable sizes, look at the Vector class, which we will cover later in the chapter. The contents of an array are called the *elements* of the array; they all have to be of the same type, although this type can either be a simple data type or a class type. When the array's type is a class, the standard object polymorphism rules apply so the array elements can contain references to instances of the class or any of its subclasses (i.e., an array of type Feline could contain references to HouseCat objects or Lion objects).

Allocating Arrays

Arrays in Java are actually objects of a special invisible array class. Although arrays are objects, they are treated specially by the compiler in the ways that they are instantiated and used. They also have limitations that other classes don't, such as not being able to be subclassed. The primary way to instantiate an array is the same way you would instantiate any class, using the new operator. Unlike other classes, the syntax for instantiating an array does not involve using a class name. Let's take a look at two different array allocations—the array of int values and the array of Integer objects:

```
int int_table[] = new int[5];
Integer int_obj_table[] = new Integer[5];
```

The first array allocation creates an array that will hold a series of five values of type int. The second array allocation is a little different in that it creates an array of objects instead of simple data types. This is important to note because when you do this, you are not actually allocating (instantiating) the objects contained in the array. An array of objects is more properly called an array of object references. When the array of objects is created, null is stored in each element of the array. A common mistake is to create an array of objects, forget that you need to instantiate an object, and store an object reference in each array element. This mistake is reinforced by the fact that an array of simple types is ready for use as soon as it is created.

Let's take a second look at the syntax for allocating an array:

```
array-type array-name[] = new array-type[array-size];
```

The array type can be any simple type or class type, the array name any valid identifier, and the array size a value greater than 0. Java also provides an alternate syntax that does the same thing:

```
array-type[] array-name = new array-type[array-size];
```

The difference is that the brackets have simply been moved after the array type instead of the array name. The first style of declaration follows C conventions; however, many Java programmers find that the second style more properly conveys the idea of an array as a class. This is especially handy when trying to return an array from a method. For example:

```
int[] CreateArray(int elem_count) {
    int[] int_table = new int[elem_count];
    return int_table;
}
```

You could move the brackets ([]) after the parameter list (i.e., int CreateArray(int elem_count)[]), but understanding it wouldn't be as intuitive when reading it.

To create a multidimensional array, you create an array of arrays. In this example we create a 16 by 16 array of type char:

```
char[][] icon = new char[16][16];
```

Strictly speaking, an array of arrays is not a true multidimensional array. It is possible to allocate them one dimension at a time. For example, we could allocate just the first dimension using the following statement:

```
short[][] graph = new short[3][];
```

We could then add other dimensions:

```
graph[0][] = new short[4];
graph[1][] = new short[2];
graph[2][] = new short[7];
```

This example shows the difference between an array of arrays and a true multidimensional array. In the example, each element of the array is a reference to a different sized array. Most of the time you will allocate an array of arrays by explicitly specifying all the dimensions of the array in the variable declaration rather than the way we've just demonstrated.

Array Declarations and Initializers

In the previous examples, we declared an array and allocated it in the same line. This is not a requirement when declaring arrays, and we did so only for the sake of brevity. For example, we could have rewritten our first example like this:

```
int int_table[];
int_table[] = new int[5];
```

Or we could use the alternate notation, like this:

```
int[] int_table;
int_table = new int[5];
```

In this case, the alternate notation better conveys that the variable int_table stores an object reference to an array of int; when we assign the reference to the array in the next line, it looks like any other object reference assignment. Remember that arrays are like any other object in the way they are declared and initialized. When we see a line like this:

```
int int_table[] = new int[5];
```

we are looking at an array declaration and initialization. The array declaration is represented by everything to the left of the assignment operator (=); the initialization, where the array object is allocated, is represented by everything to the right of the assignment operator (=). When we initialize an array this way, we are doing so just as we would initialize any other object. However, Java provides a short-cut initialization technique that can be used not only to allocate the array, but to assign the initial values for its elements. This is done by assigning the array contents directly to the array using the { and } brackets. We can see this illustrated in the following example:

```
int int_table[] = {1, 2, 3};
```

This example creates an array of three int values and initializes these values to 1, 2, and 3. We could use any other objects we wished within the brackets, provided they were of the same class (or descendants of the same class) and that class was specified as the type of the array. We see this illustrated in the following example:

```
Integer intA = new Integer(1);
Integer intB = new Integer(2);
Integer intC = new Integer(3);
Integer int_table[] = {intA, intB, intC};
```

The syntax for array initialization is as follows:

```
array-type array-name[] = {[element1, element2, ...]};
```

C users probably feel comfortable with this type of array initialization. They should be aware, however, that Java does not allow you to initialize character arrays with string literals. For example, the following line is illegal in Java:

```
char myChars[] = "test";         // Illegal in Java
```

The line would have to be rewritten as follows:

```
char myChars[] = {'t', 'e', 's', 't'};
```

Using Arrays

Using arrays means storing and retrieving values from the array elements. Elements are stored sequentially in an array and are numbered starting from 0. To get at an element in the array, you need to use the following array access syntax:

```
array-reference[array-index]
```

The array reference is a variable that contains a reference to an array, and the array index is a value from 0 to the length of the array –1. For example, we could create an array of three int elements and assign a value to each element with the following code fragment:

```
int int_table[] = new int[3];
int_table[0] = 5;
int_table[1] = 10;
int_table[2] = 15;
```

Arrays have a read-only instance variable called length that can be used to find out the size of an array at run time. This can be useful when accessing an array from a method where the array is passed to you and you don't know its length in advance. For example:

```
void FillMultiplyTable(int[] mult_table, int multiple) {
   for (int i = 0; i < mult_table.length, i++) {
      mult_table[i] = i * multiple;
   }
}
```

This method will fill any array it is passed with multiples of the value passed in multiple. Because the size of the array is determined at run time using the length variable, the method will work on any array of int that is passed to it. We can see that arrays are objects just like any other, and we can pass an object reference to the array in the parameter list of the method. This means that the array that is passed to FillMultiplyTable gets modified by the method, not a copy of the array.

Multidimensional arrays are used the same way as regular arrays. Here are some examples of assigning values to multidimensional arrays:

```
char[][] char_table = new char[2][2];
char_table[0][0] = 'a';
char_table[0][1] = 'b';
char_table[1][0] = 'c';
char_table[1][1] = 'd';
```

Using the length variable with multidimensional arrays is a little different than with single-dimension arrays. In this next example, we'll illustrate using the length instance variable to print out the contents of a multidimensional array:

```
void PrintElements(int[][] int_table) {

   // the next line loops through each row
   for (int i = 0; i < int_table.length, i++) {

      // the next line steps through each element j in row i
      for (int j = 0; j < int_table[i].length, j++) {

         // print out each element j in row i
         System.out.print(int_table[i][j]);
```

```
        // print a space between elements
        System.out.print(" ");
    }


    // print out a newline character
    System.out.println();
  }
}
```

This method takes a two-dimensional array as a parameter and prints out every element of it. The method consists of two loops. The outer loop iterates through each element of the first dimension of the array. Because this is an array of arrays, each element is a reference to another array. For each of these arrays, we iterate through each element of the array and print out its contents.

Copying Arrays

The System class provides a method called arraycopy for copying a range of elements from one array to another. The method has been overloaded so that there is a version of it for each array type that you need to copy. The method for copying Boolean arrays looks like this:

```
public static void arraycopy( boolean src[],
                              int srcpos,
                              boolean dest[],
                              int destpos,
                              int length)
```

The method copies length number of elements starting from element srcpos of the array src[] to element destpos of the array dest[]. Versions of this method exist for arrays of boolean, byte, char, short, int, long, float, double, and Object. Here's an example where we use this method to copy an array of short:

```
short[] array_1 = {1, 2, 3, 4, 5};
short[] array_2 = new array[3];
System.arraycopy(array_1, 1, array_2, 0, 3);
```

This will copy three elements starting at the second element from array_1 to the first element of array_2. After this operation has been performed, array_2 will contain {2, 3, 4}.

Strings

Most programs need to deal with text in some fashion. So far, our use of strings has been limited to the use of string literals to print out various messages in our example programs. In this section we'll take a closer look at strings and how they're used in your programs.

Strings as Classes

Like arrays, strings in Java are implemented as classes. Unlike arrays, you actually declare your strings using the String class. Strings in Java are collections of Unicode characters that are stored in an instance of the String class. The String class defines a number of useful methods that make it very easy to handle string processing tasks in Java.

Allocating Strings

String objects can be allocated in a variety of ways. A string can be allocated by assigning a string literal to a variable of type String. The compiler creates a new String object behind the scenes and stores as reference to it in the variable. For example, take a look at this line:

```
String myString = "hello";
```

This line allocates a String object that contains the character string "hello" and puts a reference to it in the variable myString. Although the new operator hasn't been used, an object allocation has still taken place.

Strings can also be allocated using the new operator and a number of constructors. The most commonly used constructors are:

```
String(String value)
```
Constructs a new string that is a copy of the string object value that is passed to it.

```
String(char[] value)
```
Constructs a new string from an array of characters passed in value.

```
String(char[] value, int offset, int count)
```
Constructs a new string from the array of characters passed in value starting with the character at offset and including the following count characters.

Here's an example where we create a string from an array of characters:
```
char[] myChars = {'h', 'e', 'l', 'l', 'o'};
String myString = new String(myChars);
```

The first line creates an array of type char and initializes it to contain the characters between the curly brackets. The second line creates a new String object from the character array using the new operator.

Working with Strings

Once you've created a String object, certain aspects of how you use them are specific to Java. For example, once you create a String object it cannot be changed. For example, in order to change the character at a specific position in a string, you need to use one of its methods to copy it to a new character array, modify the character in question, and create a new string object from the modified character array. Here's an example of this that uses the string we created in the last example:
```
char[] newChars = myString.toCharArray();
newChars[0] = 'c';
newString = new String(newChars);
```

When we create a String object, an array of characters is created as a private instance variable of the object to hold the characters in the string. If we use one of the constructors or methods that create a new String from a character array, unless the API documentation explicitly says otherwise, a new character array is not created; instead, a reference to the array you passed is stored in the String object. If you create a String object from a character array, you can't modify the array afterwards.

Another important aspect of strings is that the + operator has been modified so that it will work with strings. The + operator is used to concatenate strings; it will automatically convert operands into strings if necessary. You can also use the += operator to append a string or object to the end of an existing string. When you do this, the original string is replaced by a new string that contains the appended text.

Here's an example that shows both the + and += operator in use to create a string of a phone number:

```
int area = 415;
int prefix = 555;
int suffix = 1111;
String phone_number = "(" + area + ")";
phone_number += prefix;
phone_number += "-";
phone_number += suffix;
```

String Methods

The string class has more than 40 methods that allow you to accomplish a variety of string manipulation tasks. In addition to this, numerous classes have methods that create, manipulate, or otherwise act on strings. To make the most of this functionality, you will have to become familiar with the Java API reference and have some experience working with strings in other languages. In this section, we're going to cover some of the most commonly used string methods and look at some examples that will give you a feel for how to use them.

Converting Values to and from Strings

The String class has a static method called valueOf() that will return a String object when passed to most types of data. For example, we can easily create a string from an integer value:

```
String newString = String.valueOf(5);
```

In this example, we use the valueOf() method to create a String object from the integer literal 5. The valueOf() method is a static method, which means that you call it by referencing the class, not an object, so that you can use the method without having to instantiate an object. The method has been overloaded so that you can pass it any of the simple types as well as any object.

Every object in Java also has a toString() method, which, as the name implies, is meant to return a string representation of the object's value. For most of the provided classes, the toString() method has been overridden so that it will return an appropriate string. We see an example of this here:

```
Integer theInt = new Integer(5);
String newString = theInt.toString();
```

For classes that you create, you might want to override toString to provide a useful textual representation of your object's data; although doing this is not required, it is not a bad idea because the method is used in a number of places to print objects. For example, both the + operator, which we discussed in the previous section, and the valueOf() method in the String class that we just covered use this method to get the string value for an object. Here's an example of a toString() method that is based on the actual toString() method of the provided Boolean class although it has been modified for clarity:

```
public String toString() {
    if (value) {
        return "true";
    }
    else {
        return "false";
    }
}
```

Depending on the value of the boolean instance variable value, the method will return the string "true" or "false".

Finding Characters in Strings

The String class provides a number of methods for locating characters and substrings within string objects as well as creating new substrings of existing strings. We'll take a look at a few of these methods in this section. Before you find yourself working around these methods or trying to extend their functionality, make sure you look at the Java API reference—in many cases, a method to solve the problem might already exist.

To find a character in a string, use the indexOf() method. There are two versions of the indexOf() method:

```
public int indexOf(int ch)
```

```
public int indexOf(int ch, int fromIndex)
```

The first version of indexOf() searches the string for the first occurrence of the character passed to it and returns its position in the string. If the character can't be found, the method returns –1. Strings, like arrays, start counting character positions at 0. For example, when the following code is executed

```
String testString = "This is a test";

int a = testString.indexOf('i');
```

the variable a is set to 2, which is the position of the character 'i' in the string "This is a test". The second version of indexOf() is useful when you need to find multiple occurrences of a character in a string. In addition to taking a character as a parameter, the method also takes a starting index from where to start searching for the character. For example, with the previous example, if you were to use the second version of indexOf and pass a starting index of 3, like this,

```
String testString = "This is a test";

int a = testString.indexOf('i', 3);
```

the variable a will be set to 5, which is the position of the second 'i' in the string "This is a test". Let's take a look at how you could use this method to count the occurrences of a character within a string:

```
int CountChar(String theString, int ch) {
    int count = 0;
    int i = 0;
    while (i < theString.length()) {
        int next = theString.indexOf(ch, i);
        if (next != -1) count++
        else next = theString.length();
        i = next + 1;
    }
}
```

In this example, we count the occurrence of the character indicated in ch in the string passed in theString. First, we create and initialize to 0 variables to hold the character count and current position in the string. These variables are count and i. We then enter a loop that continues as long as the current position in the string is less than the length of the string. Within the loop, the string is searched for the next occurrence of the character ch starting from the position stored in i and stores this in a variable called next, which holds the position of the next occurrence of the character in the string or –1 if it was not found. If it is found (i.e., next is not –1), the variable count is incremented; otherwise, next is set to the value of the length of the string, which is 1, greater than the position of the last character in the string (remember, characters in strings are numbered starting from 0). Finally, the variable i is set to next + 1, which is the position after the character we just found. The loop is checked again to see if variable i is past the end of the string. If it is not, the loop continues; otherwise, the loop is done and the method ends.

Comparing Strings

Strings are compared through the use of several methods in the String class. The main ones you will use are equals and equalsIgnoreCase. You can use these with string objects or literals to compare one string with another and determine if they are equal.

Here's an example in which we make use of these methods in an extremely simplified version of a method to handle user login:

```
boolean HandleLogin() {
    String login;
    String password;
    System.out.writeln("User:");
    login = System.in.readln();
    System.out.writeln("Password:");
    password = System.in.readln();
    if (login.equalsIgnoreCase("Ed") & password.equals("Ed1A")) {
        System.out.writeln("Login accepted");
        return true;
    }
    else {
        System.out.writeln("Username or password incorrect");
        return false;
    }
}
```

In this example, we see how we can make use of both equals and equalsIgnoreCase to match strings. In the example method, we authenticate a user and password by first doing a case-insensitive comparison of the user-supplied username with the string literal "Ed" and then doing a case-sensitive comparison of the user-supplied password with the string "Ed1A" (this is not my password, so don't bother).

Substrings

The String class provides a method called substring that you can use to specify a range of characters that you would like to copy into another string. There are two versions of the substring method:

```
public String substring(int beginIndex)


public String substring(int beginIndex, int endIndex)
```

The first version of the method creates and returns a new String object containing the characters starting at beginIndex through to the end of the string. The second version copies all the characters between beginIndex and endIndex into a new String object and returns that to the caller. The following example builds on some of the techniques we saw in the last example to parse a string containing a list of items separated by commas and print out each item.

```
void PrintItems(String theText) {
    int i = 0;
    while (i < theString.length()) {
        int next = theText.indexOf(',', i);
        if (next == -1) next = theText.length();
        System.out.println(theText.substring(i, next));
        i = next + 1;
    }
}
```

The string passed in the text is expected to look something like this:

```
one,two,three
```

and the output would look like this:

```
one
two
three
```

We use a loop similar to the one in the last example, but rather than keeping count of the number of occurrences of a specific character, we use the position of the comma character to determine the ending position of the substring. An important aspect of the substring method shown by this is the fact that the ending character in the substring is the character before the ending index character position passed to the substring method.

Vectors

In an earlier section, we looked at arrays and how they can be used to maintain lists of objects. The array class is very useful in that it supports both simple and class-based types, but it is limited in that once the size of an array has been defined, it cannot be resized. While it's possible to work around this in your own programs through the clever use of temporary arrays and the System.arrayCopy method, another solution is far more optimal. Java provides a general-purpose, resizable array class called Vector that is very useful for working with collections of objects. The Vector class is designed so that it handles all the details of adding and removing elements from arrays and tries to make as efficient use of memory as it can.

Vectors vs. Arrays

Vectors have several important advantages over arrays. You would use a vector instead of an array if the following conditions were true:

1. You are dealing with a variable number of objects, and you need to add and remove objects to the collection on a regular basis.

2. The elements of your array are all objects or can be represented as objects. In order to be used in a vector, simple data types need to be converted to objects using the java.lang wrapper classes.

3. You need to determine easily whether a specific object is in an array and its position in the array.

An important consideration of using vectors instead of arrays is that you cannot directly store a simple data type in a vector; you can only store objects. As a consequence, you will need to use the data wrapper classes when storing integer and other numeric values in an array.

In other cases, arrays are preferable. For example, in the following types of situations, you would probably want to use an array:

1. You are dealing with a fixed quantity of objects; although the actual objects may change, the array will always contain the same number of them.

2. You are dealing with values that can be represented as simple types such as integers or characters, and you want the added efficiency of dealing with array elements as simple types rather than as objects.

In some cases, if you need resizable arrays using simple types, you may find it worthwhile to write your own resizable array management code. If so, you might want to look at the file Vector.java for tips on how to do this efficiently.

Using Vectors

Vectors are allocated as objects using the new operator. When a Vector is constructed, it creates an internal private array to store elements that are added to it and reallocates this array as necessary when adding an element to the vector would exceed the size of the array. The Vector class hides most of the details of this process from you although, if you care to optimize your code further, you can take a look at the optional constructors and methods available in the API reference.

Here is a basic example of allocating a Vector object:

```
Vector theVector = new Vector();
```

In this case, we used the default constructor, which is fine for most cases. You can find out about the other versions in the API reference.

Adding Elements to Vectors

Once we've created a Vector, we can add objects to it using the addElement() method. The addElement() method is defined as follows:

```
public final synchronized void addElement(Object obj)
```

This method takes an object as a parameter and adds it to the end of the Vector. Here's an example of adding three Integer objects to a Vector:

```
for (int i = 0; i < 3; i++) {
    Integer newInteger = new Integer(i);
    theVector.addElement(newInteger);
}
```

After this code is executed, the contents of theVector will be {0, 1, 2}. Vectors can be used with any type of object, and you can mix the objects stored in them. Here's another example of creating a vector, this time using String objects:

```
Vector nameVector = new Vector();
String current_name;

current_name = "Ed";
nameVector.addElement(current_name);

current_name = "Joe";
nameVector.addElement(current_name);

current_name = "Scott";
nameVector.addElement(current_name);

current_name = "Brett";
nameVector.addElement(current_name);
```

This will create a vector called nameVector with the contents {"Ed", "Joe", "Scott", "Brett"}.

Another way to add elements to a Vector is through the insertElementAt() method. This method will insert an object at a specific position in the Vector. The method is defined as follows:

```
public final synchronized void insertElementAt( Object obj,
                                                int index)
```

Here's an example where we insert a new object in the middle of the list created in the previous example:

```
String newName = "Oliver";
nameVector.insertElementAt(newName, 0);
```

After this code is executed, the contents of theVector will be {"Oliver", "Ed", "Joe", "Scott", "Brett"}.

Removing Elements from Vectors

Objects can be removed from vectors using removeElement(), removeElementAt(), or removeAllElements() methods. The removeElement() method removes the specified object from the Vector object. This method is defined as follows:

```
public final synchronized boolean removeElement(Object obj)
```

If the same object has been added to the array more than once, removeElement removes the first element, which is a reference to the object. Here's an example of using removeElement() to remove the newName object from the previous example:

```
nameVector.removeElement(newName);
```

In many cases, it will be more useful to remove an element of a vector by specifying the element number rather than the object to remove. The removeElementAt() method removes the object at the specified element number from the Vector object. This method is defined as follows:

```
public final synchronized void removeElementAt(int index)
```

Here's an example of using this to remove the first element of a vector. Assume that theVector contains {5, 0, 1, 2} before removeElementAt is called:

```
theVector.removeElementAt(0);
```

This removes the element at position 0. After the call, theVector contains {0, 1, 2}. The final method for removing elements from a Vector is removeAllElements() which, as the name implies, removes all the elements from the vector. The method is defined as:

```
public final synchronized void removeAllElements()
```

Getting and Setting Elements in Vectors

To be able to use a vector as an array, the Vector class provides two methods that provide you with the ability to get and set elements in a vector by specifying the element position, or *index*. These methods are elementAt() and setElementAt() and are defined as follows:

```
public final synchronized Object elementAt(  int index)


public final synchronized void setElementAt( Object obj,
                                             int index)
```

The method elementAt() is passed the position as a parameter and returns a reference to the object stored in that element in the vector. The method setElementAt() stores the object reference passed in the first parameter in the vector element passed in the second element. When we last left our sample name list Vector, it contained {"Oliver", "Ed", "Joe", "Scott", "Brett"}. Vector elements are numbered starting from 0 to count of objects −1. In the case of our sample vector,

```
System.out.println(elementAt(0));
```

would print out "Oliver". Let's take a look at an example where we use elementAt() and setElementAt() to swap the second and third elements of the list:

```
// Save a reference to the object at element 1 = "Ed"
Object tempObject = nameVector.elementAt(1);
// Copy element 2 "Joe" to element 1
nameVector.setElementAt(elementAt(2), 1);
// Set element 2 to tempObject which refs to String "Ed"
nameVector.setElementAt(tempObject, 2);
```

The vector now looks like {"Oliver", "Joe", "Ed", "Scott", "Brett"}. What we did in this example is first use the elementAt() method to get the object reference stored in the second element (remember, elements are numbered from 0, so the second element is at index position 1) in the vector and store that reference in the variable tempObject. In the next line, we use elementAt() and setElementAt() to copy the object reference in the third element of the vector to the second element of the vector. The last line takes the reference we stored in tempObject and stores it in the third element of the vector. When we're done with these steps, the objects at elements 1 and 2 have traded places.

Finding Objects in Vectors

One of the nice features about vectors is that they contain a number of methods that let you easily find out if an object is present in the vector and where it is located. We'll review most of these methods in this section.

```
public final boolean contains(Object elem)
```

The contains() method tests whether a vector contains a given object and returns true if the object is in the vector and false otherwise.

```
public final int indexOf(Object elem)
```

The indexOf() method searches the vector starting from element 0 and returns the element number of the specified object if it is found within the vector. If the object cannot be found, the method returns −1.

```
public final synchronized int indexOf(        Object elem,
                                              int index)
```

This second version of the indexOf() method searches the vector starting from the element number passed in index to the last element in the vector and returns the position number of the specified object if it is found within that range of elements. If the object cannot be found, the method returns −1.

```
public final synchronized int lastIndexOf( Object elem)
```

The lastIndexOf() method searches the vector backwards, starting from the last element, and returns the element number of the specified object if it is found within the vector. If the object cannot be found, the method returns −1.

```
public final synchronized int lastIndexOf( Object elem,
                                              int index)
```

This second version of the lastIndexOf() method searches the vector backwards, starting from the element number passed in index to the first element in the vector, and returns the position number of the specified object if it is found within that range of elements. If the object cannot be found, the method returns −1.

```
public final synchronized Object firstElement()
```

The firstElement() method returns the object reference stored in the first element of the arrays.

```
public final synchronized Object lastElement()
```

The lastElement() method returns the object reference stored in the last element of the arrays.

Vectors, Loops, and the Enumeration Class

In most cases where you use Vectors, you will need to perform some action using each element of the vector. One way to do this would be via a simple for loop, like this:

```
for (int i = 0; i < nameVector.size(); i++) {
    String theName = (String)nameVector.elementAt(i);
    System.out.println(theName);
}
```

This loop will print out every element of the nameVector. A second method of looping through arrays makes use of the Enumeration class, which provides a simple interface for retrieving a set of objects in a sequential manner. The Enumeration class provides two methods: hasMoreElements() and nextElement(). These methods are defined like this:

```
public abstract boolean hasMoreElements()
public abstract Object nextElement()
```

The Vector class will create an Enumeration object for you when you call the Vector's elements() method. You can then use the Enumeration object to step through the elements of the Vector with a loop like this:

```
for (Enumeration e = nameVector.elements(); e.hasMoreElements();) {
    System.out.println(e.nextElement());
}
```

This loop will print out every element of the nameVector by calling elements() to get an Enumeration object for the nameVector. The Enumeration object is stored in the variable e. The loop continues as long as the hasMoreElements() method returns true. Each time through the loop, the nextElement() is used to get the next object from the Enumeration.

The case can be made that using the Enumeration class for looping through vectors is unnecessary because the same task can be handled through conventional loops. However, it is a good idea to get into the habit of this approach because it is used to sequentially access other types of Java collection classes such as Hashtables, which cannot be stepped through in any other way.

Using the Java Wrapper Classes

The simple types are boolean, char, double, float, int, and long, and because these types are not class-based, we can't use them as is in classes like Vector (or, as we see in the next section, Hashtable). In this case, we make use of the wrapper classes, discussed earlier in the chapter.

Let's take a look at an example of using the wrapper classes with our earlier example of parsing a list of items in a string to create a method that takes a list of integers in a string and stores them in a vector that is returned to the caller:

```
Vector ParseNumberList(String theText) {
    Vector items = null;
    if (theText != null) {
        items = new Vector();
        int i = 0;
        while (i < theText.length()) {
            int next = theText.indexOf(',', i);
            if (next == -1) next = theText.length();
            String theItem = theText.substring(i, next);
            Integer theInt = Integer.valueOf(theItem);
            items.addElement(theInt);
            i = next + 1;
        }
    }
    return items;
}
```

In this example, we build on some techniques we saw in our string examples to parse a list of comma-separated items in a string. We take each item and convert it to an Integer object by making use of the static valueOf() method of the String class. Because valueOf() is a static method, we can use it with the class without having to instantiate an object first. The valueOf() class is a static method present in each of the wrapper classes (Boolean, Character, Double, Float, Integer, and Long) that takes a string as a parameter and returns a newly created instance of the wrapper class if it is able to convert the string to an acceptable value. Since the instances of wrapper classes like Integer are genuine objects as opposed to simple types like int, we can store them as elements in a vector.

Java provides a StringTokenizer class which is worth looking into if you are writing programs that need to parse through string data. In the case of our last example, we could have rewritten it to use the StringTokenizer like this:

```
Vector ParseNumberList(String theText) {
    Vector items = new Vector();
    StringTokenizer st = new StringTokenizer(theText, ',');
```

```
    while (st.hasMoreTokens()) {
       String theItem = st.nextToken();
       Integer theInt = Integer.valueOf(theItem);
       items.addElement(theInt);
    }
    return items;
}
```

You can find more information about the methods available in the StringTokenizer in the class reference.

Hashtables

Java's Hashtable class lets you create associated arrays where you can map a key to an object, then later use that key to retrieve the object quickly. Working with the Hashtable class is very similar to using the vector class, with a few differences that we will address this section.

Hashtables are based on the idea that you have keys associated with values so that when you go to retrieve the value, you can do so by referring to its key. Depending on your application, your keys might be things like employee names, which would be stored as strings. The object you associate with the string would then contain instance variables for things such as phone numbers, departments, and more.

Another use of hashtables is to hold sets of values. In this case, you would use the methods provided by the hashtable to add elements to the set, remove elements from the set, and determine whether an element was present in the set.

Using Hashtables

To store an object in a hashtable, you need to assign it a key. It is worthwhile to take a little time to determine what you will use as a key because that key is how you will retrieve objects from the hashtable. As we mentioned earlier, keys might be last names, id code, or just about any object within Java. The one caveat is that the key must be an instance of an object that implements the hashCode() method. For most purposes, you don't need to worry about this because all of the Java-supplied data classes implement hashCode() for you. You will only need to create a hashCode method() if you create your own classes for use as keys—and only then to improve the performance of the hashtable.

A hashtable creates what is referred to as a many-to-one relationship table, which means it allows you to map one or more keys to the same object. For example, suppose you were creating a glossary. You would have a list of keywords that would refer to specific entries in your glossary. In the case of our glossary of object-oriented terms, you would map the keywords "subclass", "derived class", "child class", and "descendent" to the string "A class derived from another class." Here's the code that would implement this as a hashtable:

```
HashTable glossary = new HashTable();
String definition = "A class derived from another class.";
glossary.put("subclass", definition);
glossary.put("derived class", definition);
glossary.put("child class", definition);
glossary.put("descendent", definition);
definition = "A class from which other classes are derived.";
glossary.put("superclass", definition);
glossary.put("base class", definition);
glossary.put("parent class", definition);
glossary.put("ancestor", definition);
```

In the above example, we created a hashtable and mapped strings containing the common terms to describe subclasses and superclasses to strings containing the definitions of those terms. To retrieve a definition, I could use the hashtable's get() method to return the appropriate string object. Here's an example of this:

```
String definition = (String)glossary.get("ancestor");
```

The variable definition will be set to a reference to the string holding the definition. If the object that the key is mapped to was not found, null would be returned.

Adding and Removing Objects

As we've seen in the previous examples, adding an object to a hashtable is done through the put() method, defined as follows:

```
public synchronized Object put(Object key, Object value)
```

If the hashtable already contains the specified key, the object associated with the key is returned by the method, and the new object in value replaces the old object in the hashtable.

To remove a key and its associated object from a hashtable, you make use of the remove() method:

```
public synchronized Object remove(Object key)
```

If the key is found, the object associated is returned (or null if the key is not found), and the key is removed from the table. The important thing to notice is that objects are removed from the hashtable via their keys. Because the same object could be associated with several different keys in the same hashtable, you can't assume that removing a single key will eliminate all references in the hashtable to the object.

Finding Keys

There are two methods for finding keys within a hashtable. The first, which we've seen in previous examples, is the get() method. This method is defined as follows:

```
public synchronized Object get(Object key)
```

The get() method finds the specified key in the hashtable and returns the object associated with the given key. If the key isn't found, the method returns null.

The second way of finding if a hashtable contains a key is with the aptly named containsKey method, defined as follows:

```
public synchronized boolean containsKey(Object key)
```

This method returns true if the key is contained in the hashtable and false otherwise. Although you could accomplish the same thing with the get() method and simply test whether the result was false, using the containsKey() method in situations where you don't need to retrieve the object associated with the key can make the code more readable.

A Final Example

In some cases, you may want to create a many-to-many relationship. In this case, you could store vectors into the hashtable. For example, suppose we want to map keywords to one of several definitions that contain that keyword. Depending on the size and number of keywords and definitions, we might decide that a search algorithm is appropriate to search through all the definitions and present each one that contains the keyword. In the case of a very large number of definitions, we would not want to execute this search algorithm each time someone looked up a keyword. Instead, we might build a hashtable of vectors. When the hashtable is given a key, it will return a vector that contains a list of references to definitions that contain the keyword.

An Illustration Let's take a look at a final example that combines many of the concepts we've learned in this chapter to implement a small many-to-many database that allows us to search our glossary by keyword. It will return a list of definitions that match the given search keyword.

```java
import java.util.*;

class Definition {
    String name;
    String definition;
    Vector keys = new Vector();

    Definition() {
    }

    Definition(String name, String definition) {
        this.name = name;
        this.definition = definition;
    }

    void SetName(String name) {
        this.name = name;
    }

    void SetDef(String definition) {
        this.definition = definition;
    }

    String GetName() {
```

```java
        return name;
    }

    void AddKey(String key_string) {
        keys.addElement(key_string);
    }

    Vector GetKeys() {
        return keys;
    }

    void Print() {
        System.out.println(name + " - " + definition);
    }
}

class Glossary extends Hashtable {

    Glossary(Vector entries) {
        Build(entries);
    }

    void Build(Vector entries) {
        System.out.println("Building key list...");
        for (Enumeration e = entries.elements();
                e.hasMoreElements();) {
            Definition theEntry = (Definition)e.nextElement();
            HandleDefinition(theEntry);
        }
        System.out.println();
        System.out.println("Done.");
    }

    void HandleDefinition(Definition theEntry) {
```

```
        Vector theKeys = theEntry.GetKeys();


        for (Enumeration e = theKeys.elements();
             e.hasMoreElements();) {
          String theName = (String)e.nextElement();


          StringTokenizer st = new StringTokenizer(theName, " ");
          while (st.hasMoreTokens()) {
            String theKeyWord = st.nextToken();
            Vector items = (Vector)get(theKeyWord);
            if (items == null) items = new Vector();
            if (items.indexOf(theEntry) == -1)
               items.addElement(theEntry);
            put(theKeyWord, items);
            System.out.print(theKeyWord + " ");
          }
        }
      }


  void PrintMatches(String theKey) {
     System.out.println("Searching for \"" + theKey + "\"");
     Vector items = (Vector)get(theKey);
     if (items != null) {
       System.out.println("Match(es):");
       for (Enumeration e = items.elements();
            e.hasMoreElements();) {
         Definition theEntry = (Definition)e.nextElement();
         theEntry.Print();
       }
     }
     else {
       System.out.println("No matches found.");
     }
   }
}
```

```java
class GlossaryExampleApp {
   public static void main (String args[]) {
      Vector entries = new Vector();

      Definition theDef;
      theDef = new Definition ();
      theDef.SetName("subclass");
      theDef.SetDef("A class derived from another class.");
      theDef.AddKey("subclass");
      theDef.AddKey("derived class");
      theDef.AddKey("child class");
      theDef.AddKey("descendent");
      entries.addElement(theDef);

      theDef = new Definition ();
      theDef.SetName("superclass");
      theDef.SetDef("A class from which others are derived.");
      theDef.AddKey("superclass");
      theDef.AddKey("base class");
      theDef.AddKey("parent class");
      theDef.AddKey("ancestor");
      entries.addElement(theDef);

      theDef = new Definition ();
      theDef.SetName("method");
      theDef.SetDef("An operation upon an object.");
      theDef.AddKey("method");
      theDef.AddKey("member function");
      entries.addElement(theDef);

      theDef = new Definition ();
      theDef.SetName("instance variable");
      theDef.SetDef("A variable within an object.");
      theDef.AddKey("instance variable");
```

```
        theDef.AddKey("member variable");
        theDef.AddKey("property");
        entries.addElement(theDef);


        Glossary theGlossary = new Glossary(entries);


        theGlossary.PrintMatches("class");
        theGlossary.PrintMatches("method");
    }
  }
```

This example defines a class to hold a glossary definition called Definition that holds the name and text of a glossary definition. We also define a class called Glossary based on the Hashtable class. The lengthy main method in the GlossaryExampleApp simply loads the definition data into a Glossary instance.

If you were to run the example, you would see the following:

```
Building key list...
sub class instance variable super class ancestor method descendent
derived class property parent class child class member variable base
class member function
Done.
Searching for "class"
Match(es):
subclass - A class derived from another class.
superclass - A class from which others are derived.
Searching for "method"
Match(es):
method - An operation upon an object.
```

HANDLING

EXCEPTIONS

A n exception is a condition that can occur during the execution of your code that requires the program either to stop immediately or to perform a special action to deal with the exception. Most exceptions that you encounter will occur in response to error conditions, such as dividing an integer by 0. When the interpreter encounters an error such as this, it throws an exception, which causes the code to jump to an appropriate exception handler. The exception handler that is able to deal with the type of exception that has been thrown is said to *catch* the exception. If no exception handler has been defined, the default exception handler takes over, prints out the error to the command line, and stops the program.

When you learn about exceptions, you should realize that although they are most often used to handle error conditions, exceptions are not the same thing as errors—they are thrown by errors. Like just about everything else in Java, an exception is a type of object. As we will see in this chapter, you can throw your own exceptions by allocating an Exception object and using the throw statement to throw it.

Using Exception Handlers to Handle Errors

When looking at a program and deciding when to use exception handlers, you'll want to think about your goal in catching an exception. Because the exception-handling mechanism can be used to hide errors from the rest of the system, there is a potential for misuse—your programming focus can shift from the proper debugging of code to designing graceful recoveries from error conditions without understanding what is causing those errors. If you encounter intermittent exceptions when you run your programs, you should first find out why these exceptions are occurring before you put an exception handler in place to cover them up.

Let's take a look at a basic use of an exception handler to catch the exception thrown when you try to use a null object reference as a legitimate object reference.

```
void BadMethod() {
    String myString = null;
    try {
        if (myString.equals("Test"))
            System.out.println("String matched.");
    } catch (Exception e) {
        System.out.println("An exception occurred.");
    }
    System.out.println("Method done.");
}
```

This example shows how exception handlers are defined by surrounding the code that you want to catch exceptions from with the try and catch statements. The catch statement in this example looks for an exception that is an instance of the Exception class or one of its subclasses; if it matches, it executes the code within the catch block. In the case of this example, we try to use the equals() method of the object reference by myString. The problem is that myString hasn't been assigned an instantiated object and still contains null. This will result in a NullPointerException being thrown when we make the method call to the equals() method. Because we've set up a catch statement that is watching for instances of the Exception class or its subclasses, we catch the NullPointerException object that is thrown by the error. The catch block prints out the message "An exception occurred." Because we have caught the error, the program can continue with the code outside the exception handler with the next line in the method, which is the statement System.out.println("Method done.");.

Additional catch statements can be used within an exception handler to deal with specific types of exceptions. The first catch statement that matches the exception is executed. Let's revisit the last example:

```
void BadMethod() {
    String myString = null;
    try {
        if (myString.equals("Test"))
            System.out.println("String matched.");
    } catch (NullPointerException e) {
        System.out.println("A null pointer exception occurred.");
    } catch (Exception e) {
        System.out.println("An exception occurred.");
    }
    System.out.println("Method done.");
}
```

This version first tries to catch the null pointer exception and, if it is unable to match that, it catches the generic exception.

While some exceptions are the result of bugs in your program or encountering unexpected values like null object references, events outside your control—like your program running out of memory—can also throw exceptions. Most exception objects in Java are subclasses of Exception, or RuntimeException, or Error. These classes are all descendants of the base exception class Throwable. (If you're wondering why the base exception class isn't Exception, the answer is that, for most purposes, you will use it as if it were.) RuntimeException is a subclass of Exception, and in earlier releases of Java, Exception was the ancestor of all exception classes. As Java has evolved during its alpha and beta testing phases, it became necessary to create a more robust set of classes to handle the different error conditions that could occur within programs and applets. As we examine the different types of exceptions that you can catch in your exception handlers, you will see what the issues are when using subclasses of Exception, RuntimeException, and Error. Table 11.1 lists the exceptions that are subclasses of each one of these.

Table 11.1 Subclasses of Exception, RuntimeException, and Error

RuntimeException subclasses

ArithmeticException

ArrayIndexOutOfBoundsException

ArrayStoreException

ClassCastException

IllegalArgumentException

IllegalThreadStateException

IndexOutOfBoundsException

NegativeArraySizeException

NullPointerException

NumberFormatException

SecurityException

StringIndexOutOfBoundsException

Exception subclasses

ClassNotFoundException

DataFormatException

IllegalAccessException

InstantiationException

InterruptedException

NoSuchMethodException

RuntimeException

Error subclasses

ClassCircularityError

ClassFormatError

Error

IllegalAccessError

IncompatibleClassChangeError

InstantiationError

▮▮▮▮▮▮▮ **Table 11.1** Continued

InternalError

LinkageError

NoClassDefFoundError

NoSuchFieldError

NoSuchMethodError

OutOfMemoryError

StackOverflowError

Throwable

UnknownError

UnsatisfiedLinkError

VerifyError

VirtualMachineError

▮▮▮▮▮▮▮

We will deal with some of these exceptions in more detail as the chapter progresses.

Elements of Exception Handling

As we've seen in previous examples, an exception handler is defined with the help of the try and catch statements. In this section, we'll take a closer look at these and introduce the third statement that can be used in an exception handler, the finally statement.

throw

Exceptions are often the result of an error condition that the interpreter signals by throwing an exception. However, there are times when you will want or need to throw an exception yourself. To do this, you use the throw keyword followed by an instance of a Throwable object. The form of a throw statement is as follows:

```
throw reference-to-Throwable-subclass;
```

Here is an example of throwing an object with a throw statement:

```
throw new ArithmeticException()
```

As soon as a throw statement completes, the program will jump to the first exception handler that handles exceptions of this class type.

try

The try statement starts the exception handler. The general form of the try statement is as follows:

```
try statement;
catch(Throwable-subclass e) statement;
```

Each try statement must be followed by at least one catch statement. If an exception is thrown in any of the code between the try and catch statements, it causes execution to jump to the catch statements that attempted to match its class type. If the code between the try and catch statements contains a method call, and if that method or any methods called by it throw an exception that they don't handle themselves, our handler gets an opportunity to handle it.

catch

When an exception is thrown within the try block, execution jumps to the first catch statement in the exception handler that will accept an exception object of the type thrown. The general form of the catch statement is as follows:

```
try statement;
catch(Throwable-subclass e) statement;
```

The catch statement works in a similar way to a method definition. The catch statement is passed a single parameter, which is a reference to the exception object that was thrown. This object is an instance of a class that is based on the Throwable class. If you have more than one catch statement in the exception handler, the first catch statement whose parameter type is compatible with the exception object that was thrown is executed. Let's take another look at one of our examples from the start of the chapter:

```
try {
    myString.equals("Test");
    if (myString.equals("Test"))
        System.out.println("String matched.");
    System.out.println("A null pointer exception occurred.");
} catch (ArithmeticException e) {
    System.out.println("An arithmetic exception occurred.");
} catch (Exception e) {
    System.out.println("An exception occurred.");
}
```

In this example, if the exception is an instance of NullPointerException, the first catch block will handle the exception. If not, then the exception is checked to see if it is an instance of ArithmeticException, and if so, then the second catch block handles the exception. The final catch block checks to see if it is an instance of Exception and handles that if it matches. Because most exceptions are instances of Exception or one of its subclasses, it is likely that the error will get handled by this catch block. If the exception is not caught by any of the three catch blocks, then it will be up to whoever called this method to catch the exception; otherwise, the default exception handler will respond to the exception by halting the program.

finally

After the catch blocks get their shot at handling the exception, one final element of the exception handler is executed. This is the code that makes up the finally statement block. The finally statement is defined as follows:

```
try statement;
catch(Throwable-subclass e) statement;
finally statement;
```

The code in the final block gets executed whether or not an exception is thrown in the try block. The purpose of the finally block is to execute some code that you want to occur regardless of whether errors, such as making sure that instance variables are correctly initialized, occur in the try block. Here's our example revised to use the finally statement:

```
void BadMethod() {
    String myString = null;
    System.out.println("Watching for exceptions.");
    try {
        if (myString.equals("Test"))
            System.out.println("String matched.");
    } catch (NullPointerException e) {
        System.out.println("A null pointer exception occurred.");
        System.out.println("Exception dealt with.");
    } catch (Exception e) {
        System.out.println("An unexpected exception occurred.");
        System.out.println("Exception NOT dealt with.");
        throw e;
```

```
    } finally {
        System.out.println("Exception handler done.");
    }
    System.out.println("Method done, all exceptions dealt with.");
}
```

In this example, if the try block throws a null pointer exception, the catch block for NullPointerException will be executed. The code in the finally block will then get executed, followed by the code after the exception handler. The output would look like this:

```
Watching for exceptions.
A null pointer exception occurred.
Exception dealt with.
Exception handler done.
Method done, all exceptions dealt with.
```

If an exception is thrown that is not the null pointer exception, then it is caught by the second catch block, which prints out a message and rethrows the error. In this case, the output would look like:

```
Watching for exceptions.
An unexpected exception occurred.
Exception NOT dealt with.
Exception handler done.
```

And, of course, if no exceptions were thrown, the output would look like:

```
Watching for exceptions.
Exception handler done.
Method done, all exceptions dealt with.
```

Declaring Exceptions in Method Definitions

When a method does not contain an exception handler to catch exceptions that might be thrown from within a method, the uncaught exceptions will be thrown by the method for the calling method to handle. A method can define which methods it can throw so that the calling method will know that it is possible for exceptions to be thrown to it. A method indicates which exceptions it throws using the throws parameter in the method definition:

```
return-type method-name (parameter-list) [throws exceptions] {
    [statements;]
}
```

A common point of confusion for Java programmers is when to declare exceptions and which exceptions need to be declared. First of all, you are required to declare an exception only if you don't have an exception handler in place that will catch that type of exception. Declaring an exception means that the method may throw the exception and either does not catch it or catches it and rethrows it. As a consequence, any method calling this method must be prepared to catch the exception or declare it with the throws parameter.

The second reason why you may have to declare an exception in a method definition is if the method throws certain types of exceptions. Earlier in this chapter, we listed all the exception classes (using the broad definition of exception classes as any class based on the Throwable class) and classified them as Exceptions, RuntimeExceptions, and Errors. If your method or any of the methods that it calls can throw any of the exception classes listed in the Exceptions table, and it does not have an exception handler in place to deal with those exceptions, then the exceptions must be declared with the throws parameter.

In the case of our previous examples, because we were throwing NullPointerException, which is a run-time exception, we didn't have to use the throws parameter in the method definition. However, if we were to call a method that could throw an InterruptedException, which is an exception that gets thrown when a thread gets interrupted (see Chapter 12 for more information on threads), we would need either to declare it with a throws parameter or to catch it with an exception handler, or the compiler would not let us compile the program. Either one of these would satisfy the compiler's requirement:

```
void BadMethod() throws InterruptedException {
    throw new InterruptedException();
    System.out.println("Method done.");
}
```

```
void BadMethod() {
    try {
        throw new InterruptedException();
    } catch (InterruptedException e) {
        System.out.println("A interrupted exception occurred.");
        System.out.println("Exception dealt with.");
    }
    System.out.println("Method done, all exceptions dealt with.");
}
```

Runtime Exceptions

This section will provide you with a brief description of all the exceptions that are subclasses of RuntimeException.

ArithmeticException

An arithmetic exception is thrown if you try to divide an integer by zero or take a modulus by zero.

For example, the following code causes an ArithmeticException to be thrown:

```
void BadArith() {
    int d = 0;
    int n = 4;
    int result = d/n;
}
```

ArrayIndexOutOfBoundsException

An ArrayIndexOutOfBoundsException is thrown when you try to access an element that is out of the bounds of an array, meaning that you are using an index of less than zero or greater than or equal to the size of the array.

Here's an example that would throw an ArrayIndexOutOfBoundsException:

```
void BadArrayIndex() {
    int theArray[] = new int[10];
```

```
    theArray [10] = 0;    // bad index, should be between 0 and 9
}
```

ArrayStoreException

This exception is thrown by some methods in the supplied package classes when you try to store a value into an array of an incompatible class or type. You may also choose to throw this exception in your methods when you are passed a value that you are unable to store in one of your object's arrays.

The following method results in a ClassCastException at runtime:

```
void BadArrayCopy() {
    int[] src = new int[5];
    boolean[]dst = new boolean [5];
    System.arraycopy(src, 0, dst, 0, 3);
}
```

ClassCastException

When we talked about class casting in earlier chapters, we saw that you can cast an instance of a class to its superclass, but you can't cast an instance of a class to one of its subclasses. If you attempt this cast, you will throw a ClassCastException.

The following class declaration results in a ClassCastException at run time:

```
class ClassA {
}


class ClassB extends ClassA {
    void test() { }
}


class Test {
    void BadCast() {
        Object theObject = new ClassA();
        ClassB instanceB = (ClassB)theObject;
        instanceB.test();
    }
}
```

IllegalArgumentException

This exception is thrown by some methods in the supplied package classes when you pass a parameter that is not in a valid range or value for the method. You may also choose to throw this exception in your methods when passed unacceptable values.

The following method throws an IllegalArgumentException if passed an illegal parameter value:

```
void TestForBadArg(int value) {
    if (value == 0)
        throw new IllegalArgumentException("Argument cannot be 0.");
    int something = 1 / value;
}
```

IllegalThreadStateException

This exception is thrown by some methods in the supplied package classes when you try to illegally change the state of a thread, for example, by trying to start a thread that is already running. You may also choose to throw this exception in your methods if they are requested to perform an action on one of your thread sub-classes that is not allowed when the thread is running or suspended.

IndexOutOfBoundsException

This exception is the parent class of exceptions such as ArrayIndexOutOfBoundsException. It should not be thrown by any of the supplied classes, but you may choose to throw this exception in your methods if passed an index value that is outside an acceptable range. In this case, your decision will be whether to throw this exception or IllegalArgumentException.

NegativeArraySizeException

This exception is thrown when an array with a negative size is attempted to be allocated.

The following method results in a NegativeArraySizeException at runtime:

```
void BadArraySize() {
    int theSize = -5;
    int[] badArray = new int[theSize];
}
```

NullPointerException

This exception is thrown when you attempt to use a method or variable in a variable that contains a null object reference. NullPointerException is misnamed for historical reasons; the term "reference" replaced "pointer" to describe the value used to refer to specific objects.

The following method results in a NullPointerException at runtime:

```
void BadPointer() {
    String theString = null;
    if (theString.equals("test")) {
        System.out.println("Matched.");
    }
}
```

NumberFormatException

This exception is thrown by some methods in the supplied package classes when you try to convert an invalid string to a number or vice versa.

SecurityException

This exception is thrown by some methods in the supplied package classes when you attempt to call a method that will perform an action not allowed by the current security settings of the browser within which your applet code is running. It can also be thrown if the user denies permission when prompted whether to allow an action such as writing to a file.

StringIndexOutOfBoundsException

A StringIndexOutOfBoundsException is thrown when you try to access a character that is out of the bounds of a string, meaning that you are using an index of less than zero or greater than or equal to the length of the string.

Here's an example that would throw a StringIndexOutOfBoundsException:

```
void BadStringIndex() {
    String theString = "14 char string";
    char theChar = theString.charAt(15);
    // bad index, should be between 0 and 13
}
```

Other Exceptions

This section will provide you with a brief description of all the exceptions that are subclasses of Exception. These types of exceptions occur less frequently than the runtime exceptions we listed before; when they occur they usually indicate a more serious error condition.

ClassNotFoundException

This exception is thrown by the class loader when a .class file is not found when a class is attempted to be instantiated. This could happen, for example, if a class file in a Web server was placed in the wrong directory or if the Web server—for whatever reason—was unable to send the class file when requested.

DataFormatException

This exception is the parent class of exceptions that are thrown when data being read from a stream appears to be in an invalid format.

IllegalAccessException

This exception is thrown by methods in java.lang.Class when instantiating a class by its name if the class is not public or there is no public constructor. You might encounter this exception if calling a method that, in turn, calls one of these methods.

InstantiationException

This exception is thrown when an attempt is made to instantiate an abstract class, primarily by methods in java.lang.Class when instantiating a class by its name. You might encounter this exception if calling a method that, in turn, calls one of these methods.

InterruptedException

This exception is thrown within a thread when it is interrupted by some other thread. You will most likely encounter this when calling wait() or sleep() within a thread. Because these methods declare that they throw InterruptedException, and because this exception is not classified a run-time exception, you must catch it with a try/catch exception handler. Here's an example of typical usage:

```
public void run() {
    while (true) {
        System.out.println("testing");
        try {
            sleep(100);
        } catch (InterruptedException e) {
            return;
        }
    }
}
```

NoSuchMethodException

This exception is thrown when a particular method in an object or class cannot be found. You will seldom encounter this exception because, in order for it to be thrown, several other exceptions must somehow not be thrown.

Error Classes

There are a number of exceptions that are subclasses of java.lang.Error, which are thrown in response to conditions such as running out of memory or stack over-flows. We listed these errors earlier in the chapter but won't cover them in further detail because they represent conditions from which you may not be able to easily recover without a deep understanding of the supplied packages. A good place to start is looking at the source files included with the Java release as well as online documentation at www.javasoft.com. I recommend that you do not catch these errors until you understand why they are thrown and the implications of ignoring or trying to recover from them.

CHAPTER 2

THREADS

Depending on the applications and operating systems you've used in the past, you may or may not understand what multitasking and concurrent processes mean and how they make your computer more responsive and interactive. Historically, when you used an operating system like the Macintosh OS and Windows, each application you launched was a separate process. These application processes could switch between each other (for example, most Mac users are used to having several applications open and switching between a word processor, a spreadsheet, and the Finder and, to some extent, sending messages to each other).

Within each application process, however, the applications had a single flow of control, which consisted of an event-loop; this is simply a loop that polls for events from the operating system, and depending on the event it receives, performs a task to process, such as repaginating a document. When the application asks the operating system of the event, the operating system checks to see if any of the other applications need to perform any tasks, and gives them time to perform the tasks. The OS then gives the original application the event it requested, and it is none the wiser to the fact that several other applications were just given execution time as well. As long as every application requests events from the OS on a regular and frequent basis, every application will in turn be given time to execute; as a consequence, the system is able to provide the user with the perception that several applications are executing simultaneously.

If any of the applications need to perform a lengthy task, or a task that is not comfortable letting other applications run concurrent with, it can hog the system and not allow other applications to run simply by not requesting an event from the operating system. In some cases, certain operating system-supplied services reinforce this type of situation. For example, on the Macintosh, while you hold down a menu, other applications are unable to execute (this won't happen when you use menus within an applet in the Macintosh version of Java because it uses its own menu-handling code rather than the operating system's) and anything else going on in the program, like animations that are playing, stops. The application really needs to be doing (at least) two things at the same time: dealing with events and user interaction (like the menu) and performing whatever other task or tasks that it needs to perform such as playing an animation.

Most versions of UNIX as well as new versions of the Windows and the Macintosh OS allow each application process in turn to own a number of lightweight processes or threads. An application that is written to take advantage of this feature can be thought of as consisting of a number of subprograms that execute at the same time. When the application needs to draw an animation running across the screen, it spawns a new process to handle the animation. The new process, for the most part, thinks of itself as the only program that is running, but in fact, many other processes are executing as well, such as threads to handle user interaction or downloading files from the net. The innovation of threads is not that they allow you to actually run two processes at the same time—most computers still only have one microprocessor to execute code with—but that they allow you to write the code for these processes as if they were, in fact, running simultaneously.

Where does Java come into the picture? Java defines threads as an integral part of the language and includes a number of features that allow you to easily write Java programs that create multiple threads. In addition, Java handles the differences between the way threads are handled on various platforms for you, so that you don't have to do anything special for your program to be able to create a thread on the Macintosh or under Solaris.

Understanding Threads

In Chapter 6 we talked about flow of control and the sequence in which Java executes your programs. Java also enables you to have multiple flows of control. Each flow of control can be thought of as a separate mini-program, referred to as a thread, that gets started by your application and runs in parallel to it. This thread has access to all the objects in your program and can call methods or access variables within them. In running a Java program you will often have several threads handling various activities such as tracking the mouse position, updating the position of on-screen graphical objects, or simply keeping time. The ability to have multiple threads running in a language is called *concurrency*; Java's threads are often referred to as *lightweight threads*, which means that they run in the same memory space. Because Java threads run in the same memory space, they can easily communicate among themselves because an object in one thread can call a method in another thread without any overhead from the operating system.

Concurrency and Thread Execution

When we talk about concurrency, we do not mean that threads actually run at the same time, but that the Java interpreter handles switching between threads for you to provide the appearance that they are running concurrently. Let's imagine that we have two methods (runA() and runB()) that are each running in a different thread and that the two threads were told to start execution at virtually the same time, although thread A was actually started first. Figure 12.1 shows how the two threads perceive that they are being executed by the processor.

As you can see, both threads are allowed to believe that they are running in an ideal computer that has two microprocessors. In reality, these two threads are running on a single processor system, and the flow of execution is shared between the two threads. If the flow of execution passes between the threads at certain points in the code, the output from these two threads would look like this:

```
A:Start
B:Start
A:1
B:1
A:2
B:2
A:Done
B:Done
```

Scheduling

As mentioned before, thread A was started first, and as a consequence, it will be run first by the Java thread scheduler. While thread A is run, thread B waits for control of the processor to become available for it to execute. In multithreaded programs, you think of the processor as a resource that becomes available and is lent to your thread for a certain period of time. When a thread relinquishes the processor, it is granted to the next waiting thread. With our two threads in this example, control of the processor alternates after each one prints a line and then calls the yield() method, which causes control to be passed to the next waiting thread.

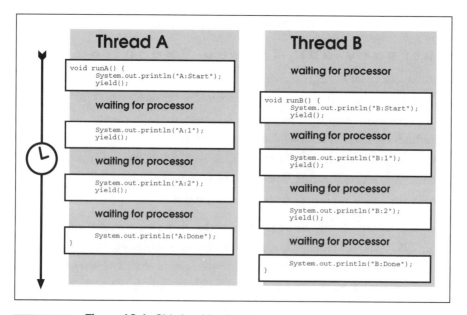

Figure 12.1 Side-by-side threads.

Priority

Each Java thread is assigned a priority, which affects how the Java thread scheduler chooses when to run a thread. The threads that we have looked at so far are of the same priority, so they share the processor on a first-come, first-serve basis. When a thread of a higher priority than any of the others comes into existence, it will get control of the processor, even if it needs to preempt a currently running thread to do so. For a thread of a lower priority then to gain control, the higher priority thread needs to go to sleep (using the sleep() method) or wait until notified (by calling the wait() method).

The Life of a Thread

Each thread is always in one of five states, as shown in Figure 12.2.

Threads move from one state to another via a variety of means. We indicate some of the most common methods for affecting a thread's state in our thread state diagram.

Newborn

When a thread is first created but not yet run, it is in a special newborn state—it has had memory allocated for it, and private data has been initialized, but the thread has not yet been scheduled. At this point, a thread can be scheduled via the

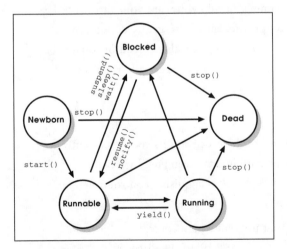

▰▰▰▰ **Figure 12.2** The five states of a thread.

start() method or killed via the stop() method. If it is scheduled, it moves to the runnable state.

Runnable

The runnable state means that a thread is ready to go and is awaiting control of the processor. Threads in the runnable state are said to be *scheduled*, which means that they are in a queue while they wait their turns to be executed. When all threads in the queue are of equal priority, control is given in a first-come, first serve manner in which the first thread in the queue is given control of the processor when the thread with control relinquishes it. Usually, the thread that relinquished control goes to the end of the queue, where it awaits its turn again.

When a thread enters the queue, it is placed in front of any lower priority threads. If the thread at the start of the queue is of a higher priority than the currently executing thread, it will preempt it and kick it back to the end of the line. Usually, these types of high-priority threads are created to perform some periodic task such as redrawing the screen. When they complete the task, they sleep for a predetermined period of time. When they wake, because they are of the highest priority, they go to the head of the line and usually preempt the currently running task, in order to again perform their task; then they go back to sleep, and the cycle repeats.

Most of the threads that you create will be of the same priority because you do not necessarily want high-priority threads running, nor do you want your threads to be disadvantaged and at the mercy of higher priority threads to get execution time. The system won't interrupt a thread to give control to another thread of equal priority, so in order for these threads to coexist, they must occasionally yield control to give other equal-priority threads a chance to execute.

Running

Running means that the thread has control of the processor. Its code is currently being executed, and it owns the processor until it gets preempted by a higher priority thread, or until it relinquishes control. A thread relinquishes control usually in one of three ways:

1. It can yield control, which means that it won't regain control until it is the next equal-priority thread in line to regain control of the processor.

2. It can go to sleep for a certain period of time, which means that it won't be entered into the queue to be run again until after a certain period of time.

3. It can wait for some event to notify it that it should be scheduled to run again.

Blocked

When a thread is *blocked*, it means that it is being prevented from entering the Not Runnable state (and subsequently the Running state). A blocked thread is essentially waiting for some event in order for it to reenter the scheduling queue. This event is dependent on what caused the thread to block in the first place. A sleeping thread is blocked until a certain amount of time has elapsed; a suspended thread is blocked until it is requested to resume; a waiting thread is blocked until it is notified of a change in the condition of another thread.

Dead

When a thread has completed execution, either by running its course or being stopped by another thread, the thread is *killed*.

Synchronization

Because threads in Java are running in the same memory space, they can share access to variables and methods in objects. In the case of an object being shared between two threads, where, for example, one thread stores data into the shared object and the other thread reads that data, there can be synchronization problems if the first thread hasn't finished storing the data before the second one goes to read it. There are a number of situations where threads will need to make use of shared objects and resources; without some synchronization facilities built into the language, things could quickly get out of hand as multiple threads try to write to the same files, read characters from the same input devices, or try to draw to a window that isn't visible yet.

Exclusion and Objects

The idea behind synchronization is to prevent two or more threads from trying to access the same resource. In an object-oriented language like Java, resources are represented in the form of objects, and Java's synchronization features serve to prevent multiple threads from performing conflicting tasks on the same object. How does Java know what is a conflicting task? The answer is that it doesn't, and when a class is designed with threads in mind, the class designer decides which methods should not be allowed to execute concurrently. This is done by indicating that a method is synchronized, and a class may have several synchronized methods.

When a class with synchronized methods is instantiated, the new object is given a monitor. To call a synchronized message in an object, a thread acquires the monitor of that object. If it is able to acquire the monitor, the thread enters the synchronized method, and while it owns the monitor, no other thread can call a synchronized method in that object. If a thread calls a synchronized method in an object and that object's monitor is owned by another thread, the calling thread is blocked until the other thread relinquishes the monitor. When the original thread exits the synchronized method where it acquired the monitor, ownership of the monitor is transferred to the blocked thread, which is now able to enter the method it was blocked on. By providing this mechanism to specify which methods can run concurrently, Java allows you to prevent situations where two threads are fighting over the same resource. We'll see how this works in practice in later sections.

Using Threads

Threads in Java are implemented in the form of objects that contain a method called run(). When the thread is started, the run() method is executed in its own thread. There are two ways of providing the run() method for a thread. The first way is to subclass the Thread class and override its run() method. The second way is to use the Runnable interface to add a run method to an existing class and then attach an instantiated thread to it. We'll take a look at both approaches in this section.

To better understand threads in action, we will step through a simple Java application that uses a subclass of Thread to perform a repetitive action. First, let's take a look at the program listing; then we'll talk about what the various elements of it mean.

```
class CountThread extends Thread {
    int maxcount;

    CountThread(int maxcount) {
        this.maxcount = maxcount;
    }
```

```
    public void run() {
      for(int count = 1; count < maxcount; count++) {
        System.out.println("The count is " + count + ".");
        try {
          sleep(10);
        } catch (InterruptedException e) {
          return;
        }
      }
    }
  }

class CountApp {
    public static void main (String args[]) {
      CountThread theCounter = new CountThread(10);
      theCounter.start();
      while (theCounter.isAlive()) {
        System.out.println("Counting...");
        try {
          Thread.sleep(10);
        } catch (InterruptedException e) {
          return;
        }
      }
    }
  }
```

If we run this application, the output will look like this:

```
$ java CountApp
Counting...
The count is 1.
Counting...
The count is 2.
Counting...
```

```
The count is 3.
Counting...
The count is 4.
Counting...
The count is 5.
Counting...
The count is 6.
Counting...
The count is 7.
Counting...
The count is 8.
Counting...
The count is 9.
Counting...
```

Let's now take a closer look at the example to understand what is happening. The code for the CountApp looks similar to other applications we've reviewed before. There are several points of interest, however. First of all, we perform the following statements that create our Thread object and call the start() method in it:

```
CountThread theCounter = new CountThread(10);
theCounter.start();
```

These commands instantiate a CountThread object. We defined the CountThread class in our listing, and we're responsible for the constructor method, which takes an integer parameter to use as the value to which it will count. After this thread has been instantiated, it is in the newborn state. New threads are assigned the same priority as the threads that created them (remember, all Java code is running in a thread, either one created by you or one created by the system).

The only other method we declare within CountThread is the run() method, so the start() method that we see being called in the above statements must be inherited from Thread. The start() method causes a newborn Thread to be scheduled, which means that it enters the runnable state and is waiting to gain control of the processor. The start() method immediately returns to the caller, which in this case is our main() method.

At this point, we have two threads in our program. The first is the one that we are currently running, which is the system-created primary thread; the second is the CountThread we just created, which is waiting for an opportunity to run. In the next statement of our main() method, we enter and repeatedly execute the following loop:

```
public static void main (String args[]) {
    CountThread theCounter = new CountThread(10);
    theCounter.start();
    while (theCounter.isAlive()) {
      System.out.println("Counting...");
      try {
        Thread.sleep(10);
      } catch (InterruptedException e) {
        return;
      }
    }
  }
}
```

The highlighted code is executed as long as the isAlive() method in theCounter returns true. The isAlive() method is defined in java.lang.Thread and returns true as long as a thread's run() method is still executing. When that run() method completes, isAlive() will return false. Our loop prints out "Counting..." as long as the CountThread is running.

There are two other interesting things in this loop. First of all, we are calling Thread.sleep(10) once every time through the loop; second, we have wrapped the call with an exception handler that catches an InterruptedException. Let's examine these one at a time.

The sleep() method in the Thread class causes the currently running thread to go to sleep by blocking for a certain period of time. This causes the next runnable thread to gain control of the processor. Because the two threads are of equal priority, Java will not preempt between them. Therefore, we need to ensure that the running thread yields time to other threads. This can be done by calling the static yield() or sleep() methods in the Thread class. The yield() method simply passes control to the next waiting thread. The sleep() method is called with the number of milliseconds that you want this thread to sleep before being scheduled to resume control. In terms of our previous illustration of the states of a thread, the thread is blocked for a certain period of time before it re-nets the runnable queue. When calling sleep() from outside a class that is a subclass of Thread(), you need to call it using the class name as you would any other static method.

The other interesting thing about the loop in our example main() method is that it is wrapped in an exception handler that catches the InterruptedException, which the sleep() method declares that it can throw. Because InterruptedException is one of the exceptions that we need to catch (from our list of exceptions in Chapter 11), we need to set up an exception handler to deal with it. You will see this type of exception handler used in many of our examples. If we had neglected to set up this handler, we would have gotten an error message from the compiler warning us of the potential for uncaught exceptions.

Inside the Thread Class

Threads in Java are created and managed through use of the Thread class. This class provides a number of methods for controlling the state, priority, and scheduling of a thread. Let's take a closer look at the Thread class and the methods we used in our last example.

Threads have several constructor methods. The most common ones you will use are the following:

```
public Thread()
```

```
public Thread(Runnable target)
```

You will find other versions of the constructor in the class reference, but these are the basic ones you will use in most cases. When called with no parameters, the constructor initializes the new thread object and places it in the newborn state. You will use this constructor when you work with classes that you have subclassed from Thread. The second version of the constructor is used when you want to make an existing object the target of a thread. Essentially this means that the code for the thread to execute is found in a separate object (the target) than the thread. This constructor is mostly used when you work with actual instances of Thread and not subclasses of it.

Thread objects can be started and stopped with the start() and stop() methods:

```
public synchronized void start()
```

```
public final void stop()
```

Starting a thread sends it to the Runnable state; stopping a thread sends it to the Dead state. These methods are usually called from outside the thread that you want to start or stop.

To ensure that other threads get time, you can yield to other threads or put the current thread to sleep for a certain period of time. Yielding a thread is done through the yield() method, and putting a thread to sleep is done through the sleep() method:

```
public static void yield()
```

```
public static void sleep(long millis) throws InterruptedException
```

Yielding control means that the next scheduled thread of equal priority gets control of the processor, while the yielding thread reenters the end of the runnable queue. If there are no threads of equal priority, the thread essentially goes to the head of the runnable queue and is once again given control of the processor. If there are no other threads of equal priority, yielding has no effect.

The sleep method puts the currently running thread into the blocked state until the time indicated expires. After that point, the thread reenters the runnable queue. The sleep() method can throw an InterruptedException so that you must catch it with an exception handler, especially if calling sleep() from within a run() method, which does not declare that it throws any exceptions, and as a consequence is prevented from throwing any exception other than run-time exceptions. Most sleep() methods will be wrapped in an exception handler like this:

```
try {
    sleep(10);
} catch (InterruptedException e) {
    return;
}


setPriority
get priority


setDaemon
isDaemon
```

The run() Method

For a thread to run, it must have a run() method either within it or in its target. The run() method is defined as follows:

```
public void run()
```

At first glance, this seems to be a very simple method to implement. The problem lies with the fact that the method does not declare that it throws any exceptions. This is a problem because exception throws are frequent in threads, especially when created by applets for HotJava. As a consequence, you will often need to include an exception handler within your run method to catch any exceptions that might be thrown by a thread becoming interrupted (for example, by the user switching to a different page). Here is an example of an exception handler that will allow your thread to exit gracefully, regardless of the exception thrown:

```
try {
    sleep(10);
} catch (Exception e) {
    return;
}
```

As you can see, this exception handler will catch any Exception subclass, which will be the case for the majority of throwable exceptions. In most cases, you want to avoid these blanket exceptions, especially when debugging your program, but in your final code you may want to consider such steps to make sure that any threads do not cause the program to halt.

Subclassing Thread

One method of making use of threads within a program is to create your own subclass of Thread that is designed to perform a specific task in its own thread. When subclassing the Thread class, you need to have a run() method within your new subclass. For example, here is the CountThread class we used in some of our earlier examples:

```
class CountThread extends Thread {
    int maxcount;

    CountThread(int maxcount) {
      this.maxcount = maxcount;
    }

    public void run() {
      for(int count = 1; count < maxcount; count++) {
        System.out.println("The count is " + count + ".");
        try {
          sleep(10);
        } catch (InterruptedException e) {
          return;
        }
      }
    }
}
```

This class demonstrates the classic design of a Thread subclass. The class is defined as extending Thread, and it had its own constructor and run() method. The constructor is not strictly required, but having it is good practice. The run() method is required, and, like most run() methods, this one consists mainly of a loop that executes a certain number of times before the method exits and the thread subsequently dies. Also, the run() method correctly wraps its call of the sleep() method in an exception handler. Most threads that you create are going to be variations of this basic implementation of a Thread subclass, although they will very likely be much more complicated.

Using the Runnable Interface

A second way to use threads is to make use of the Runnable interface. When using this approach, you will have one of your existing classes defined as implementing the Runnable interface. When you later go to create a new thread, you will define an object that was instantiated from this "runnable" class as the target of your thread, meaning that the thread will look for the code for the run() method within your object's class instead of inside the thread's class.

The Runnable interface is defined as follows:

```
public interface Runnable {
   public abstract void run();
}
```

Implementing this interface in one of your classes means that you need to have a run() method within your class. It is important that this method be defined as follows:

```
public void run()

class CircleThread extends Thread {
   int numsides;
   double radius;

   CircleThread(int numsides, double radius) {
      this.numsides = numsides;
      this.radius = radius;
   }

   public void run() {
   double incAngle = (2 * Math.PI) / numsides;
      for(int sides = 0; sides < numsides; sides++) {
         // Point on circle
         double dx = radius * Math.cos(sides * incAngle);
```

```
        double dy = radius * Math.sin(sides * incAngle);
        // print it
        System.out.println("x:" + dx + " y:" + dy);
        yield();
    }
  }
}
```

Implementing Synchronization

Earlier in this chapter we saw that every object that has synchronized methods is given a monitor. A *synchronized method* is a method that can only be entered if the thread in which the method is called is able to acquire the monitor of the object; otherwise, the thread in which the synchronized method is called will be blocked until the monitor is relinquished by another thread. A monitor can be acquired only by one thread at a time, and when another thread needs to acquire the monitor, that thread must wait for the current thread to relinquish the monitor. By marking a method or methods of an object as synchronized, you can prevent different threads from calling these methods at the same time.

Synchronized Methods and Blocks

Methods and blocks are marked as synchronized by using the synchronized keyword modifier. The following lines of code show a method that is marked as synchronized:

```
synchronized int getPipedInt() {
    // synchronized code

    ...
}
```

When a code running within a thread attempts to enter a synchronized method of an object, it will be blocked until it can acquire the object's monitor. If the monitor is in use by another thread, the method cannot be entered until the other thread relinquishes the monitor. When this happens the waiting thread is able to resume execution and enter the method.

A synchronized block works a little differently. In this case, the synchronized keyword is used to mark a block of code that can't be entered until the monitor of the specified object can be acquired. This object (or class) can be entirely different from the object whose method contains the synchronized block we are trying to enter. Once we acquire the monitor and enter the block, other threads will be unable to enter synchronized methods of the specified object until we exit the synchronized block and relinquish the specified object's monitor. Here's an example of its use:

```
synchronized (lock_object) {
   // synchronized code
   ...
}
```

wait() and notify()

Once inside a synchronized method, it is sometimes useful to relinquish the monitor temporarily and allow other threads to acquire the monitor as needed. This is done by calling the wait() method. This method can be called to wait indefinitely or until a set amount of time has elapsed. A waiting thread can reacquire the monitor if another thread calls the notify() method of the object where the wait() method was originally called. This causes the original thread to resume execution at the point where it called wait().

Figure 12.3 lists the methods for causing a thread to wait and for notifying waiting threads to resume. These methods must be called from synchronized methods.

Threadsafe Variables

Threadsafe variables are variables that are marked by the programmer to tell the compiler that they are never modified by more than one thread. This allows the compiler to perform optimizations such as using a processor register to contain the variable's value. If you mark a variable as threadsafe, you should do so only because you are certain that it will never be accessed from another thread; otherwise, situations will arise in which a thread will get an incorrect value when accessing the variable because another thread was working with a copy of the variable that had been cached in a processor register.

Object.wait

```
public final void wait(long timeout) throws InterruptedException
```

Causes a thread to wait for the specified number of milliseconds or until notified.

Object.wait

```
public final void wait(long timeout,
                          int nanos) throws InterruptedException
```

Causes a thread to wait for the specified number of milliseconds and nanoseconds or until notified.

Object.wait

```
public final void wait() throws InterruptedException
```

Causes a thread to wait indefinitely or until notified.

Object.notify

```
public final void notify()
```

Notifies a thread that is waiting within a synchronized method of this object.

Object.notifyAll

```
public final void notifyAll()
```

Notifies all threads that are waiting within a synchronized method of this object.

Figure 12.3 Methods for causing a thread to wait.

APPLET OVERVIEW

I n this chapter we start on the third and final part of this book, which deals with the use and development of Java applets. Most of your exposure to actual Java programs has probably been in the form of Java applets running within a Java-capable browser, such as HotJava or Netscape 2.0. In Part 3 of this book, we'll explore how these applets are created and what steps are necessary to place them on your HTML pages.

At the beginning of this book, we talked about how to run a Java-capable browser and access pages that contain applets. In this chapter, we'll readdress some of that material and look at how applets coexist with Web browsers.

Applets and Browsers

An applet is nothing more (or less) than a Java class that inherits from the Java API's Applet class and implements certain methods that need to be present for the applet to handle its appearance and to respond to events passed to the applet. For the most part, supporting applets in a browser is an all-or-nothing proposition, so if your browser is able to view applets, it supports the JDK.

The exception to this is some versions of Sun's HotJava, which will support only the alpha 3 release. At the time of this writing, most versions of HotJava support only alpha 3 applets. When you use HotJava alpha 3, you may go to some Web sites that claim they are Java-enhanced, but you may find that HotJava won't load the applets. Conversely, some JDK 1.0 browsers, such as Netscape 2.0, will hit some sites that make use of alpha 3 applets and won't load those applets. This is a temporary situation, and we expect that within the next couple of months all Java-enabled browsers will be JDK 1.0 compliant and most sites hosting Java applets will have converted their applets to the 1.0 standard. This book deals only with the JDK 1.0 release of applets and the Java API.

Inline Applets with HTML

When a browser loads an HTML page, it starts to format the text. If it is a graphical browser, it lays out the text around any graphical elements that are embedded in the page (as indicated by the IMG or FIG tags). Some browsers, like Netscape, may allow the HTML page to have some additional control over layout and formatting issues, but for the most part, these decisions are supposed to be made by the browser and the user. As an HTML page loads, when the browser sees certain tags that suggest the display of inline elements such as images, the browser requests that the server send the data for those elements in order that they might be properly displayed. An *inlined element* is an element that is drawn right onto the Web page, as opposed to appearing in a separate window, with the page's text wrapping around it. The most common inline element is the image, usually a GIF or JPEG bitmap file. Netscape 2.0 and a few other browsers allow a number of different types of objects to be inlined on the page.

A Java applet is handled with HTML as a type of inline element. The browser reads the HTML file and sees that it needs to load the data associated with this element. The applet element also tells the browser how much display space, in terms of pixel height and width, to reserve for the applet. Many browsers (especially the Java-capable ones) are multithreaded, so the browser will continue dealing with the rest of the HTML data in one thread, while creating a new thread to load the inline element's data. In the case of the applet, this data is a Java class. For a browser to load a Java class, it needs to implement a Java class. The class loader loads the class that is indicated by the HTML applet tag over the network; once that class is loaded, it uses the class loader to load any other classes it needs, pulling those down over the net if necessary. Java-enabled browsers also keep all the Java API classes in a local file on the hard drive, so that these are available for the applet to use. It is also up to the applet to load any images, sounds, or other data that it needs. The applet at this point is talking directly to the browser to handle these requests, so that you usually won't see any reference to these other files used by the applet in the HTML page's source. Note that all this applet loading is taking place in a separate thread, so that while this is happening, the browser is continuing to load and lay out the other traditional HTML page elements. When the applet has finished loading and initializing, the browser asks it to draw itself; from then on the applet has the responsibility for managing its display area.

Let's take a look at the HTML code for a page that loads an applet:

```
<HTML>
<HEAD>
<TITLE>Applets</TITLE>
</HEAD>
<BODY>
<H1>
My HTML page
</H1>
<P>
This is a sample html page.
Cool applets soon...
<APPLET CODE=MyApplet.class WIDTH=100 HEIGHT=100>
</APPLET>
more text
<P>
</BODY>
</HTML>
```

When the browser hits the applet tag, it will load the indicated applet class and create an applet object. Figure 13.1 depicts this process.

This illustration is presented to develop a conceptual model of how applet loading works; it does not necessarily reflect the actual technical implementation that a particular browser might use. The processes called the HTML loader and Applet loader represent the internal mechanisms in the browser for handling these activities. How the browser actually implements these is up to the browser manufacturer. In HotJava, much of the applet loading is handled by the class loader in conjunction with several other classes that implement *protocol handlers*, which allow the browser to be extended to handle any media type that a browser might want to

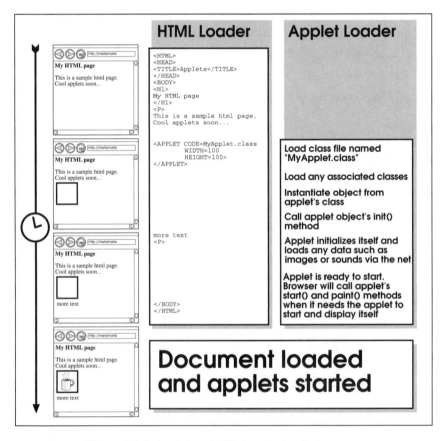

Figure 13.1 Applet and HTML page loading process.

load. While you can assume that Netscape uses a similar mechanism, all that matters is that the result is the same for any Java-enabled browser.

Figure 13.1 also infers that multithreaded applet loading is the norm. Most Internet-related applications, whether on the Mac, Windows, or UNIX, use some form of threads to handle these types of situations, but whether these threads are native threads, Java threads, or some other form of concurrency will depend on the browser's developers. Java classes, however, will always use Java threads.

Where to Go from Here?

In the next chapters, we will look at the specifics of how an applet is included in an HTML page, as well as how to write your own applets. At this point, you may also want to take a look at applets that you find at Sun's Java site at http://www.javasoft.com.

APPLET BASICS

In this chapter, we will learn how applets work—how they are used with HTML, where they are located on the Web server, and what happens when an applet class is loaded. We will also take a look at the basic methods of a single panel applet, which is an applet that does not contain any user interface elements such as buttons. Don't worry, we'll cover how to add interface elements and more in the next chapter.

Java existed as a language long before it was used within the World Wide Web. As a consequence, most of the final details of how applets interface within a variety of browsers have been only recently defined. In fact, although one of the goals of this book is to adhere as closely as possible to the JDK 1.0 standard, at the time of this writing that standard is still in pre-beta state. Some things such as the <APPLET> tag are still pending approval of the Web standards bodies, and at the moment, Netscape is the only browser that supports JDK 1.0, although a new version of HotJava is expected presently and may be available by the time you read this. The long and short of all this is that as we move into the area of applets, we run the risk of covering material that could quickly become out of date.

Several early books on Java have already been rendered useless because they assumed that Sun would not change the Java API significantly in the beta release. The final authority on the latest information of the state of the JDK will be the Java home page at http://www.javasoft.com. Wiley will also be setting up a Java resource center on its home page for its various Java-related publications at http://www.wiley.com. Now that I've made these points, let's move on to the technical information.

Java applets are simply Java classes, just like any other Java application. As we saw in Part 2 of this book, a Java application is a class that contains a main() method, which the interpreter looks for when asked to run a class as an application. Applets run within an application, sometimes written in Java, such as HotJava, that loads the Applet's class as it would load any of its own classes and calls certain methods to perform a set of defined actions that applets are expected to be able to handle in order to display themselves and respond to user interaction. In this chapter, we'll see exactly what those methods are. We'll also take a look at how a Java class can be created so that it can be used as both an applet and a stand-alone application. This will be done by simply adding a main() method to the applet class so that when the interpreter tries to run the class as a stand-alone application, it will be able to do so. The applet will also contain the required applet methods so that it can be used by a browser. This will become important for our sample applications because of the caveats about running applets from a local file system that now prevails.

The <APPLET> Tag

In order for an applet to be used within a Web page, the page must include a tag for the applet within its HTML source. In early versions of HotJava, Sun had proposed the <APP> tag as the way to accomplish this. Many HTML experts pointed out that this type of tag was an improper HTML construct for a number of reasons: it was not expressible within an SGML DTD, and the <APP> tag inherited the IMG tag's weakness for specifying text to display to users of browsers that don't display Java applets. With the release of the JDK 1.0 pre-beta, Sun replaced the <APP> tag with the <APPLET></APPLET> start and end tags, which solved many of the limitations of the previous tag.

The syntax of the <APPLET> tag is as follows:

```
<APPLET
    [CODEBASE = codebase_URL]
    CODE=classname.class
    [ALT = alternate_text]
    [NAME = applet_instance_name]
    WIDTH=pixels HEIGHT=pixels
    [ALIGN = alignment]
    [VSPACE = pixels]
    [HSPACE = pixels]
>
[<PARAM NAME=param1_name VALUE="param1_value">]
[<PARAM NAME=param2_name VALUE="param2_value">]
[alternate_HTML]
</APPLET>
```

The various attributes indicate the options that can be used when placing an applet on a Web page. Many of these options will never be necessary for most of your applets (the optional tag syntax is italicized). The minimum requirements to place an applet on a page are:

```
<APPLET CODE=classname.class WIDTH=pixels HEIGHT=pixels>
</APPLET>
```

The first thing to notice is the CODE attribute, which indicates the name of the class file from which to load and instantiate the applet. The WIDTH and HEIGHT attributes specify the dimensions of the applet's display area. These are going to be the width and height in pixels that the applet will either use on the Web page, if the browser displays applets inline, or the size of the external window in which the applet gets displayed, if the browser displays applets in a separate window or uses a helper application like Applet Viewer to display the applets.

Passing Parameters to Applets

Some applets are designed so that they can accept parameters that have been encoded as parameters within the HTML page. This is done through use of the <PARAM> tag. When the <PARAM> tag is used with the <APPLET> tag, the syntax is as follows:

```
<APPLET CODE=classname.class WIDTH=pixels HEIGHT=pixels>
<PARAM NAME=param_name VALUE="param_value">
</APPLET>
```

The <PARAM> tag has two attributes, the NAME of the parameter and the VALUE
of the parameter. The number of parameters passed to an applet is dependent on
the applet. You can specify as many parameters as you want within the HTML
source. In this example we pass two parameters to an applet:

```
<APPLET CODE=MyApplet.class WIDTH=100 HEIGHT=100>
<PARAM NAME=picture VALUE="Ed.gif">
<PARAM NAME=sound VALUE="Hello.au">
</APPLET>
```

The parameters named picture and sound are looked for by the MyApplet object
when it starts up. Parameters are passed in the form of strings, so it's necessary to
enclose their values in quotation marks. If you pass a parameter that the applet
doesn't look for, it is ignored. However, depending on the applet, the consequences
of not passing a parameter that an applet does require will vary. A well-written
applet should exit gracefully. Whether it throws an exception resulting in the
browser displaying the red broken gears icon, or it displays a message indicating that
required parameters were not provided, or it fails silently is up to the applet author.

The parameters that are passed to the applet are usually handled by the applet in its
init() method, which we will look at later in this chapter.

Providing for Browsers
That Don't Support Java

An important aspect of the World Wide Web that is often overlooked in these days
of graphic-intensive pages is that not every user of the Web will have a graphic
browser, have graphics loading turned on, or use a Java-capable browser. For any
number of reasons, people looking at your pages may not have the ability to view
Java applets. The <APPLET> tag provides two different mechanisms for this.

The first way to provide alternate text is to use the ALT attribute to specify a string
that will contain an alternate message to use when the browser understands the
<APPLET> tag, but is unable to display the applet. Here's an example of how it can
be used:

```
<APPLET CODE=MyApplet.class
   ALT="Applet loading is unsupported or turned off."
   WIDTH=100 HEIGHT=100>
<PARAM NAME=picture VALUE="Ed.gif">
<PARAM NAME=sound VALUE="Hello.au">
</APPLET>
```

The ALT attribute has the same limitations when used with applets as it does when used with the <IMG> tag: It is suitable for short messages but is not very effective for more descriptive alternate text.

The other way to provide alternate text is to place HTML text within the <APPLET></APPLET> start and end tags that will be displayed as an alternative to displaying the applet. This text will be seen by users with a text-only browser, a browser that doesn't support Java, or if they've disabled applet loading. Although not all HTML authors do so, it is extremely good practice to do this, usually for the first applet on a page. Here's our last example with alternate text added:

```
<APPLET CODE=MyApplet.class WIDTH=100 HEIGHT=100>
<PARAM NAME=picture VALUE="Ed.gif">
<PARAM NAME=sound VALUE="Hello.au">
This page is Java enhanced.<P>
You will need a Java-capable browser to view its applets.<P>
</APPLET>
```

This will let people who visit your page know that if they use a Java-capable browser they will be able to see applets on the page. You may even want to put links to places where they can find such browsers. For example:

```
<APPLET CODE=MyApplet.class WIDTH=100 HEIGHT=100>
<PARAM NAME=picture VALUE="Ed.gif">
<PARAM NAME=sound VALUE="Hello.au">
This page is Java enhanced.<P>
You will need a Java-capable browser to view its applets.<P>
Try <A HREF="http://home.netscape.com/comprod/mirror/index.HTML">
Netscape Navigator 2.0</A> or
<A HREF="http://www.javasoft.com">Sun HotJava.</A>
</APPLET>
```

At this point, we need to point out a potential problem when using this technique. Netscape 2.0b1 does not correctly ignore the text between the <APPLET></APPLET> tags, which means that any of the alternate text you include will be displayed by the Netscape 2.0b1 browser even if it displays the applet. This has been fixed in later beta versions as well as the final release of Netscape Navigator 2.09. The latest release notes for all versions of Netscape can be found at:

```
http://home.mcom.com/eng/mozilla/2.0/relnotes/
```

Classes, Objects, and the <APPLET> Tag

When the applet class is loaded, the browser looks for it in the same location where it found the original HTML document. For example, if the page URL was:

```
http://www.server.com/index.HTML
```

the class MyApplet.class loaded from the index.HTML document would be expected to be at:

```
http://www.server.com/MyApplet.class
```

Usually, it is convenient to place class files in a separate directory on the server. For example, suppose you had all your Java classes in a subdirectory called java/. The URL for the class would then be:

```
http://www.server.com/java/MyApplet.class
```

In order for the browser to find the class in this location, we need to specify a URL in the CODEBASE attribute. This can be a complete or partial URL, which means that either of the following would be able to find the class file:

```
CODEBASE = "http://www.server.com/java/MyApplet.class"
```

```
CODEBASE = "/java/"
```

```
CODEBASE = "java/"
```

For a better understanding of partial and full URLs, you probably want to refer to a good HTML text. Ian Graham's *The HTML Sourcebook* (published by Wiley) provides good coverage of the subject. Also, although the 2.0b1 beta version does not support it, there is no reason why you should not be able to load HTML files and their associated applets from local files. At the time of this writing, however, only Sun's Java Applet Viewer is able to do this, and it displays only the applet, not the HTML text, making it difficult to use to preview how an applet will look when combined with other page elements.

Once the applet class is loaded, an applet object is instantiated from the class. You can provide a name for this instance using the NAME attribute.

```
CODEBASE = "Test"
```

The main reason for naming an instance is that you can then locate the applet from within one of the methods of another applet object on the same page, using something like the following:

```
Applet theApplet = getAppletContext().getAppletName("Test");
MyApplet otherMe = (MyApplet)theApplet;
otherMe.someMethod();
```

This let's you have two applets that communicate with each other on the same page. For example, you might have an on and off switch button applet that you locate at the top and bottom of a page, and you want to have switching the button at the top of the page result in both of the applets being switched to the same state. You could have the two applet instances locate each other by name and send each other messages to make sure they each maintained the same on/off state.

Applet Display Attributes

The final attributes in the applet tag relate to how the applet is displayed with the Web page. While these attributes are part of the <APPLET> tag standard, how they are interpreted by the browser will vary between browsers from different developers, so that while you can specify settings for these attributes, you have to consider them hints rather than absolute specifications that the browser must follow (unlike the WIDTH and HEIGHT attributes that the browser must use to fit an applet on the page or create an external window for it).

The first of these attributes is ALIGN, which has the same parameters as the ALIGN attribute in the Netscape-extended version of the IMG tag. Because many

HTML authors are not familiar with Netscape's IMG tag and its alignment options, we will recap ALIGN here. Please note that although it is justifiable to avoid these parameters in the IMG tag because not all browsers have adopted these as extensions to that tag, these are not extensions to the APPLET tag but are part of its standard definition.

ALIGN=LEFT

The applet will float down and over to the left margin (into the next available space there), and subsequent text will wrap around the right side of that image.

ALIGN=RIGHT

The applet aligns with the right margin, with text wrapping around the left.

ALIGN=TOP

The applet aligns with the top of the tallest item in the line.

ALIGN=TEXTTOP

The applet aligns with the top of the tallest text in the line, which is often the same as ALIGN=TOP.

ALIGN=MIDDLE

The middle of the applet aligns the baseline of the current line.

ALIGN=ABSMIDDLE

The middle of the applet aligns the middle of the current line.

ALIGN=BASELINE

The bottom of the applet is aligned with the baseline of the current line.

ALIGN=BOTTOM

This is identical to ALIGN= BASELINE.

ALIGN=ABSBOTTOM

The bottom of the applet is aligned with the bottom of the current line.

The VSPACE and HSPACE attributes are used to specify the number of pixels surrounding an applet that separate it from other elements on the page such as text, images, or other applets. The VSPACE applet indicates the number of pixels above and below the applet's display area, and the HSPACE attribute indicates the number of pixels to the left and right of the applet's display area.

Running Applets
without a Browser and/or Server

When you test applets you can run the applet classes in several different ways, depending on what platform you are running on. As of this writing, the support development environment for writing JDK 1.0 compliant applets is SPARC work-station running Solaris 2.3 or better. It is expected that the Windows 95/NT version of the JDK will be available in the immediate future, and that it will be roughly equivalent to the Solaris version. Macintosh users have no official word as to the status of the Mac JDK, but we can only hope that it too will be forthcoming.

Because of the pressures on the Java team to complete the JDK 1.0 pre-beta release so that browser developers such as Netscape could incorporate Java support in their products, the JDK was released without a new version of the HotJava browser. This means that in order to view applets within a browser, your most likely alternative will be Netscape 2.0.

At the time of this writing, a couple of problems with the Netscape 2.0 beta release make it less than optimal for Java development. The most glaring problem is that you can't open local files that contain applets. I hope this will be fixed by the time you read this, but if it isn't, you will need to run a Web server to test applets from within Netscape. If you decide to follow this route, check out Yahoo's Web servers page at
http://www.yahoo.com/Computers_and_Internet/Internet/World_Wide_Web/HTTP/Servers/.

The JDK supplies an Applet Viewer application that can be used to test applications. If the Java tools are in your PATH, you can invoke it with the following command:

```
appletviewer page_URL
```

The applet viewer loads applets from the HTML page at the specified URL into their own windows. This URL can be a file path for loading pages from the local file system. For example, the following command, issued from within the JDK root directory, will load the ThreeD applet used in the file example1.HTML stored in the current directory:

```
appletviewer demo/WireFrame/example1.HTML
```

Figure 14.1 shows what the applet viewer looks like when running under Solaris.

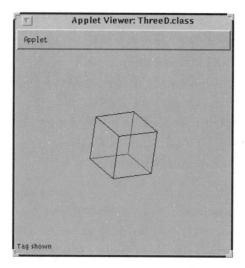

Figure 14.1 The applet viewer running under Solaris.

If there are multiple applets on a page, each will be opened in its own window. Each applet window has a menu bar that provides a couple of interesting options. The most interesting one is the Tag menu item under the Applet menu, which will display the tag that was used to generate the applet (Figure 14.2).

The Applet Class

We've spent a lot of time talking about how applet classes are loaded and where they are found on the server. In this section, we'll take a look at what goes into an applet class.

Figure 14.2 The applet HTML tag.

All applets are subclasses of java.applet.Applet. The ancestry of java.applet.Applet
is as follows:

```
java.applet.Applet → java.awt.Panel → java.awt.Container → java.awt.Component →
java.lang.Object
```

As you can see, the Applet class inherits from several classes in the AWT (Advanced
Window Toolkit) package, which we will cover in the next chapter. The
Component class deals with the issues necessary for a user-interface component to
display itself and respond to events. The Container and Panel classes provide the
ability for a component to contain other components. The Applet class takes the
user interface capabilities it inherits from these classes and adds a number of methods for interfacing with Web browsers. When we look at the essential methods for
creating applets, some of these methods will come from the Applet class, and others
will come from the ancestor classes.

The methods that we will look at in this chapter are ones that you will usually need
to override when creating applets, which we list below:

```
public void init()


public void start()


public void stop()


public void paint(Graphics g)


public boolean mouseDown(Event evt, int x, int y)


public boolean mouseDrag(Event evt, int x, int y)


public boolean mouseUp(Event evt, int x, int y)
```

You will find that you need to override a number of other methods, but in looking
at a number of different applets, we've seen that these are the most commonly overridden when creating applets. None of these methods is abstract; in fact, none of
the Applet class methods are, so that theoretically you could override none of them,
but in practice you will.

First, let's take a look at the listing for a completed sample applet that we will use to illustrate the techniques of writing applets. This applet should be saved in a file called AppletSkeleton.java. When you create your own applets, you will be able to use this applet as a starting point and flesh it out with your own code, hence the name SkeletonApplet.

Take a moment to scan the listing. At this point, you should be familiar enough with the Java language that you can understand the syntax of the language, even though other packages may be used that you are probably not yet familiar with; you won't yet understand the significance of the applet methods. Don't worry, we'll be covering those details in the next section.

```java
// AppletSkeleton.java
import java.util.*;
import java.applet.*;
import java.awt.*;


public class AppletSkeleton extends Applet {

    String TestParam = null;
    Date startDate = null;
    Date mouseDownDate = null;
    Date mouseDragDate = null;
    Date mouseUpDate = null;
    int down_x = 0;
    int down_y = 0;
    int drag_x = 0;
    int drag_y = 0;
    int up_x = 0;
    int up_y = 0;

    public void init() {
        TestParam = getParameter("test");
        if (TestParam == null)
            TestParam = "Test parameter not provided.";
    }
```

```java
public void start() {
   startDate = new Date();
   repaint();
}

public void stop() {
}

public void paint(Graphics g) {
   g.drawRect(0, 0, size().width - 1, size().height - 1);
   g.drawString("Test parameter = " + TestParam, 10, 20);

   if (startDate != null)
      g.drawString("Started at " + startDate.toString(),
         10, 40);

   if (mouseDownDate != null) {
      g.drawString("Mouse down at time: " +
         mouseDownDate.getMinutes() + ":" +
         mouseDownDate.getSeconds(),
         10, 60);
      g.drawString("X: " + down_x + " Y: " + down_y, 10, 80);

      g.drawOval(down_x - 5, down_y - 5, 10, 10);
   }

   if (mouseDragDate != null) {
      g.drawString("Mouse drag at time: " +
         mouseDragDate.getMinutes() + ":" +
         mouseDragDate.getSeconds(),
         10, 100);
      g.drawString("X: " + drag_x + " Y: " + drag_y, 10, 120);

      g.drawLine(down_x, down_y, drag_x, drag_y);
```

```
        g.fillRect(drag_x - 3, drag_y - 3, 6, 6);
    }

    if (mouseUpDate != null) {
        g.drawString("Mouse up at time: " +
            mouseUpDate.getMinutes() + ":" +
            mouseUpDate.getSeconds(),
            10, 140);
        g.drawString("X: " + up_x + " Y: " + up_y, 10, 160);
    }
}

public boolean mouseDown(Event evt, int x, int y) {
    mouseDownDate = new Date();
    mouseDragDate = null;
    mouseUpDate = null;

    down_x = x;
    down_y = y;

    repaint();
    return true;
}

public boolean mouseDrag(Event evt, int x, int y) {
    mouseDragDate = new Date();

    drag_x = x;
    drag_y = y;

    repaint();
    return true;
}
```

```
    public boolean mouseUp(Event evt, int x, int y) {
        mouseUpDate = new Date();

        up_x = x;
        up_y = y;

        repaint();
        return true;
    }

}
```

The HTML file that goes with this applet is called AppletSkeleton.HTML:

```
<!--AppletSkeleton.java-->
<HTML>
<HEAD>
<TITLE>AppletSkeleton</TITLE>
</HEAD>
<BODY>

<APPLET CODE=AppletSkeleton.class WIDTH=300 HEIGHT=300>
<PARAM NAME=test VALUE="test value">
</APPLET>

</BODY>
</HTML>
```

This applet can then be run using the Applet Viewer using the following command (assuming that the appletviewer command is in the command path):

```
appletviewer AppletSkeleton.HTML
```

This applet does a couple of simple but interesting things. First of all, it reads a parameter from the <APPLET> tag. Second, it illustrates how mouse events can be handled from an applet. When the applet is run, you will see a window similar to the one shown in Figure 14.3.

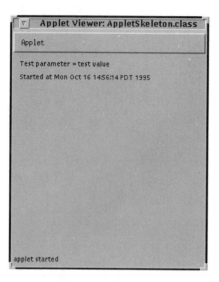

Figure 14.3 Solaris AppletViewer running the AppletSkeleton applet.

When the applet starts up, it displays the parameter specified in the <APPLET> tag, in this case the string "test value". It also displays the time that the applet's start() method was called. Clicking and dragging in the applet will result in the applet looking like Figure 14.4.

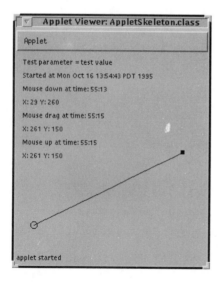

Figure 14.4 Running the AppletSkeleton applet after clicking and dragging in the applet.

The applet uses the mouse coordinates sent to it via the mouseDown(), mouseDrag(), and mouseUp() methods to display information about where the mouse was clicked and to draw a line between where the mouse button was depressed and where it was released. Take a few moments to play with the applet by clicking and dragging in different areas of the applet. You should be able to observe a few things about the coordinate system of applets and see some of the basics of how graphics are drawn with the applet's display area. If you can, you will also want to try this applet within a browser.

In the next section, we'll take a look at how an applet like this is created.

Initialization

When an applet is loaded, it has two points where initialization can take place. The first is the applet class's constructor. We don't use this in our example class, but you should keep in mind that you can provide a constructor if you choose to. If you do provide a constructor, you may want to restrict the code you place within it to initialization code that does not use any of the methods from parent class's or for accessing browser properties. The reason for this is that the constructor is called when the class is instantiated. At this point in the life of the applet, these services may not yet be available for the applet's use.

The place where applets are safe to perform most initialization tasks is within the init() method. This method is defined as follows:

```
public void init()
```

In the example applet, we used the following code for our init() method:

```
public void init() {
    TestParam = getParameter("test");
    if (TestParam == null)
        TestParam = "Test parameter not provided.";
}
```

The init() method is called by the browser so that it has an opportunity to perform any initialization tasks needed. In this method we use the init() method to load a parameter from the <PARAM> tag and if it's not present, to store a default value into the TestParam instance variable in the SkeletonApplet class.

Loading Parameter Values

As we just saw, parameters are loaded using the getParameter() method. This method takes the string name of the <PARAM> tag NAME attribute and returns the value provided from the VALUE attribute. The value is returned as a string object. If it can't be found, it returns a null string. You can test for the null value and, if it is returned, take appropriate steps to recover. In the case of our skeleton applet, we simply assign a string to the instance variable that we are using to hold the parameter value.

The question that often arises when reading attributes is how to read numerical data that is provided as parameters to the applet. When you need to pass a number to the applet, it is going to be returned to your applet as a string by getParameter(). You will need to convert this string to the desired value using one of the numeric wrapper classes. For example, if you had a parameter called radius, you could convert it to a double using the following code:

```
String paramStr = getParameter("radius");
double numParam;
if (paramStr != null) {
    numParam = Double.valueOf(paramStr).doubleValue();
}
```

What we are doing in this code fragment is calling the static valueOf() method in the Double class, which returns a Double object containing the double value of the passed string. We then call the doubleValue, which returns a double floating point value. If you still aren't following this, remember that this line:

```
numParam = Double.valueOf(paramStr).doubleValue();
```

is the same as this one:

```
Double tempDouble = Double.valueOf(paramStr);
numParam = tempDouble.doubleValue();
```

One last thing, from a practical programming standpoint, is that numeric conversion can often throw exceptions if they are unable to perform the conversion.

Remember that this is taking place within our applet's init() method, and that if we throw an exception here, the browser is going to present the user with either a broken gears icon or a cryptic error dialog. As a consequence, you may want to be on guard for exceptions and provide an exception handler to deal with possible exceptions thrown by the numeric conversion. Here's how we would write this code in a real applet:

```
String paramStr = getParameter("radius");
double numParam = 5;
if (paramStr != null) {
   try {
      numParam = Double.valueOf(paramStr).doubleValue();
   } catch (NumberFormatException e) {

   }
}
```

This way, in case of a missing or bad value, the applet will still continue. This type of error handling needs to be implemented in a case-by-case basis. In some situations, the applet should fail rather than continue with a default value, and throwing the exception to handle might be the most expeditious manner.

Basic Mouse Events

When a mouse event occurs within the display area of an applet, it is up to the applet to respond to the event. These events are delivered to the applet by the browser calling the appropriate mouse method to handle the particular event. To handle one of these events, you must override the appropriate mouse method in your applet class and provide your own version of the method to handle the event. Here's the method I used to handle mousedowns in our applet:

```
public boolean mouseDown(Event evt, int x, int y) {
   mouseDownDate = new Date();
   mouseDragDate = null;
   mouseUpDate = null;

   down_x = x;
   down_y = y;
```

```
        repaint();
        return true;
    }
```

When the user clicks in the applet, I set the instance variable mouseDownDate to refer to a new Date object. When the Data class constructor is called with no parameters, it sets the Date object to contain the current date including the current hour, minute, and second, so it can be used as a way to time-stamp the event. The event object that is passed to the mouseDown method contains a when instance variable as well that you could convert to a Date object using the following statement:

```
mouseDownDate = new Date(evt.when);
```

All mouse methods take the same parameters: an event object and the x and y coordinates of the mouse. If a mouse method handles the mouse event, it is expected to return true and if not, to return false.

```
public boolean mouseDown(Event evt, int x, int y)
```
Called when the mouse button is clicked while the mouse pointer is within the applet.

```
public boolean mouseDrag(Event evt, int x, int y)
```
Called when the mouse pointer is moved while the mouse button is depressed.

```
public boolean mouseUp(Event evt, int x, int y)
```
Called when the mouse button is released.

```
public boolean mouseMove(Event evt, int x, int y)
```
Called when the mouse pointer is moved within the applet's display area.

```
public boolean mouseEnter(Event evt, int x, int y)
```
Called when the mouse pointer enters the applet's display area.

```
public boolean mouseExit(Event evt, int x, int y)
```
Called when the mouse pointer exits the applet's display area.

Of these methods, we used only the mouseDown, mouseUp, and mouseDrag methods in our skeleton applet because they represent the types of actions that you are going to spend the most time using for things like tracking icon presses, drawing lines, and dragging objects. The mouseMove, mouseEnter, and mouseExit methods can be used to implement "roll-over" handlers for taking some action when the cursor passes over an on-screen object.

When we examine the Component class in the next chapter, we will see the other methods amiable for handling events within applets.

Applet Display Methods

When a browser needs an applet to repaint itself, it calls a series of methods that ultimately result in the applet's paint() method being called. The paint method is defined as follows:

```
public void paint(Graphics g)
```

By overriding the paint() method in your applet, you can have your own drawing code get executed when the applet is asked to draw itself. In our skeleton applet, our paint() method draws status information about when the applet was started as well as about the mouse events that have recently taken place. Let's take a quick look at the paint() method again. We'll review only the first couple of lines of the method this time:

```
public void paint(Graphics g) {
    g.drawRect(0, 0, size().width - 1, size().height - 1);
    g.drawString("Test parameter = " + TestParam, 10, 20);

    ...

}
```

When the paint method is called, it is passed a reference to a Graphics object. This object is good only for the life of the method and shouldn't be used after the paint() method exits, so don't be tempted to store it in an instance variable for later use by other methods.

All graphics operations are performed by calling one of the supplied methods in the Graphics class. In our example, we make use of the drawRect(), drawString(), drawOval(), and fillRect() methods from this class to draw the contents of the applet's display area.

Because all drawing to the screen by an applet takes place within the paint() method (or methods called from the paint() method), the question that occurs is when is the paint() method called, and can it be called directly to perform draw on-demand actions such as animation. The answer is that the browser normally causes an applet to paint itself in response to such actions as needing to update the display after the page is scrolled or an overlapping window is moved. An applet can request to be redrawn as soon as possible using the repaint() method. This method does not redraw the applet, but it schedules the thread that handles the display of the applet to redraw the applet as soon as possible. From a practical standpoint, this might not happen right away or might get combined with several other repaint requests. If you called repaint() three times in a row, it might result in the applet being painted on the screen only once.

Starting, Stopping, and Shutting Down

Applets are sent the start(), stop(), and destroy() messages in response to an applet's document being visited, left, and closed (or un-cached). These are declared as follows:

`public void start()`

Called when the applet is started. This usually means that the applet's page has just been loaded, or the page has been revisited.

`public void stop()`

Called when the applet's page is no longer on the screen. At this point, the applet may be revisited, so although threads should be stopped, other resources don't need to be cleaned up before destroy() is called.

`public void destroy()`

Called when the browser has closed or un-cached the page that the applet is on, so that if the page is revisited, the applet will be re-instantiated. Inside the destroy() method the applet can free any resources not automatically freed by the garbage collector.

Usually, an applet only needs to respond to these messages if it is performing some continuous action such as playing a sound or displaying animations, usually with the help of running threads, and needs to suspend these activities when the user leaves the page and resume them when the page is revisited.

Let's take a look at how we can combine these methods with a thread in order to have the current time continuously displayed and updated at the bottom of the applet. We would implement this by having a thread that was started in the applet's start() method and that once a second created a new Date object holding the current date and time and then asked the applet to repaint itself. Let's take a look at the changes we need to make to the skeleton applet to make this happen.

First, we need to make the applet implement the Runnable interface, like so:

```
public class AppletSkeleton extends Applet implements Runnable {
```

Next, we have to add instance variables to hold references to the current Date object and the thread object used to update it. These instance variables would be declared as follows:

```
Date currentTime = null;
Thread timeKeeper = null;
```

Now, we update our start() method, which looks like this:

```
public void start() {
    startDate = new Date();
    repaint();

    timeKeeper = new Thread(this);
    timeKeeper.setPriority(Thread.MAX_PRIORITY);

    timeKeeper.start();
}
```

This method will now allocate a new thread object with the applet as the target (meaning that the run() method will be contained in the applet). We then set the priority of the new thread to the maximum priority, which will allow it to preempt just about any other threads, and last, we start the new thread. Because this thread is of maximum priority, its likely result is that it will preempt the current thread right away, which means that the run() method is going to be executed immediately.

We don't yet have a run() method in our applet, so we need to add it. This is the run() method our thread will use to update the time once a second:

```
public void run() {
    while (timeKeeper != null) {
        currentTime = new Date();
        repaint();
```

```
        try {
            Thread.sleep(1000);
        } catch(InterruptedException e) {
            return;
        }
    }
}
```

This run() method looks like the ones we looked at in Chapter 12. The main thing to look at is that the thread creates a new Date object, calls repain(), and then goes to sleep for 1000 milliseconds (i.e., 1 second). Because this method is executed by a high-priority thread, after it has slept for 1000 milliseconds, it will preempt whatever else is going on and start up again. The net result of this is that a new Date object and an update request will happen once a second for as long as the thread is active.

Any time a new thread is started, you should have a plan for how to shut it down when appropriate. We do this in applets through the applet's stop() method.

In order to stop the timeKeeper thread we started earlier, we need to add a stop() method to our class as well:

```
public void stop() {
    if (timeKeeper != null) timeKeeper.stop();
    timeKeeper = null;
}
```

This stop() method simply checks to see if there is a valid (non-null) thread object stored in the timeKeeper instance variable, and if so, stops it.

Once these methods have been added, a continuously updated date and time display will appear in the lower left corner of the applet.

15

APPLET USER

INTERFACES

In this chapter, we will take a look at how to construct user interfaces within Java applets. Java provides a package of classes called the Abstract Window Toolkit (or sometimes the Advanced Window Toolkit or Another Window Toolkit), which we'll simply refer to as the AWT. This package allows you to place buttons, text fields, and other user interface elements within your applet's display area and to respond to events when users interact with these elements.

The AWT organizes on-screen elements into components and containers. A component is any on-screen object such as a button. A container is a type of component that can contain other components (or containers). You've already been introduced to one type of AWT container although you might not have recognized it. The Applet class is a subclass of the container class (java.awt.Container via java.awt.Panel), which is why your applet can contain other components. In the next sections, we'll see the component classes available to you for building user interfaces within applets.

The AWT Display Model

When an Applet object is instantiated by its host browser, it is sized to the dimensions specified in the <APPLET> tag and embedded within the Web page. In the case of a browser, such as HotJava, which is written in Java, the Web page is a type of container that contains several components (or containers) such as your applet and other page elements. In the case of a browser such as Netscape, you can't make any assumptions about what sort of container your applet is in. In either case, you will usually write your applet as if it were the top-level container that you need to deal with.

In Chapter 14, we saw how to draw into the applet's display area to present some information about mouse events and to provide graphical feedback in the form of a line from the mousedown to mouseup points. In that sort of simple applet, we were interested only in using the applet as a component because we didn't need to make use of any user interface components at that time.

When we need to build a user interface within an applet, we simply instantiate the user interface components we need and add them to the applet. For example, the following applet init() method would create a button component and add it to the applet.

```java
// ButtonApplet.java
import java.applet.*;
import java.awt.*;

public class ButtonApplet extends Applet {

    public void init() {
        Button testButton = new Button("Button");
        add(testButton);
    }
}
```

The resulting applet, when viewed within a Web browser, would look something like Figure 15.1 (without the labels, of course).

Just for reference, Figure 15.2 shows a screen shot of it in Netscape.

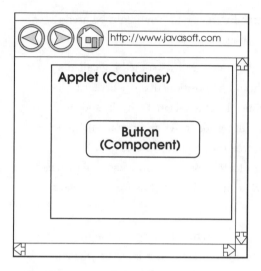

■■■■■■■ Figure 15.1

Our applet contains a single button within its display area. At this point, you're probably wondering how the applet knew where to place the button on-screen, or perhaps you're worrying that Java doesn't give you control over the placement of user interface components. Don't worry, you can control the layout of your user interface elements with as much detail as you wish, although the AWT takes an

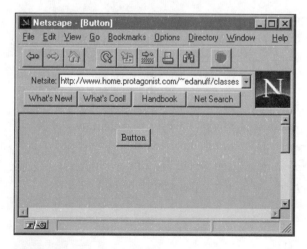

■■■■■■■ Figure 15.2

approach to managing UI layout that is a little different than you might be used to if you've been using a visual interface tool such as Visual Basic.

When a component is added to a container, the container uses something called a layout to determine where the component should be positioned and whether it should be resized. Every container has a layout object associated with it, and there are layout classes for organizing components into grids (rows and columns), compass positions (i.e., north, south, east, west), freeflow, and even cards (i.e., HyperCard style). If none of these layouts works for you, you can create your own layout classes, as we will do when we present a simple layout class for exact placement of components.

The advantage of placing components using layouts rather than specifying their exact position is twofold. First, many components represent user interface elements that are displayed using the platform's native user interface toolkit. This means that an applet button looks like a Windows 95 button when running on Windows 95 and an X Window button when running on Solaris. Because of this, it is very likely that the size and shape of these elements might differ on different platforms. If you were to place two buttons exactly next to each other on the Mac, they might overlap when the applet is run under Solaris, or they might be too far apart under Windows. The container uses the layout to space out the components so that they look correct regardless of platform.

Second, by using layouts to place components within a container, it becomes possible to resize the container and have the components still be laid out correctly. This is extremely useful when you are creating applets that you want to reuse on different pages and want the flexibility of resizing to accommodate other page elements.

Most user interfaces constructed within applets make use of several containers, each with its own layout. For example, an applet might have a row of buttons across the top and a picture in the center. The row of buttons would be contained within a panel, which is a subclass of container, and would be laid out within the panel using the FlowLayout layout. Here's what the applet's init() method would look like:

```
public void init() {
    setLayout(new BorderLayout());
```

```
Panel ledge = new Panel();
ledge.setLayout(new FlowLayout());
ledge.add(new Button("Button"));
ledge.add(new Button("Button"));
ledge.add(new Button("Button"));
ledge.add(new Button("Button"));
add("North", ledge);

IconCanvas theIcon = new IconCanvas();
add("Center", theIcon);
}
```

In this example, we first set the layout for the applet to be an instance of BorderLayout. When we add a component to a container using the BorderLayout, we specify which border we want the component to "stick" to. This is done with the following line:

```
setLayout(new BorderLayout());
```

When we later add the ledge Panel to the applet, we will specify the north border. Before we do that, however, we need to instantiate the Panel and set the layout that it will use for its components. We do this with the following lines:

```
Panel ledge = new Panel();
ledge.setLayout(new FlowLayout());
```

This will create an instance of Panel and store a reference to it in the variable ledge. We then set the layout of the new Panel object to FlowLayout, which means that components added to it are going to flow from left to right. We then add four buttons to the ledge Panel:

```
ledge.add(new Button("Button"));
ledge.add(new Button("Button"));
ledge.add(new Button("Button"));
ledge.add(new Button("Button"));
```

Now that we have set up the ledge Panel, we add it to the applet, using the following statement:

```
add("North", ledge);
```

By specifying "North" as the location of the ledge Panel, it will be positioned on the north (i.e. top) border of the applet.

Finally, we create the IconCanvas object and add it to the applet, specifying that it be placed in the "Center" position:

```
IconCanvas theIcon = new IconCanvas();
add("Center", theIcon);
```

The resulting applet would be laid out something like the one shown in Figure 15.3.

To recap, Java's AWT provides a number of user interface objects called components. Containers are components that have the ability to contain other components; Applets are a type of container, so Applets also have the capability to contain other components. When a container includes one or more components, it lays

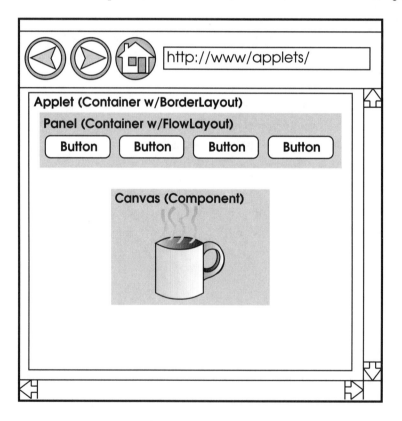

■■■■■■ **Figure 15.3**

them out within the container using a layout, which provides the logic for positioning and sizing the contained elements. Because a container is a type of component, it can be placed inside another container. In this case, the layout of the enclosing (parent) container can be different from the layout of the enclosed (child) container. The child container is positioned within the parent container using the parent container's layout. Components placed within the child container will be positioned using the child container's layout.

In the next sections, we will look at the different AWT classes for components, containers, and layouts.

Using Components

The AWT provides you with eight basic user interface components that it supports on all platforms:

- Button
- CheckBox
- Choice
- Label
- List
- Scrollbar
- TextArea
- TextField

When these components are displayed, they are drawn using the native user interface toolkit of the platform running the applet. As a consequence, they are consistent with the user interface conventions of the platform on which they are running. The AWT implements this by storing a reference to a second object called a Peer within the component. This Peer represents the platform-native on-screen control that is drawn by the component. When a component is sent a message to draw itself, or perform some display-related action (such as moving the thumbwheel on a scroll bar), it passes that message on to the Peer object, which interfaces with the operating system using native methods (Figure 15.4).

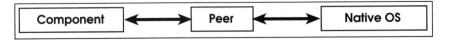

Figure 15.4

If you look through the Java API source code, which we encourage you to do, you will see numerous references to the component's peer in most of the component classes. The peer is the "go-between" of the component and the native OS and can "speak the local language" in order to translate the AWT's requests into native user interface routines and return feedback from the OS to the AWT. When Java is ported to a new platform, only the AWT peer classes need to be ported for the component classes to work.

Each component is implemented as a subclass of java.awt.Component. Components are always rectangular, although the exact location and size of the component depends on the layout being used by the container that owns the component. When using user interface components, that size is dependent first on the native OS requirements as mediated by the peer for the size of controls and second on the rules used by the layout for sizing components within the container. The result is that you will usually not know the exact size of a given component once it is added to the container.

Let's take a look at a simple applet that puts all the user interface components on-screen at the same time. The source file should be named Widgets.java. Here's the listing for the applet:

```
// Widgets.java
import java.util.*;
import java.applet.*;
import java.awt.*;

public class Widgets extends Applet {

    Label testLabel;
    Button testButton;
    Checkbox testCheckbox;
    Choice testChoice;
```

```
Scrollbar test_h_Scrollbar;
TextArea testTextArea;
TextField testTextField;
List testList;

public void init() {
    setLayout(new FlowLayout(FlowLayout.LEFT));

    testLabel = new Label("Label");
    add(testLabel);

    testButton = new Button("Button");
    add(testButton);

    testCheckbox = new Checkbox("Checkbox");
    add(testCheckbox);

    testChoice = new Choice();
    testChoice.addItem("1");
    testChoice.addItem("2");
    testChoice.addItem("3");
    add(testChoice);

    test_h_Scrollbar = new Scrollbar(Scrollbar.HORIZONTAL,
        50, 10, 0, 1000);
    add(test_h_Scrollbar);

    testTextArea = new TextArea("TextArea", 3, 30);
    add(testTextArea);

    testTextField = new TextField("TextField", 30);
    add(testTextField);

    testList = new List();
```

```
      testList.addItem("Item 1");
      testList.addItem("Item 2");
      testList.addItem("Item 3");
      add(testList);


   }


}
```

This is the HTML page that displays the applet. It is saved in a file named
Widgets.html.

```
<!--Widgets.html-->

</HTML>
<HEAD>
<TITLE>Widgets</TITLE>
</HEAD>
<BODY>

<APPLET CODE=Widgets.class WIDTH=300 HEIGHT=300>
</APPLET>

</BODY>
</HTML>
```

After saving all the files, compiling the Widgets.java file, and placing the
Widget.html and newly created Widgets.class file in the appropriate directory for
either Applet Viewer to find it, or for the Web server to find it so that you can view
it with Netscape, you are ready to try the applet out. You do not need to do this
right now, though, since we'll refer to the screen shots presented next rather than to
what you're seeing on-screen.

If you were to view the applet with Netscape 2.0, running under Windows 95, the
browser would look something like Figure 15.5.

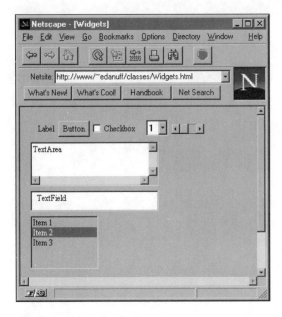

Figure 15.5

Notice that the components have been rendered as Windows 95 controls, so that on-screen components like the scroll bars for our text area component are the same as the scroll bars used by the browser for scrolling the page.

Meanwhile, if we were to fire up the applet using Applet Viewer on a SPARC machine running Solaris 2.4, we would see the window in Figure 15.6.

In this case, the components are displayed as X Window widgets.

The other thing to notice in our previous example is that we used the flow layout that resulted in the newly added components simply laying out from left to right and wrapping around when the applet's width was reached.

In the next sections, we will look at each component class that the AWT provides for creating user interface controls. When using these components, be sure to look at their entries in the API reference found in Appendix B.

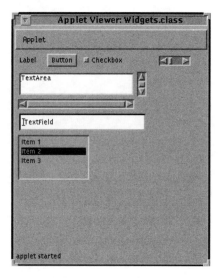

■■■■■■ Figure 15.6

Button

The button class provides a simple on-screen pushbutton, like the one shown in Figure 15.7.

The button's label is the text contained within the button. Buttons are displayed by the native user interface toolkit, so they will ignore the component's color settings for the background and foreground. Buttons can be constructed one of two ways:

- Button constructors
  ```
  public Button()
  ```
  Constructs a Button with no label.

  ```
  public Button(String label)
  ```
  Constructs a Button with a string label.

In our Widgets.java example, we created a Button component using these lines:

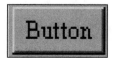

■■■■■■ Figure 15.7

```
testButton = new Button("Button");
add(testButton);
```

The button's label can be retrieved and changed using the getLabel and setLabel methods:

- Button.getLabel/setLabel
    ```
    public String getLabel()
    ```
    Gets the label of the button.

    ```
    public void setLabel(String label)
    ```
    Sets the button with the specified label.

Checkbox

A checkbox is a simple on/off toggle control. Like buttons, checkboxes can also have labels. The state of the checkbox is represented by a Boolean value: true means checked, and false means unchecked. A typical on-screen representation of a checkbox will look something like Figure 15.8.

Checkboxes will usually be constructed one of two ways:

- Checkbox constructors
    ```
    public Checkbox()
    ```
    Constructs a Checkbox with no label and initialized to a false state.

    ```
    public Checkbox(String label)
    ```
    Constructs a Checkbox with the specified label and initialized to a false state.

In the Widgets example, the following lines of code were used to create a checkbox object:

```
testCheckbox = new Checkbox("Checkbox");
add(testCheckbox);
```

The label of the checkbox can be retrieved and set using the getLabel and setLabel methods that we used with the button in the previous section.

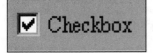

Figure 15.8

CheckboxGroup

Checkboxes can be organized into groups to implement radio-button style functionality in your programs. To do this, you need to create a new CheckboxGroup object and attach checkboxes to it. For example, the following lines of code (which you could add to the init() method of Widgets.java) would create a new CheckboxGroup and attach three CheckBox components to it:

```
CheckboxGroup theRadioGroup = new CheckboxGroup();
Checkbox checkbox1 = new Checkbox("A", theRadioGroup, false);
Checkbox checkbox2 = new Checkbox("B", theRadioGroup, false);
Checkbox checkbox3 = new Checkbox("C");
checkbox3.setCheckboxGroup(theRadioGroup);
add(checkbox1);
add(checkbox2);
add(checkbox3);
theRadioGroup.setCurrent(checkbox2);
```

The CheckboxGroup is not a component or a container, but an object that is used to manage the relationship between several CheckBox objects. Consequently, you can't add a CheckboxGroup to a container.

Choice

A Choice component represents a pop-down menu of choices with the current choice indicated in a read-only text box to the left of the pop-down menu icon. A typical representation of a Choice component will look something like Figure 15.9.

There is only one constructor for the Choice component:

- Choice constructor
    ```
    public Choice()
    ```
    Constructs a new Choice.

■■■■■ **Figure 15.9**

In our Widgets.java example, we create a Choice component using the following lines:

```
testChoice = new Choice();
testChoice.addItem("1");
testChoice.addItem("2");
testChoice.addItem("3");
add(testChoice);
```

As we see in this example, items are added as strings to the Choice component using the Choice class addItem() method. Here's the definition of addItem()

- Choice.addItem
  ```
  public synchronized void addItem(String item)
  ```
  Adds an item to this Choice.

You can find the current item that has been chosen by the user by using the getSelectedItem() method, which will return the string of the currently selected menu choice:

- Choice.getSelectedItem
  ```
  public String getSelectedItem()
  ```
  Returns String of the currently selected item.

Finally, you can select a specific item by name using the select() method:

- Choice.select
  ```
  public void select(String str)
  ```
  Selects the item with the specified String.

More information about the Choice class can be found in the java.awt.Choice entry in the API reference.

Label

Labels are lines of static text that are not editable by the user and can be used for messages, titles, or any other textual information. The text within a Label can be left, center, or right justified. Figure 15.10 shows a typical representation of a Label.

■■■■■■ **Figure 15.10**

Labels will usually be constructed one of two ways:

- Label constructors
  ```
  public Label()
  ```
  Constructs Label component with empty label text.

  ```
  public Label(String label)
  ```
  Constructs Label component with specified label text.

In our Widgets.java example, we create a Label component using the following lines:

```
testLabel = new Label("Label");

add(testLabel);
```

Once you've created a label, you can change its text using the setText() method:

- Label.setText
  ```
  public void setText(String label)
  ```
  Sets the label text.

More information about the Label class can be found in the java.awt.Label entry in the API reference.

List

Lists are scrolling lists of text items. If there are more items in the list than are visible, a scrollbar is displayed, allowing the user to scroll through the list items.

Lists are constructed using one of these constructors:

- List constructors
  ```
  public List()
  ```
  Default constructor for empty list with 0 visible rows, which means use the size of the container.

  ```
  public List(int rows,

              boolean multipleSelections)
  ```
  Constructs new scrolling list with the specified number of visible lines and with multiple selections enabled to the specified state.

In our Widgets example, we used the following code in the init() method to create the list:

```
testList = new List();

testList.addItem("Item 1");
```

```
testList.addItem("Item 2");
testList.addItem("Item 3");
add(testList);
```

Because we didn't specify the number of rows, the List allows the container's layout manager to size the List as necessary, attempting to resize itself to the size of the container. Because there are other components in this container, the List was arbitrarily sized to fit within the component. If we had specified rows in the constructor, the number of visible rows would have been used to calculate the size for the List. The layout manager does not always satisfactorily resize components that resize themselves to the size of their containers, especially when the component is the only item in a container. If you are concerned about how the layout is going to resize a List, you should explicitly specify the number of visible rows or experiment to see which layout provides the best results for you.

Items are added to the end of the list with the List class addItem() method, which is defined as follows:

- List.addItem
  ```
  public synchronized void addItem(String item)
  ```
  Adds the specified item to the end of the list.

The default behavior is for the List to allow only single selections. If you turn on multiple selections, either via the constructor or with the setMultipleSelections() call, the user will be able to select multiple lines of the list, usually using the shift key to extend the selection, although this behavior is platform-dependent.

When using single selections, you can find the current item that has been chosen by the user by using the getSelectedItem() method, which will return to you the string of the currently selected menu choice:

- List.getSelectedItem
  ```
  public String getSelectedItem()
  ```
  Returns string of the currently selected item.

And you can select a specific item by name using the select() method:

- List.select
  ```
  public void select(String str)
  ```
  Selects the item with the specified string.

When using multiple selections, the getSelectedItem() method will return null if there is more than one selection. To get the selected items in a list with multiple selections enabled, you can use the getSelectedItems() method, which will return a string array of the selected items:

- List.getSelectedItems

  ```
  public synchronized String[] getSelectedItems()
  ```
  Returns an array containing the item strings of the selected list items.

More information about the List class can be found in the java.awt.List entry in the API reference.

Scrollbar

Scrollbars are the typical horizontal and vertical scrollbar controls present in most windowing environments. The Scrollbar class is used to create a stand-alone scrollbar that will scroll through a predetermined range of values. Scrollbars will typically look something like the one shown in Figure 15.11.

There are three Scrollbar constructors:

- Scrollbar constructors

  ```
  public Scrollbar()
  ```
  Default constructor for vertical scrollbar.

  ```
  public Scrollbar(int orientation)
  ```
  Constructs new scrollbar with the given orientation ID.

  ```
  public Scrollbar(int orientation,
                   int value,
                   int visible,
                   int minimum,
                   int maximum)
  ```
  Constructs new scrollbar with the given orientation ID, current value, visibility per page, and minimum and maximum values.

■■■■■■ **Figure 15.11**

In our Widgets example, we used the following code to construct our scrollbar:

```
test_h_Scrollbar = new Scrollbar(Scrollbar.HORIZONTAL, 50, 10, 0, 1000);
add(test_h_Scrollbar);
```

This sets up our scrollbar to be horizontal, have a current value of 50, increment or decrement by 10 when the user clicks in the paging area, and have a minimum value of 0 and a maximum value of 1000.

At any given time, you can find out the current value of the scrollbar using the getValue() method:

- Scrollbar.getValue
  ```
  public int getValue()
  ```
  Returns the current value.

Refer to the API reference in Appendix B for information about the java.awt.Scrollbar class and its methods.

TextArea

The text area class represents a scrolling area for editing and displaying multiline text. It will typically look something like Figure 15.12.

TextArea (and TextField in the next section) are subclasses of TextComponent, which is the abstract base class for all AWT text components. As a consequence, you will want to refer to the methods within TextComponent for information about manipulating the selection and inserting and replacing text, since TextArea inherits the methods for these operations from TextComponent.

TextArea provides four constructors for creating TextArea objects. Two of them use a row and column value to specify the fixed size of the TextArea. The other two allow you to omit these parameters, in which case the TextArea will size the object

Figure 15.12

to the size of the TextArea's container. Some layout managers, such as FlowLayout, resize the container depending on the size of their components. These will produce unexpected results when used with TextAreas that have 0 rows and columns. The BorderLayout has been found to produce good results when used with 0 row and column text areas if the TextArea is added to the center. We recommend that you use this layout with the TextArea's container when you want to create a TextArea that will automatically resize to the size of its container.

Here are the TextArea constructors:

- TextArea constructors

  ```
  public TextArea()
  ```
  Default constructor for a new empty TextArea. When this constructor is used, the visible rows and columns are set to 0, which means use the size of the container.

  ```
  public TextArea(int rows,
                      int cols)
  ```
  Constructs new TextArea using the specified rows and columns.

  ```
  public TextArea(String text)
  ```
  Constructs new TextArea and sets initial contents to the specified text. When this constructor is used, the visible rows and columns are set to 0, which means use the size of the container.

  ```
  public TextArea(String text,
                      int rows,
                      int cols)
  ```
  Constructs new TextArea using the specified rows and columns and specified initial text.

In our Widget example, we constructed our TextArea with the following lines:

```
testTextArea = new TextArea("TextArea", 3, 30);
add(testTextArea);
```

You can get and set the text from a TextArea using the getText() and setText() methods found in the TextArea's super class, TextComponent:

- TextArea.getText/setText

  ```
  public String getText()
  ```
  Returns the TextComponent text.

```
public void setText(String t)
```
Sets the text of the TextComponent.

More information about the TextArea class can be found in the java.awt.TextArea entry in the API reference. Make sure you also look at the java.awt.TextComponent class, which provides a number of methods that TextArea inherits. For example, TextComponent provides several methods for getting and setting the selection.

TextField

The TextField class represents a single text-entry field for editing and displaying a single line of text. It will typically look something like Figure 15.13.

As mentioned in the previous section, TextField (and TextArea) are subclasses of TextComponent, the abstract base class for all AWT text components. As a consequence, you will want to refer to the methods within TextComponent for information about manipulating the selection and inserting and replacing text because TextField inherits the methods for these operations from TextComponent.

There are four constructors for TextField:

- TextField constructors
  ```
  public TextField()
  ```
  Default constructor for text field with a column count of 0, meaning that it will attempt to size to the width of its container.

  ```
  public TextField(int cols)
  ```
  Constructs new TextField with the specified columns.

  ```
  public TextField(String text)
  ```
  Constructs new TextField and sets initial contents to the specified text. The TextField will have a column count of 0, meaning that it will attempt to size to the width of its container.

TextField

▐██████████ **Figure 15.13**

```
public TextField(String text,
                          int cols)
```
Constructs new TextField with the specified columns and sets initial contents to the specified text.

In our Widget example, we constructed our TextField with the following lines:

```
testTextField = new TextField("TextField", 30);
add(testTextField);
```

As with the TextArea, you can get and set the text from a TextField using the getText() and setText() methods found in the TextArea's super class, TextComponent:

- TextField.getText/setText

```
public String getText()
```
Returns the TextComponent text.

```
public void setText(String t)
```
Sets the text of the TextComponent.

TextFields have a couple of methods that can be used when implementing a password entry system, where you don't want the characters entered to be echoed on the screen. You probably are familiar with password entry systems where the system displays a character, such as *, instead of the characters of your password. You can use the following methods to set an echo character for the TextField that will mask any characters entered in it:

- TextField echo character methods

```
public boolean echoCharIsSet()
```
Returns true if this TextField has a character set for echoing. Typically used for entering passwords.

```
public char getEchoChar()
```
Returns the character to be used for echoing.

```
public void setEchoCharacter(char c)
```
Sets the echo character for this TextField for entering characters such as passwords that shouldn't be visible on-screen. Call with a value of 0 to clear the echo character.

More information about the TextField class can be found in the java.awt.TextField entry in the API reference. Make sure you also look at the java.awt.TextComponent class which provides a number of methods which TextField inherits. For example, TextComponent provides several methods for getting and setting the selection.

Using Containers

If you use any of the component classes in your applets, you will need to deal with containers. Because the applet is a type of container, you will need to understand how containers work and how to use them with layouts to construct all but the simplest of interfaces. In previous sections, we introduced you to the basics of containers. In this section, we'll go into further detail about what you need to know about containers and layouts in order to construct applet user interfaces.

A container is a type of component that can contain other components. Because containers are subclasses of components, it also follows that some of the components inside a container can be other containers. Containers provide a rectangular display area in which components are positioned. Figure 15.14 shows how components are drawn with the display space of a container.

The actual position of a component within a container is highly dependent on the layout associated with the container. Most of the system-supplied layouts will prevent components from being positioned so that they are outside the component's bounds.

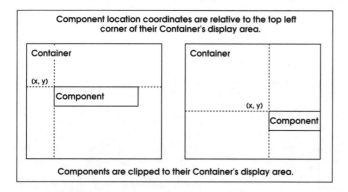

Figure 15.14

Each component (and container) has its own coordinate space. Components within a container are positioned relative to the top left corner of the container and are located using the container's coordinate space. When drawing takes place within a component, graphics operations use the coordinate space of the component. In the following diagram, we have a container that has within it another container, which in turn contains a component. The specified coordinates of each component/container's positions illustrate the relationships between the coordinate spaces of components and subcomponents (Figure 15.15).

We'll see more of graphics operations within components in the next chapter.

Components are added to layouts using the add() method. We saw this method used earlier in our Widgets example. There are two forms of the add() method, which are defined as follows:

- Component.add
    ```
    public synchronized Component add(Component comp)
    ```
    Adds the specified component to this container. The current layout manager will later be called to position and size the component.

    ```
    public synchronized Component add(String name,
                                    Component comp)
    ```
    Adds the specified component to this container. Calls the addLayoutComponent() method of the current layout manager with the name string and component as arguments. The name string is used by some layout managers such as BorderLayout to indicate that special rules need to be used in positioning and sizing the new component.

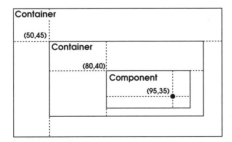

Figure 15.15

The first version of the method adds the component to the container and let's the current layout manager handle positioning the component when it is called to lay out any unpositioned components before the next redraw. The second version of the method takes a string parameter and calls the layout manager's addLayoutComponent() method to specially handle the positioning of the layout. Most layout managers have an empty method for addLayoutComponent(), which means that they ignore it. We've mentioned that BorderLayout is an exception to this, as is CardLayout. In the case of the BorderLayout, the layout allows you to position at the north, south, east, and west borders of the container. To specify that a component should be placed on one of these borders, the name of the border is passed as a string to add(). Because all layout managers implement addLayoutComponent() even if they don't use it, you can call add() with a string parameter even if the current layout doesn't support it; the result will be that the name string is ignored. Some of the JDK example code, such as CardTest.java, makes use of this fact, so if you're trying to make sense of layouts by looking at these examples, keep this in mind.

There are three principal methods for dealing with the positioning and sizing of components with containers:

- Component.move

```
public void move(int x,
                        int y)
```

Moves the Component to a new x, y location in the parent container's coordinate space.

- Component.resize

```
public void resize(int width,
                        int height)
```

Resizes the Component to the specified width and height. If you don't get the results you expect from this call, the parent container's layout manager is likely to be interfering.

- Component.reshape

```
public synchronized void reshape(int x,
                                    int y,
                                    int width,
                                    int height)
```

Moves the component to the specified location and resizes it to the specified dimensions. If you don't get the results you expect from this call, the parent container's layout manager is likely to be interfering.

All of these methods use the coordinate system of the component's container to position the component. The move() method locates the component at a given coordinate, the resize() method sizes the component to a given width and height, and the reshape() method combines the two and positions and sizes the component in a single method call. As the method definitions indicate, these methods are likely to have no effect if the container's layout manager handles these properties for the container's components.

Layouts

The positioning of components within a container is handled by the container's layout manager. Every container has a layout attached to it. If you don't specify a layout, most containers assign the border layout as the default layout. In this section we'll learn more about layouts and how they work.

A layout manager is a class that implements the LayoutManager interface. This interface requires that the class implement the following five methods:

- LayoutManager interface methods

```
public abstract void addLayoutComponent(String name,
                                                Component comp)
public abstract void layoutContainer(Container parent)
public abstract Dimension minimumLayoutSize(Container parent)
public abstract Dimension preferredLayoutSize(Container parent)
public abstract void removeLayoutComponent(Component comp)
```

The specifics of the implementation of these methods can be found in the API reference and in the source files of the AWT package, which are included in the JDK. These methods are invoked by methods in the component and container classes in order to manage the layout of components. The method that does most of the work is the layoutContainer() method. This method is invoked by the AWT after you have added and sized your components, but before they are drawn. This means that the layout will have the last word on reshaping your components before they are drawn. The key to creating Java user interfaces is figuring out which layout class will provide the desired results. In the case where none of the layouts will do the trick, we will show you a simple custom layout that let's you position components with exact coordinates. There are some caveats to its usage, and this type of technique goes against the spirit of Java user interface design, so we encourage you to stick with the supplied layout classes.

FlowLayout

The FlowLayout class will draw the subcomponents of a container starting from the top left and will continue to lay out components horizontally until the right edge of the container is reached. At this point the layout manager will skip down to the next row and again start laying out components from left to right. FlowLayout is instantiated with one of the following three constructors:

- FlowLayout constructors

  ```
  public FlowLayout()
  ```
  Default constructor. New FlowLayout object will use centered alignment.

  ```
  public FlowLayout(int align)
  ```
  Constructs new FlowLayout object using the specified alignment ID.

  ```
  public FlowLayout(int align,
                          int hgap,
                          int vgap)
  ```
  Constructs new FlowLayout object using the specified alignment ID and gap values.

The FlowLayout class can have an alignment specified for it, in which case it will use this alignment to left, center, or right align the components on a given row. This alignment is specified with one of the following codes:

- FlowLayout alignment codes

  ```
  public final static int CENTER
  public final static int LEFT
  public final static int RIGHT
  ```

Figures 15.16–15.18 show how the alignment of a FlowLayout affects the layout of components.

Figure 15.16 shows essentially the same layout that we used in the Widgets example. We choose a left-aligned layout using the following line:

```
setLayout(new FlowLayout(FlowLayout.LEFT));
```

If we instead used the CENTER alignment, the components would have laid out like Figure 15.17.

We'd use the code:

```
setLayout(new FlowLayout(FlowLayout.CENTER));
```

Finally, right alignment would use the following code and would look like Figure 15.18.

```
setLayout(new FlowLayout(FlowLayout.RIGHT));
```

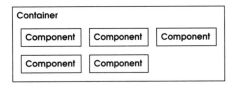

Figure 15.16 Left aligned.

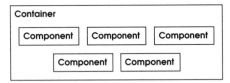

Figure 15.17 Center aligned.

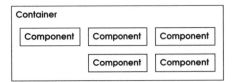

Figure 15.18 Right aligned.

BorderLayout

The BorderLayout is a versatile layout that can be used as the base container for most common types of application user interfaces. A drawing program with a tool palette on the left-hand side of the applet, scroll bars on the right and bottom, and a draw area in the center would be one type of layout that the BorderLayout could implement. A word processing program would be a small variation of this, with a text area instead of a drawing area, and a tool bar at the top of the container. Figure 15.19 shows the basic form of the layout of components using the BorderLayout.

The key to using the BorderLayout is specifying the position of components when they are added to a container using the container's add() method. As we pointed out earlier, the add() method can take a string name parameter. If this name string is "North", "South", "East", "West", or "Center", the component will be assigned the corresponding position in the layout.

Here's an example of using the BorderLayout in an applet. We'll also make use of the FlowLayout as the layout of a subcontainer:

```
// ScrollBorderApplet.java
import java.util.*;
import java.applet.*;
import lava.awt.*;

public class ScrollBorderApplet extends Applet {

    Scrollbar h_scroll = null;
    Scrollbar v_scroll = null;
    Panel document_area null;
```

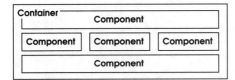

Figure 15.19

```
public void init () {
    setLayout(new BorderLayout());

    h_scroll = new Scrollbar(Scrollbar.HORIZONTAL, 50, 10, 0, 100);
    v_scroll = new Scrollbar(Scrollbar.VERTICAL, 50, 10, 0, 100);

    add("South", h_scroll);
    add("East", v_scroll);

    document_area = new Panel();
    add("Center", document-area);

    document_area.setLayout(new FlowLayout());

    document_area.add(new Label("label 1"));
    document_area.add(new Label("label 2"));
}
}
```

GridLayout

The GridLayout, as the name suggests, is used for constructing grids of components. A GridLayout is constructed with a number of rows and columns specified in the constructor, and as components are added to the container, they are assigned positions on the grid. Figure 15.20 shows how components would be laid out in a three-by-three grid.

The GridLayout has the following basic constructors:

- GridLayout constructors
  ```
  public GridLayout(int rows,
                        int cols)
  ```
  Constructs grid layout with the specified rows and specified columns.

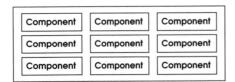

■■■■ **Figure 15.20**

```
public GridLayout(int rows,

                  int cols,

                  int hgap,

                  int vgap)
```
Constructs grid layout with the specified rows, columns, horizontal gap, and vertical gap.

When adding components to containers that use this layout, you use the basic add() method without the optional name parameter. The column specification for the grid is more important than the row specification in that the grid fills each row from left to right with the number of components specified for the columns before moving to the next row. You don't need to fill every cell of the grid; in that case the layout will look somewhat like the left-aligned FlowLayout, but with precise alignment of the components. Current versions of the GridLayout allow you to exceed the specified number of rows and the layout will still work. However, this behavior is "undefined," meaning that it may throw an exception in future versions, so you shouldn't count on it to work. Some of the Sun example applets do this, though, so if you're scratching your head over why one of their GridLayout examples works, this is the probable reason.

Here's a simple example of a phone pad created with a GridLayout:

```java
// TouchPad.java
import java.awt.*;
import java.applet.*;

public class TouchPad extends Applet {

  public void init() {
    setLayout(new GridLayout(4, 3, 5, 5));
    add(new Button("1"));
    add(new Button("2"));
    add(new Button("3"));
    add(new Button("4"));
    add(new Button("5"));
    add(new Button("6"));
    add(new Button("7"));
```

```
        add(new Button("8"));
        add(new Button("9"));
        add(new Button("*"));
        add(new Button("0"));
        add(new Button("Button"));
    }

}
```

CardLayout

The CardLayout is different from the previous layout classes in that it is not designed to lay out components so much as it is meant to lay out other containers. A container that uses the CardLayout as its layout manager will display only one component at a time, and this component will usually be a container that contains the contents of a "card." Every component in a CardLayout is a "card" and is organized into a stack. The CardLayout is very useful for implementing HyperCard-style applets that have a number of screens that can be flipped through. For example, control panels, address books, and file cards could all be implemented using the CardLayout interface.

To use the CardLayout, you will typically perform the following steps in your program. First, you will create the card container that will use the CardLayout. In many cases, this will be the applet itself. If not, then you will need to add the card container to another container (i.e., the applet); you should make sure that the container being added to is set up with a compatible layout. You will then create an instance of CardLayout and assign it as the layout for the card container. These steps are illustrated by the following lines of code:

```
setLayout(new BorderLayout());
Panel card_stack = new Panel();
CardLayout cl = new CardLayout();
card_stack.setLayout(cl);
add("Center", card_stack);
```

Once the CardLayout object has been instantiated and set as the layout for the card container, the individual "cards" must be added. Each card should be a container, such as Panel, although this is not required. The following lines of code will set up three panels:

```
Panel card_1 = new Panel();
card_1.setLayout(new FlowLayout());
card_1.add(new Label("Card 1"));
card_1.add(new Button("One"));
card_stack.add("One", card_1);

Panel card_2 = new Panel();
card_2.setLayout(new FlowLayout());
card_2.add(new Label("Card 2"));
card_2.add(new TextField("Two", 30));
card_stack.add("Two", card_2);

Panel card_3 = new Panel();
card_3.setLayout(new FlowLayout());
card_3.add(new Label("Card 3"));
card_3.add(new Checkbox("Three"));
card_stack.add("Three", card_3);
```

When the applet is fired up, it's going to show the first card in the card container.

The CardLayout is also one of the few layouts you will call directly. To specify which card is shown, you must use several methods present in the CardLayout:

- CardLayout.first
  ```
  public void first(Container parent)
  ```
  Display first "card."

- CardLayout.last
  ```
  public void last(Container parent)
  ```
  Display last "card."

- CardLayout.next
  ```
  public void next(Container parent)
  ```
  Display "next" card.

- CardLayout.previous
  ```
  public void previous(Container parent)
  ```
  Display "previous" card.

- CardLayout.show
  ```
  public void show(Container parent,
                       String name)
  ```
  Display named "card."

Let's take a look at an expanded version of our card example, which adds some buttons for moving from page to page:

```java
// SimpleCard.java
import java.awt.*;
import java.applet.*;

public class SimpleCard extends Applet {
    Panel card_stack;
    CardLayout cl;

    public void init() {
        setLayout(new BorderLayout());
        card_stack = new Panel();
        cl = new CardLayout();
        card_stack.setLayout(cl);
        add("Center", card_stack);

        Panel card_1 = new Panel();
        card_1.setLayout(new FlowLayout());
        card_1.add(new Label("Card 1"));
        card_1.add(new Button("One"));
        card_stack.add("One", card_1);

        Panel card_2 = new Panel();
        card_2.setLayout(new FlowLayout());
        card_2.add(new Label("Card 2"));
        card_2.add(new TextField("Two", 30));
        card_stack.add("Two", card_2);

        Panel card_3 = new Panel();
        card_3.setLayout(new FlowLayout());
        card_3.add(new Label("Card 3"));
```

```
        card_3.add(new Checkbox("Three"));
        card_stack.add("Three", card_3);

        Panel button_bar = new Panel();
        button_bar.setLayout(new FlowLayout());
        button_bar.add(new Button("First"));
        button_bar.add(new Button("Previous"));
        button_bar.add(new Button("Next"));
        button_bar.add(new Button("Last"));
        add("South", button_bar);
    }


    public boolean action(Event evt, Object arg) {
        if ("First".equals(arg)) {
            cl.first(card_stack);
        } else if ("Previous".equals(arg)) {
            cl.previous(card_stack);
        } else if ("Next".equals(arg)) {
            cl.next(card_stack);
        } else if ("Last".equals(arg)) {
        cl.last(card_stack);
        }
        return true;
    }

}
```

The main differences between this and our previous example are the addition of a panel of buttons at the bottom of the applet and an action() method that uses these buttons to navigate from card to card using the CardLayout methods. We'll learn more about event handling and the action() method in the next section. Here's a look at what the final version of our SimpleCard.java example looks like, as shown in Figure 15.21.

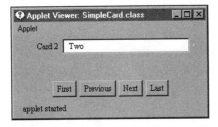

■■■■ **Figure 15.21**

Event Handling

In the previous example we saw how the action() method can be used to handle events. In this section, we'll take a look at how events are handled by the AWT.

At a basic level, events are generated by the system in response to a user or system activity. User actions such as clicking within an applet, or system activities such as notification of the fact that a window needs to be closed, are delivered to the AWT in the form of events. Once the system event is converted to a java.awt.Event object, it needs to be delivered to the appropriate component, which decides how best to respond to it. This is done using the java.awt.Component deliverEvent() method. Let's take a look at how this works with a hypothetical example. Imagine a top-most container that contains a number of subcomponents. In a real program, this might be an applet with a number of panels and buttons. In this example, we have an event, in this case a mousedown, occur within the container (Figure 15.22).

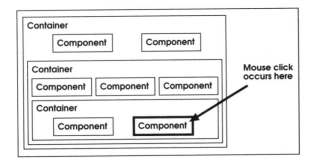

■■■■ **Figure 15.22**

At this point, the AWT basically knows two things: the coordinates of the mouse and the fact that its button has just been pressed. This information is used to construct a mousedown event object. In order for this to be of any use to us, we have to find out what component this event belongs to and deliver the event to it. This is done by traversing down the component tree using the deliverEvent() method.

The AWT calls the deliverEvent() method of the top-most component, which is usually the browser or appletviewer main window. The deliverEvent() method determines whether that component should handle the event or deliver it to one of its subcomponents by calling the subcomponent's deliverEvent() method. The subcomponent does the same thing and checks to see whether it should handle the event or pass it down to one of its subcomponents. In this way, an Event "falls" down until it reaches its target component, as illustrated by Figure 15.23.

When a component finally determines that the event belongs to it, the Event gets bounced back up the component tree until it finds a component that will handle the event. This is done through the use of the postEvent() method. When a component's deliverEvent() method determines that it is the owner of an event and should not try to send the component to any further subcomponents, it instead calls its postEvent() method. To a certain extent, postEvent() is the opposite of deliverEvent(). The postEvent() method calls the component's handleEvent() method to see whether the component should handle the event. If it does not, it responds by returning false to postEvent(), which then calls the postEvent() method of the parent component. The

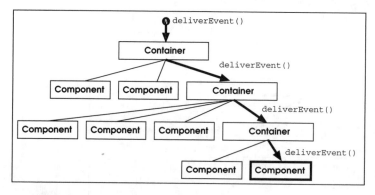

Figure 15.23

parent component does the same thing, trying to handle the event with its handleEvent() method and sending it to its parent component if the event is not handled. In this way, the event "bounces" up the component tree until it reaches a component that handles it. The process is illustrated in Figure 15.24.

In some cases, an event is handled by the component that owns it. For example, dragging objects, selecting text, and drawing lines are all operations that make sense to be handled by the component that owns them. In these cases, the event would not get sent back up the component tree. However, many user interface components, such as buttons, checkboxes, and choice menus, usually are more easily managed from higher up the event tree. For example, if you have an applet that contains a number of buttons in a subcontainer, you probably will want to handle the response to button choices in a single applet method rather than in each button instance. That way, you don't need to create a subclass of button for each button in your program in order to respond to its being pressed. You only need to override an event-handling method in your applet, and let the component class's default behavior pass the event up to your applet.

There are several ways that a component can implement event handling code, depending on the needs of your component. The important thing to understand is that handleEvent() is the central event dispatcher for a component. The handleEvent() method is defined as follows:

- Component.handleEvent
  ```
  public boolean handleEvent(Event evt)
  ```

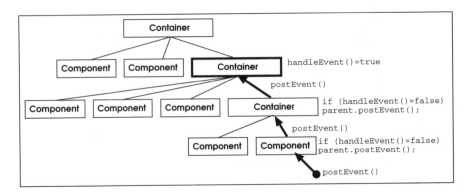

Figure 15.24

Called by postEvent to handle the event. The default behavior is to determine whether this is a mouse event, key event, or action event using the contents of evt.id, and call mouseEnter(), mouseExit(), mouseMove(), mouseDown(), mouseDrag(), or mouseUp() to handle the mouse event, keyDown() to handle key events, or action() to handle action events. The method is expected to return true if the event is handled and false if the event is not handled. Unhandled events are passed to the parent container of this component via postEvent so that they can have a chance to handle the event. If you override this method, remember to return true if you handle the event, and call super.handleEvent(evt) if you want the default event handling to be invoked.

Figure 15.25 shows the logic that the handleEvent() method follows when figuring out what to do with an event that is passed to it.

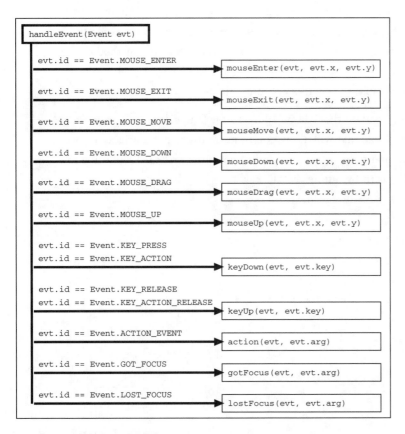

Figure 15.25

In order for a component to handle an event, its appropriate method must be over-ridden. We saw in Chapter 14 that if we override one of the mouse methods (mouseDown(), etc.) that we can have our code called when mouse events take place in components, such as the user clicking within it. Typically, you will override one of these methods to use the coordinates passed to perform some action such as drawing lines or other mouse tracking activities.

Keyboard Events

Usually, keyboard events will be directed at components such as TextField or TextArea, which will handle the keyboard events themselves. Sometimes, you'll want a component or applet to receive and respond to keyboard events. In order for a component to be sent keyboard events, it must have the focus. Having the focus means that the component is the focus of keyboard events. Only one compo-nent can have the focus at a time. A component can request the focus using the requestFocus() method, which will eventually cause the gotFocus() method of the component to be called when the component is given the focus. A click inside a component will also cause the component to get the focus.

Here's a keyDown() method that can be added to the SimpeCard.java program from our earlier example that will allow you to move to the previous and next cards using the left and right arrow keys and to go to the first card by hitting the "f" key and the last card by hitting the "l" key:

```
public boolean keyDown(Event evt, int key) {
    if (key == 'f') {
      cl.first(card_stack);
    } else if (key == Event.LEFT) {
      cl.previous(card_stack);
    } else if (key == Event.RIGHT) {
      cl.next(card_stack);
    } else if (key == 'l') {
      cl.last(card_stack);
    }
    return true;
}
```

The Event class has a number of static final variables (i.e., constant values) for key codes and event IDs. Among these are the key codes for the left and right arrow keys that are defined as Event.LEFT and Event.RIGHT, and that we use in the above method. You'll want to take a closer look at the Event class in the API reference for more information.

If you add the above method and try to run the applet, you'll find that it doesn't respond to the keyboard as you would expect. In order for this to work, you'll need to add the following line to the end of your init() method:

```
requestFocus();
```

This causes the component to request that it be the focus of future keyboard events. If the component loses the focus, for example due to the user's clicking in a text field and the text field's gaining the focus, the component will need to regain the focus in order to get keyboard events sent to it again.

You can find out if the user has held down any of the modifier keys such as the control key by calling the controlDown(), metaDown(), or shiftDown() methods of the event object. These methods will return true if their respective modifier keys are held down.

Action Events

Action events are generated in response to the user's performing some action with one of the supplied user interface components. When an event is passed to HandleEvent whose id instance variable is set to ACTION_EVENT, the event is routed to the component's action() method. The action() event is defined as follows:

- Component.action
  ```
  public boolean action(Event evt,
                            Object arg)
  ```
  Called by HandleEvent if action occurs in the component. Returns true if the component handles the action. Override this method to handle actions in this component or (when this component is a container) any of its child components.

Different user event component's respond in different ways to events that occur within them. In the case of components such as buttons, checkboxes, and choice objects, the response is in the form of an action event. The action() method is called with an Event instance and a reference to an object containing information about the component where the action occurred. Table 15.1 lists what you can expect the contents of the object to be when the action method is called.

With this in mind, let's take a look at the action() method we used in the last example:

```
public boolean action(Event evt, Object arg) {
    if ("First".equals(arg)) {
      cl.first(card_stack);
    } else if ("Previous".equals(arg)) {
      cl.previous(card_stack);
    } else if ("Next".equals(arg)) {
      cl.next(card_stack);
    } else if ("Last".equals(arg)) {
      cl.last(card_stack);
    }
    return true;
  }
```

What we're doing in this method is testing which button was chosen by the user, so we can move to the appropriate card. This is done with the following kind of test:

```
if ("First".equals(arg)) {
```

To explain how this simple test works, we will quickly review some of the properties of Java strings and objects. Remember, the variable arg contains a string repre-

■■■■■ **Table 15.1** Action() Method Arguments for Component Classes

Component Class	Argument Class	Argument Contents
Button	String	Button name
Checkbox	Boolean	Checkbox state
Choice	String	Menu choice
List	String	List item double-clicked on
TextField	String	Text field contents when Return is pressed

sentation of the Button label if the component that generated the action event was a Button component. Let's say it wasn't a Button component, and arg does not contain a string. In these types of string comparisons, what's happening behind the scenes is that the toString() method is being called to get a string representation of arg. Because the toString() method is present in the java Object class, which as Java classes implicitly are descendants of, every object in a Java program can respond to toString(). Some of you might be confused by this part of the line:

```
if ("First".equals(arg)) {
```

What's happening here is that all strings in Java are objects, including those used as string literals, which is what "First" is. So when we say "First".equals(arg), we are calling the equals() method of the string object that contains the string "First" with the object referenced in arg as a parameter. If you want to test if a button has been hit, you can use a test like this to determine which button was hit by comparing the string of the button's label to the button pressed. The second way to do comparisons is by object reference. If you store the Button object reference in instance variables, you can do a comparison like this:

```
Button  first_button;


public void init() {
   ...
   first_button = new Button("First");
   ...
}


public boolean action(Event evt, Object arg) {
   if (evt.target = first_button) {
   ...
}
```

Other Events

The handleEvent() method takes care of routing the appropriate event types; however, some events don't make it past handleEvent() without some help from you. For example, scroll bar events must be handled within the handleEvent() method to be dealt with in your code. To deal with these types of events, you will need to override the handleEvent() method. Normally, you want to avoid doing this because the default inherited handleEvent() method takes care of calling the appropriate methods, such as mouseDown(). However, if you follow the rules, you can safely override handleEvent()to catch the events you're interested in and still have it pass on the rest. What follows is an example of a well-behaved handleEvent() override:

```
public boolean handleEvent(Event evt) {
    if (evt.target == vert_scrollbar) {
        scroll_pos = ((Integer)evt.arg).intValue();
        return true;
    }
    else return super.handleEvent(evt);
}
```

What's happening here is that if the target of the event is a scrollbar for which we've saved a reference in an instance variable, we handle the event ourselves; otherwise, we call the handleEvent() method in the superclass. As long as we remember to call the default handleEvent() method, we can be sure that methods like keyDown() will get called.

Creating Your Own Components

Most of the time, you will be able to find a user interface component that suits your needs. Sometimes, however, you'll need to create your own component. In this section, we will go through the steps involved, and show a sample component that responds to the basic events.

When you create a new component class, you do so by subclassing Canvas instead of Component. This is important to note because it is a common mistake among new Java programmers. Canvas is a subclass of Component that is designed for use by your subclasses.

You will want to subclass Canvas for a number of reasons. You may simply want a subcomponent that you can use as a drawing area, or you may want to implement button-like functionality. In the next chapter, you'll see the graphics commands at your disposal for drawing in components, although we'll use a few of them here.

The following listing demonstrates an applet that uses a custom button component:

```java
// CustomButtonTest.java
import java.util.*;
import java.applet.*;
import java.awt.*;

class CustomButton extends Canvas {

    String label;

    boolean button_is_up = true;
    boolean mouse_is_down = false;

    public CustomButton() {
        this("");
    }

    public CustomButton(String label) {
        this.label = label;
    }

    public void paint(Graphics g) {
        if (button_is_up)
            paintUp(g);
        else
            paintDown(g);
    }

    public void paintUp(Graphics g) {

    g.setColor(Color.white);
    g.fillRect(0, 0, size().width-1, size().height-1);
    g.setColor(Color.black);
    g.drawRect(0, 0, size().width-1, size().height-1);
```

```
        int theWidth = g.getFontMetrics().stringWidth(label);

        int theHeight = g.getFontMetrics().getHeight();

        int theAscent = g.getFontMetrics().getAscent();

        int theLeading = g.getFontMetrics().getAscent();

        int hMargin = (size().width - theWidth) / 2;

        int vMargin = (size().height - theHeight) / 2;

        g.drawString(label,

                    hMargin,

                    vMargin + theAscent + theLeading);


    }


    public void paintDown(Graphics g) {

        g.setColor(Color.black);

        g.fillRect(0, 0, size().width-1, size().height-1);

        int theWidth = g.getFontMetrics().stringWidth(label);

        int theHeight = g.getFontMetrics().getHeight();

        int theAscent = g.getFontMetrics().getAscent();

        int theLeading = g.getFontMetrics().getAscent();

        int hMargin = (size().width - theWidth) / 2;

        int vMargin = (size().height - theHeight) / 2;

        g.setColor(Color.white);

        g.drawString(label,

                    hMargin,

                    vMargin + theAscent + theLeading);


        g.setColor(Color.black);

    }


    public boolean mouseDown(Event evt, int x, int y) {

        set_button_is_up(false);

        mouse_is_down = true;

        return true;

    }
```

```
public boolean mouseUp(Event evt, int x, int y) {
   set_button_is_up(true);
   if (mouse_is_down) buttonClicked();
   mouse_is_down = false;
   return true;
}

public boolean mouseEnter(Event evt, int x, int y) {
   if (mouse_is_down) set_button_is_up(false);
   return true;
}

public boolean mouseExit(Event evt, int x, int y) {
   if (mouse_is_down) set_button_is_up(true);
   return true;
}

public void set_button_is_up(boolean state) {
   if (button_is_up != state)
     {
        button_is_up = state;
        repaint();
     }
}

public void buttonClicked() {
   Event theEvent = new Event(this, Event.ACTION_EVENT, label);
   postEvent(theEvent);
}

public String getLabel() {
   return label;
}
```

```
    public void setLabel(String label) {
        this.label = label;
        repaint();
    }


    protected String paramString() {
        return super.paramString() + ",label=" + label;
    }


}


public class CustomButtonTest extends Applet {

    public void init() {
        setLayout(new FlowLayout(FlowLayout.LEFT));

        CustomButton testButton = new CustomButton("Button");
        add(testButton);
        testButton.resize(200,30);
        testButton.list();

    }


    public boolean action(Event evt, Object arg) {
        System.out.println(evt);
        System.out.println(arg.getClass().getName());
        System.out.println(arg);
        return true;
    }
}
```

This listing would be saved in a file called CustomButtonTest.java. If you are trying this listing out for yourself, you'll need an .html file to use with it. Here's one that will do the trick:

```
<!--CustomButtonTest.html-->
<HTML>
<HEAD>
<TITLE>CustomButtonTest</TITLE>
</HEAD>
<BODY>

<APPLET CODE=CustomButtonTest.class WIDTH=300 HEIGHT=300>
</APPLET>

</BODY>
</HTML>
```

The listing for the CustomButtonTest is fairly straightforward. The applet uses a
Canvas subclass to simulate the behavior of a button control. The key things to look
at are code for the mouseDown(), mouseUp(), mouseEnter(), and mouseExit() methods. These methods keep track of whether the button is pressed and update the component's instance variables accordingly. This information is used by the paint()
method to determine whether to draw the button highlighted or not. The final result
is not much to look at. The button is a simple rectangle with the label text drawn in
the center. However, you could easily take this code and combine it with the image
drawing methods that we will introduce in the next chapter to let you create picture
buttons that alternate between two images depending on whether they are pressed.

The CustomButtonTest applet simply instantiates the CustomButton component
and waits for action events to occur. When the CustomButton up occurs within its
display area, it posts an action event with the component as the target. This allows
the action() method of the applet to receive the event, and in our example, print out
information about the event contents.

Frames, Windows, and Dialogs

Most applets are concerned only with the display area given to them by the
browser. You might wonder what options are available to you for creating windows
and dialogs. This section will briefly discuss this issue. We'd like to point out that

this is considered an advanced topic; if you plan to build applets that use these capabilities, you will need to spend some time looking at the API reference as well as going through the on-line resources available on comp.lang.java USENET newsgroup and the java.sun.com Web site. We'll give you enough information here to get started, but there are a number of issues raised by different implementations of the Java classes on assorted platforms and within a variety of browsers.

The top-level component of every Java application is the Frame. A Frame is what the AWT calls a typical user interface window, which usually has a title bar at the top and can be moved by the user. What the AWT refers to as a Window is something a little different. An AWT Window is a borderless display area that has no adornments, such as title bars and the like. We'll continue to use the term "window" to refer to its more common meaning, so keep in mind that when we use "window" in lowercase, we are referring to regular user windows, which are represented in Java using the Frame class.

Finding the Current Frame

When you run an applet within AppletViewer or a browser, you usually don't worry much about the components that contain your applet and its subcomponents. There are times, however, when you need to determine the top-level Frame that contains your applet's components, such as when displaying a Dialog whose constructor requires you to pass a reference to a Frame and a parameter.

If you look through the API, you'll see that no method is provided for determining the top-level Frame container. To find it, you'll need to understand a few more details about the AWT component hierarchy. Every component contains a reference to its parent component that can be obtained using the component's getParent() method; if you follow the chain of component parents up far enough, you will always come to a Frame component. The following method can be used to obtain a reference to the frame component that contains your applet (or any other component). Simply pass it the component whose Frame you wish to locate, and it will return a reference to it if it exists:

```
class ComponentUtil {

    public static Frame getFrame(Component theComponent) {
```

```
Component currParent = theComponent;
Frame theFrame = null;

while (currParent != null) {
    if (currParent instanceof Frame) {
        theFrame = (Frame)currParent;
        break;
    }
    currParent = currParent.getParent();
}

return theFrame;
    }
}
```

We've made it a static method and wrapped it in a class so that you can use it from within a variety of components. For example, within an applet's init() method:

```
public void init() {
    Frame theFrame = ComponentUtil.getFrame(this);
}
```

When using the Frame object obtained from this method, remember that you might not be able to use it as you would Frames that you constructed yourself. If the applet is running within a Java application such as AppletViewer, then there should be no problems. However, if you try to attach menu items to the Frame returned by this method, and your applet is running within Netscape or another non-Java application, you can't assume that the application's authors designed the application to support all the methods available to Frames.

Displaying Dialogs

Let's now take a look at how you would put up a Dialog box from an applet. The following listing uses the ComponentUtil class we just saw to find an applet's frame, and it uses that in the constructor of a dialog:

```
// DialogTest.java
import java.applet.*;
import java.awt.*;
```

```java
public class DialogTest extends Applet {
   Frame dFrame = null;
   Dialog dDialog = null;

   public void init() {
      dFrame = ComponentUtil.getFrame(this);
      dDialog = new AlertDialog(dFrame, "This is a test.");
      dDialog.reshape(100, 100, 200, 100);
      dDialog.show();
   }
}


class AlertDialog extends Dialog {
   public AlertDialog(Frame parent, String message) {
      super(parent, "Alert!", true);
      add("Center", new Label(message));
      Panel thePanel = new Panel();
      thePanel.add(new Button("Ok"));
      add("South", thePanel);
   }


   public boolean action(Event evt, Object arg) {
      if ("Ok".equals(arg)) {
         dispose();
      }
      return true;
   }
}


class ComponentUtil {
   public static Frame getFrame(Component theComponent) {
      Component currParent = theComponent;
      Frame theFrame = null;
```

```
    while (currParent != null) {
       if (currParent instanceof Frame) {
          theFrame = (Frame)currParent;
          break;
       }
       currParent = currParent.getParent();
    }

    return theFrame;
    }
 }
```

Here's the .html file to use with it:

```
<!--DialogTest.html-->
<title>DialogTest</title>
<hr>

<applet code=DialogTest.class width=100 height=100>
</applet>

<hr>
<hr>
<a href="DialogTest.java">The source.</a>
```

This applet will display a modal dialog that contains a message string and an OK button which, when pressed, will dismiss the dialog. The exact representation of the dialog will be platform-dependent. Figure 15.26 shows what it looks like when run with Windows 95.

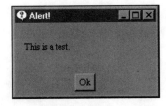

Figure 15.26

Displaying Frames

Creating Frames is done through the same process, except that the Frame constructor doesn't require a reference to an existing Frame. Let's take a look at the listing for a simple applet that puts up an external Frame:

```java
// FrameTest.java
import java.applet.*;
import java.awt.*;

public class FrameTest extends Applet {

    public void init() {
      add(new Button("New Window"));
    }

    public boolean action(Event evt, Object arg) {
      if ("New Window".equals(arg)) {
        TestWindow theWindow = new TestWindow();
      }
      return true;
    }

}

class TestWindow extends Frame {

   TestWindow() {
      super("Test Frame");
      setLayout(new FlowLayout(FlowLayout.CENTER));

      reshape(10, 10, 150, 50);

      add(new Button("Test"));
```

```
    add(new Button("Test"));
    add(new Button("Test"));


    show();
}


public boolean handleEvent(Event e) {
    switch (e.id) {
        case Event.WINDOW_DESTROY:
            dispose();
            return true;
        default:
            return super.handleEvent(e);
    }
}


}
```

Here's the .html file to use with it:

```
<!--FrameTest.html-->
<title>FrameTest</title>
<hr>


<applet code=FrameTest.class width=300 height=50>
</applet>


<hr>
<hr>
<a href="FrameTest.java">The source.</a>
```

When executed, this will present an applet that contains a single button titled "New Window". When clicked on, it will create and display an external window. The result will look something like Figure 15.27.

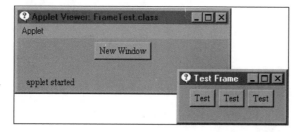

■■■■■■■ **Figure 15.27**

One important thing to notice is that we've overridden the handleEvent() method of our TestWindow Frame subclass, and we're testing for the WINDOW_DESTROY Event type. This event is generated by a user clicking on a window's close box (or closing the window using whatever the native UI conventions are for a particular OS). If we don't handle this message, the window won't go away, which is sure to frustrate the user. Even though in some cases, such as password validation, you might not want the user to be able to dismiss a window, usually you will want the window to behave correctly. As a consequence, if you subclass Frame, you should use a handleEvent() override similar to the one we've presented here.

Now that you've seen how to construct Frames, there's one last thing to show you. It's possible to turn an applet into a stand-alone application by adding a main() method to it if the main() method puts up a window in which the applet can reside. The following main() method would be added to our FrameTest applet class from the above example:

```
public static void main(String args[]) {
    Frame theAppWindow = new Frame("FrameTest");
    FrameTest theApplet = new FrameTest();
    theApplet.init();
    theApplet.start();

    theAppWindow.add("Center", theApplet);
    theAppWindow.resize(100, 100);
    theAppWindow.show();
}
```

When the FrameTest class is started as an applet, the main() method is ignored. When it's started as a stand-alone Java application, the main() method is called and it creates a Frame window for the applet to reside in, instantiates the applet, and calls its init() and start() methods. The applet is then added to the Frame, and the Frame is made visible. Before you knock yourself out converting all your applets to stand-alone applications, remember that your Java application will not have certain services available to it when run this way, such as the ability to show a Web document through showDocument(). If something doesn't work as a stand-alone app that does work as an applet in AppletViewer, it is very likely that your applet is making use of browser services that aren't available.

At this point, we'll wrap up the chapter. There are a lot more things you can do with the AWT and the component system, and we encourage you to experiment. Look through the API reference, and check out sample applets on the Web for more examples of the types of user interfaces that can be built with Java. In the next chapter, we'll take a closer look at methods for graphics and images.

GRAPHICS

In this chapter, we will look at how to perform drawing and graphics operations within Java programs and how to work with images. Our goal in this chapter is to help you understand the foundations of the Java graphics model. If you've worked with other graphics environments such as the Windows GDI or Macintosh QuickDraw, you shouldn't have any problems with the Java graphics model.

One thing that is fairly unique to Java is the way it deals with image data. Because applets need to work in low-memory situations, as well as the fact that images such as GIFs might still be loading from the net when you try to draw them, the AWT implements an image producer/consumer system that decouples the methods that display images from those that create or load them. You'll see what we mean when we get to that section of the chapter. First, though, we will cover the basics of how AWT handles drawing the component display area and then deal with how to use the methods of the Graphics class to perform most drawing operations.

Drawing in Components Revisited

While your applets or programs are running, a thread called the Screen Updater is running whose task is to call the update() method of each component that needs to be redrawn. This is important to know because it will affect the types of things you will want to do in your component's (or applet's) update() and paint() methods. There is only one Screen Updater thread, so if you do something in the paint() method that causes it to block (see Chapter 12), repainting of all components will be frozen. When running in a Java application such as AppletViewer, which uses the same Screen Updater thread as your applet for redrawing its components, the results aren't pretty.

We've started this section by talking about the Screen Updater for a reason. Many Java programs have no need to create their own threads, and as a consequence, new Java programmers will gloss over the topic. Unfortunately, threads are used in a number of places in the JDK, and understanding their usage is essential for dealing correctly with images, and, as we've just pointed out, ensuring that your paint() methods are properly behaved. If you skipped Chapter 12, on threads, now would be a good time to jump back to it. As this chapter progresses, we'll assume that you understand the basics of threads.

As we saw in previous chapters, a component indicates that it needs to be redrawn using the component repaint() method. This method does not actually repaint the component, but sets an instance variable in the component that indicates that the Screen Updater thread needs to redraw the component on its next pass. As a consequence, there is an indeterminate amount of time between when repaint() is called and when the component is redrawn.

When the Screen Updater gets around to drawing the component, it does this by calling the update() method of the component. The update() method is defined as follows:

- Component.update
  ```
  public void update(Graphics g)
  ```
  Called by the Screen Updater thread to update the component in response to a repaint request. The background at this point has not been cleared, so when double-buffering, override this method to draw an image buffer to the screen.

The default behavior for this method is very simple; in fact, it performs only four basic steps:

1. Set the current color to the component's background color:

```
g.setColor(getBackground());
```

2. Fill the component's display area with the current color:

```
g.fillRect(0, 0, width, height);
```

3. Set the current color to the component's foreground color:

```
g.setColor(getForeground());
```

4. Call the component's paint() method:

```
paint(g);
```

For most components, drawing will take place in the component's paint() method, which is defined as follows:

- Component.paint
  ```
  public void paint(Graphics g)
  ```
  Paints the component. Override to implement display code in your component (Canvas) subclasses.

We've just seen that by the time your paint() method has been called, the component display area has been cleared to the component background color. When the paint() method is called, it's passed a reference to a graphics object. Your component paints itself by using the methods provided by the Graphics class to draw to the screen. We'll take a look at the Graphics class in the next section.

If some cases, you'll want to override the update() method as well. Why? In cases where your paint() method paints over the display area itself, for example, when drawing an image that fills the component display area, you won't want the update() method to erase the display area before calling your paint() method. This causes unnecessary flicker when components redraw themselves. To avoid this, some components and applets override the update() method so that it calls the paint() method without first overriding the display area, like so:

```
public void update(Graphics g) {
    paint(g);
}
```

This causes the update() method to call the paint() method directly.

Using the Graphics Class

Whenever you draw anything to the screen, you do so by using a Graphics object. You do not instantiate the Graphics object; instead it is passed to you via the update() or paint() methods or obtained by a method call such as getGraphics() or create(). The object that you are returned is of a subclass of the Graphics class that is adapted to the local graphics system.

A Graphics object is used to manage a graphics context, which is essentially the same thing as what is referred to as a grafport on the Macintosh or a device context under Windows. Each Graphics object draws to a specific image surface, and it is possible for several Graphics objects to draw to the same image surface. This surface can be a screen display, off-screen bitmap, or a printer buffer. In many cases the surface for a given Graphics object will not be known to you, so you won't know whether you are drawing to the screen or preparing an image for printing, which is actually a plus because it allows you to use the same drawing code without concern for where the output is going. The most common exception to this is when drawing to off-screen Images, as we will see later in this chapter.

Most of the time, your drawing code is going to be inside a paint() method, but in fact, you can draw within other methods as well. To do this, call the getGraphics() method of the component your code is executing within. This method is defined as follows:

- Component.getGraphics

  ```
  public Graphics getGraphics()
  ```
  Returns a Graphics context for this component, or null if the component is not on-screen.

It is recommended that you make sparing use of the getGraphics() method and instead place your drawing code inside a paint() method, where you'll be passed a Graphics object. The drawing methods in the next section assume you have a valid Graphics object.

Colors

Whenever any drawing takes place, the current color of the Graphics object is used as the color for whatever is being drawn. To set the color, you use the setColor() method, which is defined as follows:

- Graphics.setColor

  ```
  public abstract void setColor(Color c)
  ```
  Sets the current color for subsequent operations.

To set the color, you need a color object. The Color class provides several static variables that contain the commonly used colors shown in Table 16.1.

▪▪▪▪ **Table 16.1** Commonly Used Colors in the Color Class

Variable	Value
Color.black	(R:0, G:0, B:0)
Color.blue	(R:0, G:0, B:255)
Color.cyan	(R:0, G:255, B:255)
Color.darkGray	(R:64, G:64, B:64)
Color.gray	(R:128, G:128, B:128)
Color.green	(R:0, G:255, B:0)
Color.lightGray	(R:192, G:192, B:192)
Color.magenta	(R:255, G:0, B:255)
Color.orange	(R:255, G:200, B:0)
Color.pink	(R:255, G:175, B:175)
Color.red	(R:255, G:0, B:0)
Color.white	(R:255, G:255, B:255)
Color.yellow	(R:255, G:255, B:0)

You can use these with setColor() or any other method that takes a Color object as a parameter like this:

```
setColor(Color.red);
```

If you want to create a Color object, you have several constructors available. The most commonly used are as follows:

- Color constructors

  ```
  public Color(int r,
               int g,
               int b)
  ```
  Constructs a 24-bit color with the specified red, green, and blue values. RGB values must be in the range (0 – 255).

```
public Color(int rgb)
```
Constructs a color from a 24-bit color value (0x00rrggbb).

The first constructor is used to build the Color object using the values passed for the red, green, and blue components. The second method constructs the color from a 24-bit pixel value. Once you have a color object, you can use a couple of useful methods in the Color class on it. For example, the brighter() and darker() methods take the color values in the Color object and use them to create lighter or darker representations. These methods are defined like this:

- Color.brighter/darker
  ```
  public Color brighter()
  ```
  Constructs and returns new Color object with a brighter version of this color.

  ```
  public Color darker()
  ```
  Constructs and returns a new Color object with a darker version of this color.

In addition to these methods, there are a number of other useful methods in the Color class which you might want to use. Make sure you refer to the API reference for more information.

Drawing Methods

The Graphics class provides methods for drawing lines, shapes, and fonts. Drawing takes place using the current color, origin, scale, clipping rectangle, and painting mode. This section will cover the basics of drawing to a graphics object.

Lines

In one of our earlier example applets, we used the drawLine() method to draw lines in the applet's display area. The drawLine() method is defined as follows:

- Graphics.drawLine
  ```
  public abstract void drawLine(int x1,
                                int y1,
                                int x2,
                                int y2)
  ```
  Draws a line from x1,y1 to x2,y2.

Here's a simple applet that shows how to use the drawLine() method by drawing a grid within its display area:

```java
// LineTest.java

import java.awt.*;
import java.applet.*;

public class LineTest extends Applet {

   public void paint(Graphics g) {
     Rectangle r = bounds();

     for (int x = 0; x < r.width; x = x + 10) {
       g.drawLine(x, 0, x, r.height);
     }
     for (int y = 0; y < r.height; y = y + 10) {
       g.drawLine(0, y, r.width, y);
     }


   }
}
```

The output in AppletViewer looks like Figure 16.1.

Shapes

The Graphics class provides an assortment of methods for drawing basic shapes such as arcs, rectangles, and circles. The following simple applet demonstrates the use of these methods:

```java
// GraphicsTest.java

import java.awt.*;
import java.applet.*;

public class GraphicsTest extends Applet {
```

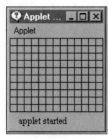

■■■■■ **Figure 16.1**

```
public void init() {
}

public void paint(Graphics g) {
    Rectangle r = bounds();

    g.setColor(Color.white);

    g.fillRect(r.x, r.y, r.width, r.height);

    g.setColor(Color.black);

    g.drawOval(10, 10, 50, 50);
    g.fillOval(70, 10, 50, 50);

    g.drawArc(130, 10, 50, 50, -90, 270);
    g.fillArc(190, 10, 50, 50, -90, 270);

    g.drawRect(10, 70, 50, 50);
    g.fillRect(70, 70, 50, 50);

    g.drawRoundRect(130, 70, 50, 50, 10, 10);
    g.fillRoundRect(190, 70, 50, 50, 10, 10);

    Polygon thePoly = new Polygon();
```

```
        thePoly.addPoint(10, 130);
        thePoly.addPoint(70, 150);
        thePoly.addPoint(120, 130);
        thePoly.addPoint(120, 180);
        thePoly.addPoint(70, 170);
        thePoly.addPoint(10, 180);
        thePoly.addPoint(10, 130);
        g.drawPolygon(thePoly);

        thePoly = new Polygon();
        thePoly.addPoint(130, 130);
        thePoly.addPoint(190, 150);
        thePoly.addPoint(240, 130);
        thePoly.addPoint(240, 180);
        thePoly.addPoint(190, 170);
        thePoly.addPoint(130, 180);
        thePoly.addPoint(130, 130);
        g.fillPolygon(thePoly);

        g.setColor(Color.gray);

        g.draw3DRect(10, 190, 50, 50, true);
        g.fill3DRect(70, 190, 50, 50, true);

        g.draw3DRect(130, 190, 50, 50, false);
        g.fill3DRect(190, 190, 50, 50, false);


    }
  }
```

Here's the .html file used to display it:

```
<!--GraphicsTest.html-->
<title>GraphicsTest</title>
<hr>
```

```
<applet code=GraphicsTest.class width=250 height=250>
</applet>


<hr>
<hr>
<a href="GraphicsTest.java">The source.</a>
```

The resulting applet will look something like Figure 16.2.

The following methods are available when using the Graphics class to draw shapes:

- Graphics shape methods

    ```
    draw3DRect(int x, int y, int width, int height, boolean raised)
    drawArc(int x, int y, int w, int h, int startangle, int arcangle)
    drawOval(int x, int y, int w, int h)
    drawPolygon(Polygon p)
    drawRect(int x, int y, int w, int h)
    drawRoundRect(int x, int y, int w, int h, int arcW, int arcH)


    fill3DRect(int x, int y, int width, int height, boolean raised)
    fillArc(int x, int y, int w, int h, int startangle, int arcangle)
    ```

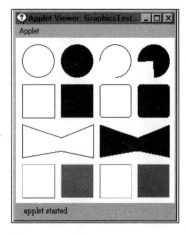

■■■■■■ **Figure 16.2**

```
fillOval(int x, int y, int w, int h)
fillPolygon(Polygon p)
fillRect(int x, int y, int w, int h)
fillRoundRect(int x, int y, int w, int h, int arcW, int arcH)
```

Fonts

Java provides you with a set of five universal fonts that all ports of the JDK will recognize. These fonts are:

- Dialog
- Helvetica
- TimesRoman
- Courier
- Symbol

Before you can use a font, you need to have a Font object. You can do this by creating a new Font object like this:

```
Font theFont = new Font("TimesRoman", Font.PLAIN, 24);
```

The above line creates a new Font object for the font TimesRoman with a style of plain and a point size of 24. The constructor for the Font class is defined as follows:

- Font constructor
  ```
  public Font(String name,
              int style,
              int size)
  ```
  Creates a new Font object using the specified name, style, and point size.

Once you have a Font object you can use it by calling the Graphics object's setFont() method:

```
setFont(theFont);
```

The setFont() method is defined like this:

- Graphics.setFont
  ```
  public void setFont(Font font)
  ```
  Sets the font for subsequent text operations.

Typically, you will draw text with the Graphic's objects drawString() method, which will draw the specified string using the current font. The drawSting() method is defined as follows:

- Graphics.drawString
  ```
  public abstract void drawString(String str,
                                      int x,
                                      int y)
  ```
  Draws the specified String starting at the baseline specified at the x and y coordinates.

When drawing text with the drawString() method, it's important to note that multi-line strings are not supported (i.e., strings with line breaks and carriage returns), and if you try to draw one of these strings, the characters will appear all on one line.

When drawing with a font, it is sometimes useful to be able to find out information about the metrics of the font (i.e., the height of the font, its spacing, etc.). To accomplish this, you need to use a FontMetrics object. You can obtain a FontMetrics object for the current font by using the getFontMetrics() method of the Graphics object. This method is defined as follows:

```
Font.FontMetrics

public FontMetrics getFontMetrics()

Returns current font metrics.
```

There is also a second version of getFontMetrics() that takes a Font object as a parameter and returns the FontMetrics for it. In the last chapter, we made use of FontMetrics information to draw centered text in a Canvas. This is the method we used:

```
public void paintUp(Graphics g) {

  g.setColor(Color.white);
  g.fillRect(0, 0, size().width-1, size().height-1);
  g.setColor(Color.black);
  g.drawRect(0, 0, size().width-1, size().height-1);
  int theWidth = g.getFontMetrics().stringWidth(label);
  int theHeight = g.getFontMetrics().getHeight();
  int theAscent = g.getFontMetrics().getAscent();
  int theLeading = g.getFontMetrics().getAscent();
  int hMargin = (size().width - theWidth) / 2;
```

```
int vMargin = (size().height - theHeight) / 2;
g.drawString(label,
             hMargin,
             vMargin + theAscent + theLeading);


}
```

To understand our example, we need to take a look at what the various types of information that can be obtained from a FontMetrics object mean. Figure 16.3 illustrates these values.

In the previous code example, we first used the FontMetrics stringWidth() method to determine the pixel width of the label string. We used that to determine the horizontal centering of the label by subtracting the width from the canvas width and dividing the result by 2. This gives us the pixel margin on either side of the string when centered on the Canvas, and we use this value as the left coordinate when drawing the string.

To calculate the vertical centering of the String, we have to be a little more clever. The vertical coordinate passed to drawString() refers to the baseline coordinate, which we can see in our illustration is at the bottom of the font line. To find out where the baseline should be positioned, we first get the height of the font and subtract it from the height of the Canvas and divide the result by 2. This gives us the number of pixels above and below the string when it is centered on the canvas. However, we can't use this value as the vertical parameter to drawString() because strings are drawn from the font baseline, not the font top. By adding the font ascent and leading to the font top, we end up with a good value to use for the baseline.

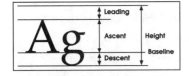

▬▬▬▬▬ **Figure 16.3**

Clipping

Clipping refers to setting a rectangular area that can be drawn within. Anything that is attempted to be drawn outside of this area is clipped to the boundaries of the clipping rectangle: You can set a clipping rectangle using the clipRect() method, which is defined as follows:

- Graphics.clipRect

```
public abstract void clipRect(int x,
                              int y,
                              int width,
                              int height)
```
  Sets the clipping area to the intersection of the current clipping area and the specified area.

All subsequent graphics operations will be clipped to the given coordinates. Once you define a clipping rectangle for a Graphics object, it can't be undone. This can present a problem when your goal is to clip a series of graphics operations and then restore the clipping rectangle to what it was before you called clipRect(). As a consequence, calls to the clipRect() method are usually preceded by a call to the create() method, which creates a duplicate of a given Graphics object. The following method shows how this is done:

```
public void paint(Graphics g) {
    Graphics clipped_g = g.create();
    clipped_g.clipRect(10, 10, 50, 50));
    clipped_g.drawLine(0, 0, 70, 70)
    clipped_g.dispose();

    g.drawLine(0, 50, 70, 50)
}
```

In this paint() method, we take the Graphics object that is passed to us and create a copy of it by calling its create() method. This returns a new Graphics object that draws to the same image surface as the original Graphics object. We can do anything we want with our copy, though, including setting its clipping rectangle, which is exactly what we do in the preceding example code. When we are done with this new Graphics object, we can dispose() of it and resume using the original Graphics object. The create() method is defined as follows:

- Graphics.create
  ```
  public abstract Graphics create()
  ```
  Creates and returns a copy of the current Graphics object. The new Graphics object will draw to the same surface (i.e., screen, pixmap, printer buffer) as the original Graphics object.

The Graphics class also has an all-in-one version of the create() method that creates a copy of the Graphics object and sets its clipping rectangle to the specified coordinates, as well as translating the origin (which we'll talk about next). The version is defined as follows:

- Graphics.create
  ```
  public Graphics create(int x,
                         int y,
                         int width,
                         int height)
  ```
  Creates and returns a copy of the current Graphics object. The new Graphics object will draw to the same surface (i.e., screen, pixmap, printer buffer) as the original Graphics object. The x,y coordinate is translated to the origin (0,0) of the new Graphics object, and the clipping area of the new Graphics object is set to (0, 0, width, height).

Moving the Origin Point

Normally, the coordinates of the origin (0,0) of a Graphics object correspond to the top-left corner of the component or image bitmap. It is often useful to move the origin point so that 0,0 will refer to a different point on the image surface. This is done through the use of the translate() method, which will move the origin point by the specified horizontal and vertical pixels. The translate() method is defined as follows:

- Graphics.translate
  ```
  public abstract void translate(int x,
                                 int y)
  ```
  Sets the new origin of the graphics context to the specified coordinates.

One of the uses for the translate() method occurs when scrolling a display area. The following example takes our GraphicsTest.java example from earlier in the chapter and updates it to use scrollbars to allow the user to scroll the image. Here's the listing of the revised GraphicsTest.java source file:

```java
// GraphicsTest.java
import java.awt.*;
import java.applet.*;

public class GraphicsTest extends Applet {

    GraphicsCanvas theCanvas;
    Scrollbar hscroll;
    Scrollbar vscroll;

    public void init() {
        setLayout(new BorderLayout());
        hscroll = new Scrollbar(Scrollbar.HORIZONTAL, 0, 0, 0, 100);
        vscroll = new Scrollbar(Scrollbar.VERTICAL, 0, 0, 0, 100);
        add("South", hscroll);
        add("East", vscroll);

        theCanvas = new GraphicsCanvas();
        add("Center", theCanvas);
    }

    public boolean handleEvent(Event evt) {
        if (evt.target == hscroll) {
            theCanvas.offset_x = ((Integer)evt.arg).intValue();
            theCanvas.repaint();
            return true;
        }
        if (evt.target == vscroll) {
            theCanvas.offset_y = ((Integer)evt.arg).intValue();
            theCanvas.repaint();
```

```
            return true;
        }
        return super.handleEvent(evt);
    }
}

class GraphicsCanvas extends Canvas {

    int offset_x = 0;
    int offset_y = 0;

    public void paint(Graphics g) {
        Rectangle r = bounds();

        Graphics new_g = g.create();
        new_g.translate(-offset_x, -offset_y);

        new_g.setColor(Color.white);

        new_g.fillRect(r.x, r.y, r.width, r.height);

        new_g.setColor(Color.black);

        new_g.drawOval(10, 10, 50, 50);
        new_g.fillOval(70, 10, 50, 50);

        new_g.drawArc(130, 10, 50, 50, -90, 270);
        new_g.fillArc(190, 10, 50, 50, -90, 270);

        new_g.drawRect(10, 70, 50, 50);
        new_g.fillRect(70, 70, 50, 50);

        new_g.drawRoundRect(130, 70, 50, 50, 10, 10);
        new_g.fillRoundRect(190, 70, 50, 50, 10, 10);
```

```
        Polygon thePoly = new Polygon();
        thePoly.addPoint(10, 130);
        thePoly.addPoint(70, 150);
        thePoly.addPoint(120, 130);
        thePoly.addPoint(120, 180);
        thePoly.addPoint(70, 170);
        thePoly.addPoint(10, 180);
        thePoly.addPoint(10, 130);
        new_g.drawPolygon(thePoly);

        thePoly = new Polygon();
        thePoly.addPoint(130, 130);
        thePoly.addPoint(190, 150);
        thePoly.addPoint(240, 130);
        thePoly.addPoint(240, 180);
        thePoly.addPoint(190, 170);
        thePoly.addPoint(130, 180);
        thePoly.addPoint(130, 130);
        new_g.fillPolygon(thePoly);

        new_g.setColor(Color.gray);

        new_g.draw3DRect(10, 190, 50, 50, true);
        new_g.fill3DRect(70, 190, 50, 50, true);

        new_g.draw3DRect(130, 190, 50, 50, false);
        new_g.fill3DRect(190, 190, 50, 50, false);

        new_g.dispose();
    }
}
```

Looking at the code, you can see that we make use of the technique we introduced when we showed how to set clipping rectangles of creating a copy of the current Graphics object and applying our new clip rectangle to the copy instead of the original. In this example, we do the same thing, but with the translate() method. All the graphics methods are now used with the copy of the Graphics object instead of the original; since the copy has had its origin point moved, all of the drawing will appear at a different position in the component's display area, effectively scrolling the drawing. Figure 16.4 shows what the applet looks like when run.

Setting the Scale

One last thing that's worth looking at is how to set the scale. The scale() method lets you set a scale factor for the horizontal and vertical directions that will affect all subsequent drawing operations. This scale factor applies only to the coordinate space; it will not affect the graphics pen size. The scale() method is defined as follows:

- Graphics.scale

```
public abstract void scale(float sx,
                                    float sy)
```
Sets horizontal and vertical scale factors for subsequent operations. Note that this does not affect the pen size, just the distance between points.

If you were to take our last example and add the following line after the line containing the translate() method:

```
new_g.scale((float)0.5, float)0.5);
```

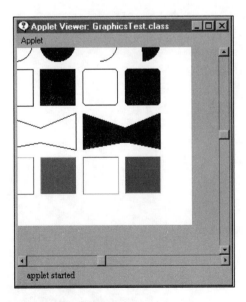

████████ **Figure 16.4**

the subsequent drawing operations would be scaled accordingly, and the output would look something like Figure 16.5.

Working with Images

The AWT allows you to draw images to a Graphics object as well as use images for off-screen drawing. Although the basics of using images in Java are similar to those for other systems, because the AWT is designed to work in network and low-memory situations, even experienced graphics programmers will have to deal with a number of unfamiliar issues. We'll try to separate the basics of image usage from the advanced topics, but even when performing simple image operations, you need to understand what the AWT is doing "under the hood" when it loads and draws images to get the results you expect.

An Image's data (i.e., its pixels) is obtained from one of several sources, such as from image data retrieved over the net, as in the case of GIF images, or from an array of pixel bytes created by a program. The AWT uses a system for managing images that is designed around the idea that image data is produced synchronously,

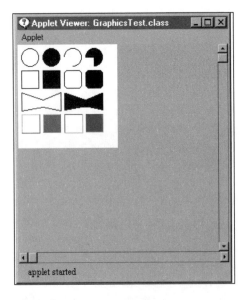

■■■■■■ **Figure 16.5**

meaning that at any given point in time, some or all of the pixels for an image may not yet be ready for drawing. This is essential in the case of image data that is loaded from the Web because it can take a while for the image data to be loaded over the network. What the AWT does to accommodate this fact is decouple the Image objects that you work with (i.e., pass to methods and send messages to) from the underlying pixel data. Because an image's pixel data is often being loaded asynchronously, you may have an Image object available for use with image drawing routines and the like, without having all the pixel data loaded. Image objects in the AWT are not containers for the pixel data, but conduits for requesting pixel data from an image source such as the net, and delivering it to an image consumer, such as a method that draws images on the screen.

There are four types of objects that you will need to deal with or at least understand when dealing with Images. These are *images* (java.awt.Image class), *image observers* (java.awt.image.ImageObserver interface), *image producers* (java.awt.image.ImageProducer interface), and *image consumers* (java.awt.image.ImageConsumer interface and java.awt.image.ImageFilter class). You will usually need to deal only with the first two of these, images and image observers; we'll spend the majority of our discussion of images looking at how to use these two.

The basic class for dealing with images is the Image class. You will obtain instances of this class from one of several sources. The most common way to do this is through the use of the getImage() method of the java.applet.Applet class, which allows you to create an Image object that obtains its pixel data from a specific URL. There are two forms of this method:

- Applet.getImage
  ```
  public Image getImage(URL url)
  ```
  Returns an Image object given a URL.

  ```
  public Image getImage(URL url,
                          String name)
  ```
  Returns an Image object given a base URL and file name.

For example, the following init() method will get an image named title.gif from the same directory from which the HTML file that loaded the applet was retrieved:

```
public void init() {
    Image theImage = getImage(getDocumentBase(), "title.gif");
}
```

The important thing to realize is that the getImage() method is going to return immediately when it is called. The Image object that is returned will refer to pixel data that is still being loaded. One way to think about this is that an Image object does not contain pixel data, but instead contains the instructions for retrieving pixel data. When a method goes to draw an Image object, it requests that the Image object retrieve the pixel data and return it to the caller. In some cases, the pixel data that an Image retrieves is already in memory; in other cases, the pixel data needs to be either loaded from the net or produced by a routine that generates the pixel data algorithmically. In the latter cases, the Image object may not be able to deliver the pixel data immediately. This is where the ImageObserver interface comes in.

A typical routine for drawing images is the Graphics class drawImage() method, which is defined as follows:

- Component.drawImage

```
public abstract boolean drawImage(Image img,
                                  int x,
                                  int y,
                                  ImageObserver observer)
```
Draws the specified image object at the specified x, y coordinate. Returns true if image was ready to be drawn. Because images may be loaded asynchronously over the net, the image data might not be available at the time drawImage() is called. By providing a reference to an instance of a class that implements the ImageObserver interface, you can have the imageUpdate() method of the object passed as observer called when the image is loaded and ready to be drawn. The Component class implements ImageObserver, so in most cases, when calling this method from within any class that is a subclass of component, you can simply pass the variable this as the observer.

As we can see from the method definition, the drawImage() method takes both an Image object and an ImageObserver object. In the case of the ImageObserver object, because ImageObserver is an interface, you need to pass a reference to an instance of a class that implements the ImageObserver interface. Classes that implement the ImageObserver interface are required to have an imageUpdate() method, which is called when the pixel data referred to by the Image object becomes available. So a typical scenario is that you call drawImage() without all the pixel data being available. At some point, the imageUpdate() method of the object passed as the observer will be called. This method is defined as follows:

- ImageObserver.imageUpdate

```
public abstract boolean imageUpdate(Image img,
                                    int infoflags,
                                    int x,
                                    int y,
                                    int width,
                                    int height)
```

Called by the AWT to notify the observer that additional information about an image has become available. The method is called with a reference to the image that the supplied information pertains to, and an information flags value constructed by combining flags with the | (or) operator such as WIDTH | HEIGHT. Depending on the specified flags, the value passed in the position and dimension parameters can be used to obtain specific information about an image or to draw a partial representation of the image. If no more information is required about the image, this method should return false; otherwise, it will continue to be called until no more information about the image is available (i.e., all the bits of the image have been delivered or an error occurs).

Before you get nervous about the prospect of writing your own imageUpdate() method, remember that several shortcuts are built into the AWT to simplify the usage of images. Some of these shortcuts were added to the AWT in the final beta of the JDK, so if you are looking at older sample code, how images are managed might be unnecessarily complex.

It is important to know that the Component class implements the ImageObserver interface. This means that every component has an imageUpdate() method. This imageUpdate() method simply requests that the component be redrawn by calling the repaint() method. The importance of the Component class providing an imageUpdate() method is that when calling methods like drawImage() from within a component, you can pass the special variable this as the image observer, and the default imageUpdate() method of the component will be called as needed. Let's take a look at a very simple applet that loads and draws an image:

```
// ImageApplet.java
import java.awt.*;
import java.applet.*;

public class ImageApplet extends Applet {

    Image theImage = null;

    public void init() {
        theImage = getImage(getDocumentBase(), "title.gif");
    }

    public void paint(Graphics g) {
        g.drawImage(theImage, 0, 0, this);
    }
}
```

Let's take a look at what happens when this applet is run. First, in the init() method, a new Image object is stored in the instance variable theImage. This image refers to the pixel data retrieved from the specified URL and file name. When the paint() method is called, the image is attempted to be drawn. The first time drawImage() is called, the Image object checks to see if it has the pixel data it needs; if not, a new thread is created that starts to load the pixel data from the URL.

When drawImage() is called, it attempts to draw however many pixels of the image have been retrieved and are ready to be drawn. In this case, it might be just the first few lines of the image; drawImage() draws those and returns immediately. However, when more image data becomes available, the imageUpdate() method of the image observer is called.

In this example, we pass this as our image observer, which means that the default imageUpdate() method provided by the component class is called when more information about the Image becomes available. As we have covered, this imageUpdate() method will call repaint(), which will cause the paint() method to eventually be called again. The drawImage() method is again called, and it again draws all the pixel data it has loaded so far, which at this point should be more than had been loaded the last time drawImage() was called.

The partial image is again drawn, and this time, because more pixel data has been loaded, more of the image is drawn and appears on the screen. The applet component is again registered as an observer by passing this to drawImage. When more pixel data is loaded, imageUpdate() is again called, and the cycle repeats itself, until all the pixel data has been loaded and the complete image has been drawn.

What users see when they try this applet is the image slowly (or quickly, depending on the size of the image and the speed of the net connection) get drawn from top to bottom as the image loads from the net. While this appears to be a slowly executing single image draw operation, it is accomplished by the paint() method being repeatedly called to redraw the image; because each time it is called, a little more pixel data has been loaded, more of the image can be drawn.

In many cases, if your applet is producing a simple display or using relatively static images, this is the desired effect. You can use variations of our previous code example for most image drawing.

Using the MediaTracker

As you've surfed to different Java-enhanced Web sites, you've undoubtedly seen some more impressive uses of images than what we showed you in the previous section. At this point, you may be wondering how you can produce interesting image effects such as animation when you never know if an image's pixel data is in memory or en route from a Web server somewhere across the world. If you've guessed that the answer has something to do with the ImageObserver interface and imageUpdate() method that we glossed over in the last section, you'd be partially correct. In previous versions of the JDK, applets that made use of asynchronously loaded images (i.e., anything pulled from a URL) had to make use of the imageUpdate() method and some cumbersome image management code to know when an image was completely loaded so that rapid-fire image drawing would not be hampered because pixel data was not ready.

In the final beta version of the JDK, a new class was introduced in the java.awt package called the MediaTracker, which is designed to provide an easy interface for determining whether an image has loaded as well as getting information about loading images. We'll take a look at this class in this chapter.

As you attempt to learn more about Java programming techniques by studying sample code you find on the Web, or even included with the JDK release, you will most likely come across applets that do animation or other image operations and use custom imageUpdate() methods rather than the MediaTracker. In a few cases, this will occur because the programmer determined that he or she could get more performance or implement some functionality that the MediaTracker would give, but more often than not, the code you are looking at was written before the MediaTracker class was made available. There are really very few reasons to implement your own imageUpdate() method for dealing with asynchronous images, so when you see examples of this being done, investigate why the programmer chose to do this. Did he or she write the code before the MediaTracker became available?

Let's look at the previous image example and see how we might use the MediaTracker class to ensure that an image had been fully loaded before we used it:

```
// ImageApplet.java
import java.awt.*;
import java.applet.*;

public class ImageApplet extends Applet {

   Image theImage = null;
   MediaTracker theTracker = null;

   public void init() {
      theTracker = new MediaTracker(this);
      theImage = getImage(getDocumentBase(), "title.gif");
      theTracker.addImage(theImage, 0);
   }

   public void paint(Graphics g) {
      if (theTracker.isErrorAny()) {
         g.setColor(Color.red);
```

```
        g.drawString("Image error!", 10, 10);
        return;
    }


    if (theTracker.checkAll(true)) {
        g.drawImage(theImage, 0, 0, this);
    }
    else {
        g.setColor(Color.green);
        g.drawString("Image loading...", 10, 10);
        repaint(100);
    }
  }
}
```

We'll take a closer look at the MediaTracker class in a moment; right now, let's go through the listing step by step. First, in our init() method, we create a MediaTracker object for this component. We then call getImage() to create a new Image object for the GIF image at the given URL. Next, we add the image object to the MediaTracker and assign it an ID code of 0. Because we're working with only one image in this example, we don't need to be too concerned with the code we use. The addImage() method is defined as follows:

- MediaTracker.addImage

```
  public void addImage(Image image,
                            int id)
```
  Adds the specified image to the image group indicated by the specified ID. The ID code indicates the order in which images will be loaded; lower IDs are loaded before higher ones. You can assign the same ID to several images, in which case they will all need to be loaded for the image group to be considered fully loaded.

When we get to the paint() method, we first call the isErrorAny() method of the MediaTracker object to see if any errors occurred while loading images. If there was an error, we draw an error string in red and return from the paint() method. If there are no errors reported by isErrorAny(), we proceed and check to see if the image has finished loading by calling the MediaTracker object's checkAll() method, which will return true if the image has finished loading. If so, then we draw it, confident that it's going to be blasted to the screen from memory.

If the checkAll() method returns false, we draw a green message string that informs the user the image is still loading, and we call repaint() with a parameter of 100, which indicates that an update should be scheduled to occur in 100 milliseconds. When we called checkAll() we passed it a parameter of true, which indicates that image loading should be initiated if not done already. It is essential that image loading be initiated by a MediaTracker method; otherwise, the MediaTracker will not correctly report on the status of images via methods like checkAll(). We bring this up because sometimes image loading will be initiated by other means, such as calling the getWidth method() of an Image object; even though the image may be loaded in this way, if none of the MediaTracker methods has been asked to load the image, the MediaTracker will not be notified of the completion of image loading. Typically, you either will request that image loading be initiated via checkAll() or checkID() or will wait until image loading is complete using waitForAll() or waitForID(). These methods are defined as follows:

- MediaTracker.checkAll

  ```
  public boolean checkAll()
  ```
  Checks to see if all images that have been added to the MediaTracker either have been loaded or have encountered errors that halted the image-loading process. This method does not initiate any image loading that is not already in progress.

  ```
  public synchronized boolean checkAll(boolean load)
  ```
  The same as the previous method, but allows you to pass a Boolean value that, if true, initiates image loading if necessary. This method will not wait for images to complete loading before returning.

- MediaTracker.checkID

  ```
  public boolean checkID(int id)
  ```
  Checks to see if images that have been added to the MediaTracker with the specified ID code either have been loaded or have encountered errors that halted the image-loading process. This method does not initiate any image loading that is not already in progress.

  ```
  public synchronized boolean checkID(int id,

                                      boolean load)
  ```

The same as the previous method, but allows you also to pass a Boolean value that, if true, initiates asynchronous image loading if necessary. This method will not wait for images to complete loading before returning.

- MediaTracker.waitForAll

  `public synchronized void waitForAll() throws InterruptedException`
  Blocks the currently executing thread until all images that have been added to the MediaTracker either have been loaded or have encountered errors that halted the image-loading process. Do not call this method from a paint() method or other system-called method, or you risk blocking a system thread such as the Screen Updater.

- MediaTracker.waitForID

  `public synchronized void waitForID(int id) throws InterruptedException`
  Blocks the currently executing thread until all images that have been added to the MediaTracker with the specified ID code either have been loaded or have encountered errors that halted the image-loading process. Do not call this method from a paint() method or other system-called method, or you risk blocking a system thread such as the Screen Updater.

The second ImageApplet example was an improvement over the previous one in that it gave us a lot more information about the state of the image with only a very slight increase in program complexity. However, a couple of things about the example could still use some improvement. The most prominent is the fact that the applet is constantly repainted until the image is loaded. This happens because we call repaint() in our paint() method if the image is not ready (as indicated by a return value of false from the checkAll() method). When using the MediaTracker, you will typically do things a little differently than we did in this example. Let's take a look at the "recommended" way of using the MediaTracker:

```
// ImageApplet.java
import java.awt.*;
import java.applet.*;

public class ImageApplet extends Applet implements Runnable {

    Image theImage = null;
    MediaTracker theTracker = null;
    Thread init_thread = null;
```

```java
public void init() {
    theTracker = new MediaTracker(this);
    theImage = getImage(getDocumentBase(), "title.gif");
    theTracker.addImage(theImage, 0);
    init_thread = new Thread(this);
    init_thread.start();
}

public void run() {
    try {
        theTracker.waitForID(0);
    } catch (InterruptedException e) {
        return;
    }
    repaint();
}

public void paint(Graphics g) {
    if (theTracker.isErrorAny()) {
        g.setColor(Color.red);
        g.drawString("Image error!", 10, 10);
        return;
    }

    if (theTracker.checkID(0)) {
        g.drawImage(theImage, 0, 0, this);
    }
    else {
        g.setColor(Color.green);
        g.drawString("Image loading...", 10, 10);
    }
}
```

This applet does virtually the same thing as our previous example, with slightly more complexity. You can see why we chose the simplified version before. This example requires a little more typing and asks you to refresh your memory about the use of threads. In the previous example, we asked that the MediaTracker checkAll() method initiate loading the image, and we then essentially polled the MediaTracker every 100 milliseconds to see if image loading was complete by having repaint() cause the paint() method to be called again. Remember the rule of thumb: If you are doing this type of polling, you may want to reexamine your thread usage, or in this case, our lack thereof.

We have spawned a new thread that uses our applet as its target. This means that it uses the run() method from the applet as the code to execute within the thread. In this case, the run() method contains the request to the MediaTracker to load the images. We've also changed this request from being a request to initiate image loading via checkAll(true) from the previous example, to a request to block the current thread until image loading is complete by using the waitForID() method. This method blocks the current thread until the image is ready to be drawn. Why didn't we use waitForID() in our paint() method? The answer is that the paint() method is called by the Screen Updater thread, which we talked about earlier in this chapter. This thread should never be blocked by any of your code, and for that matter, it should not be held up in any of your paint() methods through the use of any computation-intensive activities such as long executing loops. These types of things should be moved into their own threads, which is exactly what we do here.

The run() method waits at the call to waitForID() until the image has finished loading, an error occurs, or an exception is thrown for any reason. If the waitForID() method throws an exception, the thread concludes by the run() method returning. If not, then the method continues to the next step, which is to call repaint(). This will cause the paint() method to eventually be called by the Screen Updater. This time, when the paint() method is called, the image will be ready to be drawn (or an error will have occurred, which is flagged by the call to isErrorAny()). When we call checkForID(0), it will return true because the image is ready, and drawImage() will display the image. The number of times the paint() method is called in this applet() is potentially as few as two times (once when it is first displayed, and once in response to the repaint() call in our run() method), compared to the hundred or more times that you could see when loading the image over a slow connection.

In Chapter 17, we will look at how you can combine the image-loading capabilities provided by using the MediaTracker with off-screen drawing, which we talk about in the next section, to accomplish animation in your applets.

Creating Offscreen Image Surfaces

When we looked at Graphics objects earlier in the chapter, we discussed how a given Graphics object will draw to an image surface, and that in most cases, this image surface was the screen display. In this section, we'll look at how we can create an Image object that can be used as the image surface of a Graphics object. You would want to do this to perform a number of drawing operations with this Graphics object and then transfer the results to the screen in one operation using the drawImage() method. This technique is often used to eliminate flicker when animating images or to perform complex and time-consuming drawing in a separately running thread and then transfer the results when the final picture is done.

To create an image, you call the component class's createImage() method, which is defined as follows:

- Component.createImage

```
public Image createImage(int width,

                          int height)
```
Creates an off-screen drawable Image. Usually used for double-buffering by drawing into the image and then drawing the image to the screen in the component's paint() method.

This method returns a new Image object that is different from the types of Image objects that you get returned to you by getImage() in that the createImage() also allocates the pixel data for the Image object in memory—there is no question that this Image will be ready to draw when you need it. You could create this image in an applet's init() method with something like this:

```
Image appletImg;


public void init() {
   appletImg = createImage(size().width, size().height);
}
```

Once you have created the Image object, you need a Graphics object to draw to it. This is accomplished by calling the Image's getGraphics() method, which will return a Graphics object that you can use to draw to the Image. The getGraphics() method is defined as follows:

- Image.getGraphics

  ```
  public abstract Graphics getGraphics()
  ```
  When used with off-screen images, this will return a Graphics object that can be used to draw onto the Image. Will throw a ClassCastException if used with an Image object that was not created with createImage().

Here's a revised version of our init() method that uses this to get a Graphics object:

```
Image appletImg;
Graphics appletG;

public void init() {
    appletImg = createImage(size().width, size().height);
    appletG = appletImg.getGraphics();
}
```

This time around, we allocate the image and get the Graphics object for it using getGraphics().

Now, we need set up our paint() and update() method:

```
public void paint(Graphics g) {
    appletG.setColor(getBackground());
    appletG.fillRect(0, 0, size().width, size().height);
    appletG.setColor(getForeground());

    appletG.fillOval(10, 10, 50, 50);
    appletG.fillArc(70, 10, 50, 50, -90, 270);
    appletG.fillRect(130, 70, 50, 50);

    g.drawImage(appletImg, 0, 0, this);
}

public void update(Graphics g) {
    paint(g);
}
```

The paint() method first clears the off-screen image to the background color. Newly created images are cleared to white, but in most cases, the applet's background color is set to gray. By painting the bitmap with the background color, we make sure that the image will blend in. We then perform our drawing operations, in this case an oval, arc, and circle. In your applets, you would substitute your drawing code here.

Also, notice that we overrode the update() method so that it calls the paint() method directly. Since the off-screen image is the same size as the applet's display area, the image will draw over anything already on-screen when it gets painted to the screen. If we had used the default update() method, it would have cleared the display area before calling the paint() method; this would have resulted in unnecessary flicker.

Here's an example where we use an off-screen image in the preparation of a more complex image:

```java
// CircleImageApplet.java
import java.awt.*;
import java.applet.*;
import java.lang.*;


public class CircleImageApplet extends Applet implements Runnable{

    Thread draw_thread = null;
    int numsides = 300;
    double radius = 50;
    Image appletImg;
    Graphics appletG;
    boolean circle_done = false;

    public void init() {
        appletImg = createImage(size().width, size().height);
        appletG = appletImg.getGraphics();
        draw_thread = new Thread(this);
        draw_thread.start();
    }
```

```
public void run() {
    appletG.setColor(getBackground());
    appletG.fillRect(0, 0, size().width, size().height);
    appletG.setColor(getForeground());

    double incAngle = (2 * Math.PI) / numsides;
    double last_dx = 0;
    double last_dy = 0;
    for(int side = 0; side <= numsides; side++) {
        // Point on circle
        double dx = radius * Math.cos(side * incAngle);
        double dy = radius * Math.sin(side * incAngle);

        // draw it
        if (side > 0) {
            int x1 = (int)(100 + last_dx);
            int y1 = (int)(100 + last_dy);
            int x2 = (int)(100 + dx);
            int y2 = (int)(100 + dy);
            appletG.drawLine(x1, y1, x2, y2);
        }

        last_dx = dx;
        last_dy = dy;

        Thread.yield();
    }

    circle_done = true;
    repaint();
}

public void paint(Graphics g) {
    if (circle_done) {
```

```
            g.drawImage(appletImg, 0, 0, this);
        }
        else {
            g.setColor(getBackground());
            g.fillRect(0, 0, size().width, size().height);
            g.setColor(getForeground());
            g.setColor(Color.green);
            g.drawString("Calculating...", 10, 10);
        }
    }


    public void update(Graphics g) {
        paint(g);
    }
}
```

In this example, the applet creates an off-screen image and then starts a thread that draws a circle onto the image. For this example, instead of simply calling drawOval() we do it the hard way, calculating points along the circumference of the circle and using those to draw the circle into the image. When the circle is completely drawn, the run() method sets the circle_done flag to true and calls repaint(). When the paint() method is invoked by the Screen Updater, it sees that the flag has been set and draws the image to the screen. The user sees the completed image draw to the screen in one pass, instead of seeing each point on the circle being drawn. In applets where you need to perform computation-intensive graphics, you can use this example as a starting point and replace the circle drawing code with code for whatever you need to draw.

Later, we will show you how to combine this example and our previous one that used the MediaTracker so that you can load GIF images from a URL and use those images as sprites, which are rendered into an off-screen image and, in turn, drawn to the screen. We'll take a look at this and other multimedia techniques in Chapter 17.

Advanced Image Concepts

In the preceding sections we covered the major aspects of using images in your applets; how to deal with asynchronously loading image and how to use images for off-screen drawing. In this section, we'll take a closer look at what image producers and consumers do and how pixel data is passed between them.

Every Image object has an image producer associated with it. This image producer delivers the image's pixel data so that it can be drawn or used in some other way. An image producer is an object that implements the java.awt.image.ImageProducer interface, which means that it implements a set of methods that are used to request that the image producer deliver the pixel data.

In order for an object to be able to receive pixel data from an image producer, it must be an image consumer. In other words, it must implement the java.awt.image.ImageConsumer interface, which means that it implements the methods that the image producer will call to deliver pixel data to the image consumer. An image consumer is attached to an image producer, and when the image consumer requests that the image producer start production of the image, the image producer responds by calling the image consumer's setPixels() method to deliver pixels to the consumer.

An image producer is sometimes called an image source because it delivers pixel data from a specific source such as the net or from an array of pixels in memory. When an Image object is passed to a method such as drawImage so that it can be drawn, the AWT sets itself up as an image consumer for the Image object's image producer. In the case of an image that is being loaded from a URL, the image's image producer is an instance of a special AWT class called URLImageSource. This image producer is designed to deliver pixels, as they become available, from image data that is being loaded over the net. Inside the drawImage() method, the AWT sets itself up as a consumer for the image's producer and uses the delivered pixels to draw the image onto the screen.

For most uses of images, the system-supplied producers and consumers do their work behind the scenes whenever you draw an image to the screen, or they make use of an image for off-screen drawing. However, in some cases, you may want to use your own image producer or consumer objects to implement some specific image-processing routines, such as those used to manipulate alpha channels, for example. It's beyond the scope of this book to go too deeply into the implementation of image consumer and producers, although we'll cover a few useful aspects of these in the remainder of the chapter.

Using the FilteredImageSource

One type of image producer that is worth looking into is the FilteredImageSource. The FilteredImageSource takes the pixels of an existing image producer and uses a special type of image consumer called an ImageFilter to process these pixels. You can create a new image object that uses the FilteredImageSource producer to filter an existing image object, and this new filtered image can be drawn to a Graphics object.

To make use of the FilteredImageSource, you need to have an ImageFilter to use with it. There are two ImageFilter classes supplied with the JDK: CropImageFilter and RGBImageFilter. The CropImageFilter is used to create a cropped version of an image and can be used by simply instantiating the CropImageFilter class and using it with a FilteredImageSource. Let's take a look at another variation of our original ImageApplet.java listing:

```
// ImageApplet.java
import java.awt.*;
import java.awt.image.*;
import java.applet.*;


public class ImageApplet extends Applet {

    Image newImage;

    public void init() {
        Image theImage = getImage(getDocumentBase(), "title.gif");
        ImageProducer theSource = theImage.getSource();


        CropImageFilter cropFilter = new CropImageFilter(10, 10, 40, 40);
```

```
        newImage = createImage(new FilteredImageSource(theSource, cropFilter));
    }


    public void paint(Graphics g) {
        g.drawImage(newImage, 0, 0, this);
    }

}
```

The preceding example draws a rectangular subsection of the original image. You might wonder why you would go to the trouble of using an image filter to accomplish the same thing that could be done by setting a clipping rectangle. When you use the CropImageFilter, only the image data necessary for drawing the cropped version is loaded into memory, which makes it useful for dealing with subsections of very large images.

In the preceding example, we used the following methods:

- Image.getSource
  ```
  public abstract ImageProducer getSource()
  ```
  Returns the ImageProducer source object.
- FilteredImageSource constructor
  ```
  public FilteredImageSource(ImageProducer orig,
                                  ImageFilter imgf)
  ```
  Filters the specified ImageProducer image source with the given ImageFilter.
- CropImageFilter constructor
  ```
  public CropImageFilter(int x,
                              int y,
                              int w,
                              int h)
  ```
  Uses the specified rectangle to construct an image source (ImageProducer) from an existing image.
- Component.createImage
  ```
  public Image createImage(ImageProducer producer)
  ```
  Creates an image using the specified image producer.

To use the RGBImageFilter, you need to create a subclass of it and override its filterRGB() method. Let's take another look at our image applet, this time modified to use the RGBImageFilter. Our goal in this example is to filter the pixel data so that it is partially transparent:

```java
// ImageApplet.java
import java.awt.*;
import java.awt.image.*;
import java.applet.*;

public class ImageApplet extends Applet {

    Image newImage;

    public void init() {
        Image theImage = getImage(getDocumentBase(), "title.gif");
        ImageProducer theSource = theImage.getSource();

        TransparencyFilter transFilter = new TransparencyFilter();

        newImage = createImage(new FilteredImageSource(theSource, transFilter));
    }

    public void paint(Graphics g) {
        g.drawImage(newImage, 0, 0, this);
    }
}

class TransparencyFilter extends RGBImageFilter {

    int opacity = 128;

    public TransparencyFilter() {
        canFilterIndexColorModel = true;
    }
```

```
public int filterRGB(int x, int y, int rgb) {
    int alpha_channel = (rgb >> 24) & 0xFF;
    alpha_channel = alpha_channel * opacity / 255;
    return ((rgb & 0x00FFFFFF) | (alpha_channel << 24));
}
}
```

If you compare this example with the previous one, you'll see that the main difference is that we use a subclass of RGBImageFilter instead of CropImageFilter. Our TransparencyFilter is subclassed from RGBImageFilter and overrides the filterRGB method so that it modifies the alpha channel of the pixels to make them transparent.

Looking at the filterRGB() method, we can see that it takes three steps. First, the alpha channel value of the RGB pixel is obtained by shifting the pixel right by 24 bits. The leftover 8 bits are the alpha channel value, and, since the int type can hold more than 32 bits, we use the and (&) operator to strip out all but the lowest 8 bits. This makes sure that the value we have for the alpha channel is an 8-bit value between 0 and 255. We take this value and multiply it by the opacity value and divide the product by 255. This has the result of scaling the alpha channel value by the opacity value. The new alpha channel is then combined with the original pixel values for the red, green, and blue channels and returned to the caller.

When the image is drawn, all the original image pixels will be filtered using the filterRGB() method, which will modify their alpha channel values so that the final image will be drawn at about 50% opacity. If you've followed the calculations in the filterRGB() method, you've probably realized that the level of opacity is controlled by the instance variable of the same name. A value of 0 means the pixel is completely transparent, and a value of 255 means that the pixel is completely opaque. You might think that it would have been more intuitive to use a floating point number as the opacity factor, with, for example, 0 being transparent and 1 being opaque. The rationale is that on most computers the integer operation will be faster than a floating point operation, and the filterRGB() method gets called for every single pixel in an image, so efficiency counts.

The only new method introduced in this example was the filterRGB() method, which is defined below:

- filterRGB

```
public abstract int filterRGB(int x,
                              int y,
                              int rgb)
```

Called to filter the given RGB value that is located at the specified coordinates of the source image. If the x and y coordinates are equal to –1, the RGB value came from a color lookup table.

17

JAVA MULTIMEDIA

In this chapter, we will look at some of the techniques you can use to add multimedia elements such as animation and sound to your applets. Java has a number of aspects that facilitate its use for multimedia applications. Among these are support for threads, audio, and off-screen graphics. We'll take a closer look at these capabilities in this chapter. Even if you are not interested in multimedia per se, the techniques shown in this chapter will be applicable for creating smoother graphics (we'll build on the off-screen drawing techniques we developed in Chapter 16), or providing audio feedback to your users.

By the time you read this, several companies might have also announced additional multimedia support for Java. High-level tools may be available to help you construct multimedia applications with Java more quickly. When deciding whether to use an off-the-shelf solution or build one by hand, you should consider a number of factors. A "hand-rolled" Java multimedia applet has the advantage of being about the fastest solution for downloading from the Web. Java's asynchronous image model allows image data to be streamed from the net, which means that the applet can start working with the image as the data becomes available. Without this capability, the user would have to wait for multimedia data to finish downloading before it could be used in an applet.

Also, some Web-based multimedia technologies, even some of those that are Java-based, require special driver software or native classes to be installed on the user's machine before being able to handle multimedia content from a given Web page. Although, in many cases, the extra capabilities provided by these drivers is worth the effort, this can be a problem for Web sites that are targeted at casual visitors, who might not be interested in taking the extra steps to find, download, and install special drivers. A basic multimedia Java applet has the advantage of being able to be played back automatically with any Java-capable browser without any additional effort on the part of the user.

The remainder of this chapter will deal with what you need to know to use Java to create basic Java multimedia applets, and it will provide you with the foundation needed to build more elaborate multimedia applets.

Sound

In previous versions of Java, programmers were given more control over the playback of audio data. However, for Java to be able to play back audio data over a wide range of platforms, some of the capabilities had to be streamlined somewhat. The effect is that the audio support in the current release of Java is very simple to use, but it does not necessarily have all the features that you may be used to having if you've used sound APIs on other platforms. The benefit of cross-platform playback, we hope, will overcome some of these limitations. In any event, Sun has indicated that future versions will feature a more robust sound API, possibly including the same kind of asynchronous streaming support we've seen in the image classes. To make the most of Java, you should regularly check the Sun Java home page for new Java releases, and watch the comp.lang.java newsgroup for the latest updates on audio support and other capabilities.

Sound data in the current release of Java always comes from a URL, which will point to an .au audio file. In order to use existing sounds in formats such as .wav or .aiff, you will need to convert these to .au using a sound program that supports audio conversion. If you try to use a .wav file, or some other format that Java does not currently support, you will see the sun.audio.NativeAudioStream class throw an InvalidAudioFormatException, which will not halt your applet, but the audio won't get played either. The .au file refers to an 8-bit, 8,000 Hz, ulaw encoded audio file. This format doesn't represent the state of the art in audio fidelity, but is adequate for most sound clips.

There are two ways to play a sound file from your applet, and your choice for which method to use will depend on whether the sound is a one-shot occurrence or whether you plan to use the sound in a number of places or wish to have it continuously loop for an indeterminate length of time.

The first way to play a sound is through the play() method of the Applet class. This method comes in two versions, both of which take a URL for a sound file, load the file, and play the sound once. The advantage of using this method is the ease of setting it up. The method succeeds and plays the sound, or it fails and the user doesn't hear anything, but it catches any exceptions that occur, such as not finding the file, thus making it ideal for alert sounds or other optional audio feedback.

The play() method is defined as follows:

- Applet.play

```
      public void play(URL url)
```
Plays an audio clip if the audio clip referred to by the URL is found.

```
      public void play(URL url,
                       String name)
```
Same as the previous method but uses a base URL and file name to locate the audio file.

Typically, you will use the second form of the play method to play back a sound located relative to the .html file that loaded your applet. For example, the following applet plays a sound when a button is pressed:

```
// SoundPlayTest.java
import java.applet.*;
import java.awt.*;


public class SoundPlayTest extends Applet {
```

```
public void init() {
    setLayout(new FlowLayout(FlowLayout.CENTER));

    Button testButton = new Button("Play");
    add(testButton);
}

public boolean action(Event evt, Object arg) {
    if ("Play".equals(arg)) {
        play(getDocumentBase(), "audio/bell.au");
    }
    return true;
}
}
```

This applet simply plays the audio file bell.au, which is located in the audio subdirectory of the directory of the .html file that loaded the applet. The audio file is cached in memory so that it won't have to be downloaded again the second time the play() method is called.

Using AudioClip Objects

The disadvantage of using the play() method is that the first time you call it with a given audio file, it will have to download the file if it hasn't been used before. This can hamper responsiveness in cases like the previous example, where we want to play the sound in response to a user action, and the user ends up waiting for the sound to load in response to hitting a button. Also, the play() method is present only in the applet, which means that to use it from a component, or from within a thread, you need to have a reference to the applet (in and of itself not that big a deal to do, but again hampers its convenience somewhat). Last, the play() method plays a sound once and must be called to play the sound again. Given that there is no way to find out if a sound has completed playing in Java, it is very difficult to play a repeating or looping music clip with the play() method. The AudioClip interface solves many of these limitations (although it still won't tell you when a sound is done playing).

When you work with AudioClip objects, you are actually working with an object of some other class that implements the AudioClip interface. This class is usually a native class that knows how to play audio on your OS platform. Consequently, you will never actually instantiate an AudioClip object yourself, but you will have one returned by an API method.

To obtain an AudioClip object, you call the Applet's getAudioClip() method, which is defined as follows:

- Applet.getAudioClip

```
public AudioClip getAudioClip(URL url)
```
Returns an AudioClip object. This method will not return until the AudioClip has been loaded from the specified URL, so you should consider placing it in a separate thread if the file is expected to take a while to download.

```
public AudioClip getAudioClip(URL url,
                                  String name)
```
Same as the previous method, but finds the audio file using the base URL and file name.

As the definition text mentions, this method can take some time to return. It loads the audio file from the given URL and constructs and returns an AudioClip object. Once you have this AudioClip, you can use it from anywhere in your applet. The AudioClip interface specifies three methods, which are defined below:

- AudioClip.loop

```
public abstract void loop()
```
Plays the clip in a continuous loop.

- AudioClip.play

```
public abstract void play()
```
Starts playing the clip from its beginning.

- AudioClip.stop

```
public abstract void stop()
```
Stops the clip if it is currently playing.

Audio played by the AudioClip is played back asynchronously, which means that when you call the AudioClip's loop() or play() methods the sound will play in its own thread until explicitly stopped, in the case of sound played with loop(), or the sound reaches the end of the audio data, in the case of play(). An active AudioClip can be stopped by calling its stop() method; there is no penalty for calling the stop() method if the sound is not already playing.

Here's an example of an applet that plays a soundtrack loop as long as the applet is on-screen, or until the stop button is hit:

```java
// AudioClipTest.java
import java.applet.*;
import java.awt.*;

public class AudioClipTest extends Applet {

    AudioClip snareHit;
    AudioClip musicLoop;

    public void init() {
        setLayout(new FlowLayout(FlowLayout.CENTER));

        Button testButton = new Button("Snare Drum");
        add(testButton);

        testButton = new Button("Start Loop");
        add(testButton);

        testButton = new Button("Stop Loop");
        add(testButton);

        snareHit = getAudioClip(getDocumentBase(),"snare.au");
        musicLoop = getAudioClip(getDocumentBase(),"loop.au");
    }
```

```
public void start() {
    musicLoop.loop();
}

public void stop() {
    musicLoop.stop();
}

public boolean action(Event evt, Object arg) {
    if ("Snare Drum".equals(arg)) {
        snareHit.play();
    }
    if ("Start Loop".equals(arg)) {
        musicLoop.loop();
    }
    if ("Stop Loop".equals(arg)) {
        musicLoop.stop();
    }
    return true;
    }
}
```

When this applet is run, it will look like Figure 17.1.

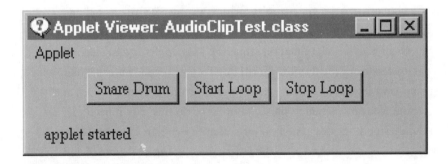

Figure 17.1

The applet loads two AudioClips in its init() method. The first is the snare drum sound, and the second is the music loop. Because sounds are loaded synchronously, the init() method will not finish until the sounds have been loaded. When the applet's start() method is called, it starts the music loop; similarly, when the applet's stop() method is called, in response to the user going to a different Web page, for example, the stop() method stops the music loop from playing. If you use AudioClips that continuously loop like this, you should remember to stop them in the applet's stop() method; otherwise, they will continue playing while the user visits other pages, no doubt to his or her annoyance.

An interesting thing to note about this example is that multiple audio clips can be played at the same time, with the limit being the polyphonic capabilities of the platform. Most platforms can support at least two channels of audio, and many can support at least four, but you should be careful about going too far beyond this if you want your applets to sound as you intended when played on any platform. The second audio clip in this example is played in response to the user clicking on the snare drum button. If the music loop is playing, it will continue without interruption, while the snare drum sound plays along with it.

Animation

Many applets on the Web make use of Java applets to add animation to their pages. There are a number of ways to create animated effects within a Java applet, and we'll take a look at a few of them in this section. The fastest way of using Java for animation is to make use of a premade applet for the purpose. We've created an animation applet that we'll take a look at that let's you take a series of existing images and play them back as an animation sequence. This applet is designed to be driven from parameters from the .html file's <APPLET> tag so you can use it as-is by supplying your own images as parameters to it. The second way to produce animation is by writing your own code to do so. In order to do this, you'll need to have read and understood our discussion on off-screen drawing in Chapter 16. We've taken the concepts we looked at in the last chapter and used them to build an applet that allows you to create sophisticated sprite animation. Before we do this, we need to talk a little bit about how animation works.

Basics of Animation

Classical animation is accomplished by showing a series of cells in rapid succession. If the drawings on each of the cells are done right, the viewer will see the illusion of motion. You've probably seen basic animations of a cartoon character walking and know that animation is created by a series of drawings, each of which has the character's arms and legs in slightly different positions that, when played back over time, appear as fluid motion.

Simple computer animation replicates this by flipping through a series of images. These images are often output by painting, animation, or 3D modeling software, or in some cases are scanned from paper drawings. Regardless of the source, the series of images needs to represent some sort of motion, or instead of animation, what you will have is a rapid-fire slide show (which can also be an interesting effect).

Because of the challenges of producing frame-based animation, a second type of computer animation is frequently seen, called path-based animation. Anytime you have an image (or cycle of images) that moves along an on-screen path over time, you have a path-based animation. Animated spaceships that fly across the screen, tickertape applets, and bouncing images are all examples of path-based animation. In some cases, the path is a predetermined series of coordinates; in other cases, it is determined programmatically or in response to user actions.

A number of metaphors are used to create path-based animations. Typically, an image or series of images is attached to a sprite. The sprite has a position within an area sometimes referred to as a stage. Sprites typically can move along a predetermined path on this stage, or they can be made to move in response to a mouse position. The advantage of path-based animation is that motion can be created independently of whatever is in the sprite's images. For example, an animated logo can be created by having a sprite with the single logo image move along a path across the screen.

In the next two sections, we will look at how to support both types of animation in Java. Our AnimationApplet is a useful tool for animations that consist of a series of images. The SpriteApplet, which we will show later in the chapter, demonstrates how to create sprite animations within Java. The SpriteApplet can be used as a starting point for building elaborate multimedia applets.

Using the AnimationApplet

At the end of this section is the listing for an applet that you can use to play back a series of images with an optional audio clip as accompaniment. This applet builds from several of the techniques we've looked at in earlier chapters. First of all, the applet makes extensive use of parameters passed via the applet <PARAM> tag. This allows the same applet to be used for entirely different purposes simply by supplying different parameters to the applet. We also make use of the MediaTracker to load images. When the applet is used, a series of image files are specified as frames for the animation, and these image files are used to create image objects that are stored in a Vector object. These images are also added to a MediaTracker object, and that MediaTracker is used to load the images into memory. Last, we optionally load an audio file as an AudioClip, using the same techniques we saw in the previous section.

In Chapter 16, we saw that the MediaTracker can be used to load images by creating a new thread and having the image loading take place in that thread. We do the same thing in this applet. When the applet is started, a new thread is created that loads the images using the MediaTracker's waitForAll() method. In our previous MediaTracker examples, once the image was loaded, that was pretty much the end of the story. The thread called repaint() and then exited. In this applet, we keep the thread around and use it to keep time for the animation.

The applet maintains a frame counter that is used to determine which image in the Vector to display next. The frame counter is updated by the timer thread at regular intervals. This is done by having the thread sleep for a certain period of time, then updating the frame counter when the thread wakes up. After the frame counter is updated, the thread calls repaint() and goes to sleep again. This continues until the frame counter reaches the final frame count, or infinitely if the applet is told to loop the animation.

Meanwhile, in response to the repaint() requests being made in the timer thread, the applet's update() and paint() methods are being called. The update() method is overridden to eliminate flicker, and the paint() method uses the current value of the frame counter to retrieve an image object from the Vector and display it on the screen.

You'll want to study the code of the applet more closely. It's basically a variation of code we've looked at in earlier chapters, so there shouldn't be anything that you can't figure out. Because it uses a number of different techniques in one applet, you may need to refer back to a couple of different sections to understand it. Consider this a sort of Java final exam.

The best part about this applet is that even if you didn't know how it worked, you could still use it. Because the applet is designed to be configured via tags, you won't have to recompile this applet again to use it for different animations. Let's take a look at the parameters that can be passed to the applet:

framerate   optional, default = 10, number of frames per second

imagebase   optional, default = getDocumentBase()

imagename   file name prefix, will have number and format suffix appended to it (i.e., if set to frame, files would be frame1.gif, frame2.gif, etc.)

imagesuffix   optional, default = .gif

startnum   optional, default = 1, first image num in file sequence

imagecount   either this or lastnum must be set, number of images in animation

lastnum   either this or imagecount must be set, last image num in file sequence

loopimages   optional, default = true

audiofile   optional, if present load and play the audio file

audiobase   optional, default = getDocumentBase()

loopaudio   optional, default = true

stopaudio   optional, default = true, stops audio when animation is done

The following is the HTML code necessary to play back the tumbling Duke images that are included with the JDK distribution. These images are named T1.gif through T17.gif, and in order to be used with this applet, they must be moved into a subdirectory of the directory from which this HTML file loads. In the distribution, the images are stored in a directory named tumble that is, in turn, within a directory named images (java/demo/TumblingDuke/images/tumble/). In our example, we've assumed that the images directory is in the same directory as our HTML file. Feel free to change the HTML code to point to whatever directory you choose. We've also moved the audio directory from the BouncingHeads example (java/demo/BouncingHeads/audio/) to the HTML document directory. Here's the HTML document that loads the applet and obtains the images and audio file from these directories:

```html
<!--AnimationApplet.html-->
<title>AnimationApplet</title>
<applet code=AnimationApplet.class width=200 height=200>
<param name=imagename value="images/T">
<param name=startnum value="1">
<param name=lastnum value="17">
<param name=loopimages value="true">
<param name=audiofile value="audio/spacemusic.au">
</applet>
```

When you use this applet, you could make a few improvements. First, the images are being drawn directly to the screen, and each image overrides the previous one. This means that you cannot use this applet with images that use transparency. This applet could be modified to draw into an off-screen buffer, which is cleared to the background color each time before the image is drawn. This would allow you to use images with transparency because we would no longer need to use the image of the current frame to overwrite the on-screen pixels drawn by the previous image. It's actually very easy to modify this applet to use an off-screen image buffer; if you decide to try to do this, you will want to take a look at our sprite applet example in the next section, where we make use of off-screen bitmaps to allow for multiple overlapping sprites.

Here is the source listing for the AnimationApplet:

```java
// AnimationApplet.java
import java.applet.*;
import java.awt.*;
import java.util.*;
import java.net.*;
```

```java
public class AnimationApplet extends Applet implements Runnable
{

    MediaTracker theTracker;
    Vector frames = new Vector();
    int start_frame;
    int cur_frame;
    Thread timer;
    boolean loop_images;
    int frame_delay;
    boolean loop_music;
    AudioClip music;
    boolean show_frames;
    boolean stop_music;

    public void init() {
        URL base = null;

        theTracker = new MediaTracker(this);

        frame_delay = 100;
        String framerate = getParameter("framerate");
        if (framerate != null)
            frame_delay = 1000 /
                    Integer.valueOf(framerate).intValue();

        base = getDocumentBase();
        String imagebase = getParameter("imagebase");
        if (imagebase != null)
            base = new URL(imagebase);

        String name = getParameter("imagename");

        String suffix = getParameter("imagesuffix");
```

```
if (suffix == null)
   suffix = ".gif";

int start_frame = 1;
String startnum = getParameter("startnum");
if (startnum != null)
   start_frame = Integer.valueOf(startnum).intValue();

int count = 1;
String imagecount = getParameter("imagecount");
if (imagecount != null)
   count = Integer.valueOf(imagecount).intValue();

loop_images = true;
String loopimages = getParameter("loopimages");
if (loopimages != null)
   loop_images = loopimages.equals("true");

int last = start_frame + count;

String lastnum = getParameter("lastnum");
if (lastnum != null)
   last = Integer.valueOf(lastnum).intValue();

for (int i = start_frame; i < last; i++) {
   Image img = getImage(base, name + i + suffix);
   theTracker.addImage(img, 0);
   frames.addElement(img);
   }

base = getDocumentBase();
String audiobase = getParameter("audiobase");
if (audiobase != null)
   base = new URL(audiobase);
```

```java
        loop_music = true;
        String loopaudio = getParameter("loopaudio");
        if (loopaudio != null)
            loop_music = loopaudio.equals("true");

        stop_music = true;
        String stopaudio = getParameter("stopaudio");
        if (stopaudio != null)
            stop_music = stopaudio.equals("true");

        String audiofile = getParameter("audiofile");

        if (audiofile != null) {
            showStatus("Loading audio");
            music = getAudioClip(base, audiofile);
        }

    }

public void start() {
    timer = new Thread(this);
    timer.start();
}

public void stop() {
    if (timer != null)
        timer.stop();
    timer = null;
    if (music != null)
        music.stop();
}

public void run() {
```

```
showStatus("Loading images");

try {
    theTracker.waitForAll();
} catch (InterruptedException e) {
    return;
}

showStatus("Starting audio");
if (music != null) {
    if (loop_music)
        music.loop();
    else
        music.play();
}

showStatus("Playing animation");

cur_frame = start_frame;

while (timer != null) {
    try {
        Thread.sleep(frame_delay);
    } catch (InterruptedException e) {
        break;
    }

    repaint();

    if (cur_frame >= (frames.size() - 1)) {
        if (loop_images) cur_frame = start_frame;
        else break;
    }
```

```
        else cur_frame++;

        if (show_frames)
            showStatus("Frame:" + cur_frame);
    }

    if ((music != null) & stop_music) {
        music.stop();
    }

    showStatus("Animation done");

}


public void paint(Graphics g) {
    if (theTracker.isErrorAny()) {
        g.setColor(Color.red);
        g.fillRect(0, 0, size().width, size().height);
        return;
    }

    if (!theTracker.checkAll())
        return;

    Image img = (Image)frames.elementAt(cur_frame);
    if (img != null)
        g.drawImage(img, 0, 0, this);
}

public void update(Graphics g) {
    paint(g);
}
}
```

Advanced Java Animation Techniques

In the last section, we looked at an applet for flipping through a series of images to display an animation. The applet we presented was designed to be used easily for a variety of applications. In this section, we'll take a look at a more complicated example that can be used to create more sophisticated, path-based animations.

The idea behind this applet is to define three types of classes. The first is the StageCanvas, which is a subclass of the Canvas component, where all the action takes place. The second class is the Sprite class. Each Sprite can contain one or more images and can be positioned anywhere on the StageCanvas. The last class is the Mover class. Mover objects are used by the Sprite class to determine where it should be at a given point in time. The Mover class itself is a generic class that must be subclassed to be useful. In our example, we subclass the Mover class to create the PathMover class, which moves Sprites along a series of points.

Here are the basic steps that an applet will take in its init() method to create an animation with the classes contained in this applet.

First of all, you will create a StageCanvas. Several constructors are available to do this:

- StageCanvas constructors
  ```
  StageCanvas(Applet theApplet)
  ```
  Construct a StageCanvas with 100 frames and a frame count of 10 frames per second.
  ```
  StageCanvas(Applet theApplet, int framecount)
  ```
  Construct a StageCanvas with a specified number of frames and a frame count of 10 frames per second.
  ```
  StageCanvas(Applet theApplet, int framecount, int framerate)
  ```
  Construct a StageCanvas with specified number of frames and specified frames per second.

If you want to, you can set a background image for the StageCanvas. This is done using the setBackground() method.

- StageCanvas.setBackground
  ```
  public void setBackground(Image theBackground)
  ```
  Constructs a StageCanvas with a specified number of frames and a frame count of 10 frames per second.

Next, for each sprite you wish to use, you need to create a Sprite object. The Sprite object has the following constructors:

- Sprite constructors

  ```
  Sprite()
  ```
  Default constructor. Sprite appears on frame 0 and leaves on frame 100.

  ```
  Sprite(int startFrame, int endFrame)
  ```
  Constructs a Sprite that appears on the stage at the specified starting frame and leaves the stage on the specified ending frame.

Once you have a Sprite object, you need to add images to it. You can do this through one of the following methods:

- Sprite.addImage

  ```
  public void addImage(Image theImage)
  ```
  Adds the specified Image as a new frame of the sprite.

  ```
  public void addImage(Image theImage, int num_frames)
  ```
  Adds the specified Image to the sprite for the indicated number of frames.

- Sprite.addGIFSequence

  ```
  public void addGIFSequence(URL base,
                     String name,
                     String suffix,
                     int img_count,
                     Applet theApplet)
  ```
  Adds the specified numbered sequence of image files to the sprite. Each file name is determined by taking the name string and adding a number between 1 and the value passed as the image count and tacking the suffix at the end. For example, if the name was "frame" and the suffix was ".gif," this method would load the images named "frame1.gif," "frame2.gif," etc.

Next, you need to construct a mover for the sprite. If you don't, then the sprite will remain stationary for the duration of the animation. In our example, we construct a new PathMover so that we can move our sprites along paths. Here are the constructors for PathMover:

- PathMover constructors

  ```
  PathMover()
  ```
  Default constructor. Constructs an empty path.

  ```
  PathMover(boolean loop)
  ```
  If the loop flag is set, the path will start again at the first point after it reaches the end of the path.

A path needs to have points added to it to be useful for moving a sprite. The PathMover class provides these methods for adding points to the path:

- PathMover.addPoint

  ```
  public void addPoint(int x, int y)
  ```
  Adds the specified coordinates as a new path point that corresponds to one frame of the animation.

  ```
  public void addPoint(int x, int y, int frames)
  ```
  Adds the specified coordinates as new path points for the indicated number of frames.

- PathMover.addPointRange

  ```
  public void addPointRange(int x1, int y1,
                            int x2, int y2,
                            int frames)
  ```
  Adds the necessary path points to move the sprite from the coordinates specified by (x1, y1) to (x2, y2) over the specified number of frames.

Once the PathMover object has been filled with the desired path points, you need to add it to the Sprite object. This is done by using the setMover() method:

- Sprite.setMover

  ```
  public void setMover(Mover theMover)
  ```
  Sets the specified Mover object to be the Mover for the Sprite.

Last, the Sprite needs to be added to the StageCanvas. This is done with the addSprite() method:

- StageCanvas.setMover

  ```
  public void addSprite(Sprite theSprite)
  ```
  Adds the specified Sprite to the StageCanvas.

These steps are repeated for all the Sprites you want to add to the StageCanvas. Once you have done that, you can start the animation using the StageCanvas start() method and stop it using the StageCanvas stop() method. You will usually want to put these in the start() and stop() methods of your applet. The StageCanvas start() and stop() methods are defined below:

- StageCanvas.start

  ```
  public void start()
  ```
  Starts the animation contained in this StageCanvas. Uses the MediaTracker to load images if necessary.

- StageCanvas.stop

  ```
  public void stop()
  ```

  Stops the animation that is playing within the StageCanvas.

The SpriteApplet listing demonstrates an example animation set up in its init() method. When using this applet for your own animations, you could modify the code in the init() method to suit your needs. The rest of the classes in the applet can be left alone.

If you are so inclined, you could move the Sprite, Mover, PathMover, and StageCanvas classes to a separate package. You might also want to create an AudioSprite that plays audio clips at specific frames in the animation. A very easy area of exploration is to create different subclasses of the Mover class to make Sprites follow the mouse cursor or other Sprites. Last, try to find a way to have events triggered by clicking on sprites. You might want to use the fact that someone clicked on an animated character to trigger the playback of a sound, such as a digitized voice.

We'll end this chapter with the source file listing for the SpriteApplet:

```java
// SpriteApplet.java
import java.applet.*;
import java.awt.*;
import java.util.*;
import java.net.*;


public class SpriteApplet extends Applet {

    StageCanvas theStage;

    public void init() {
        setLayout(new BorderLayout());


        theStage = new StageCanvas(this);
        add("Center", theStage);
```

```
            Image bg = getImage(getDocumentBase(),"bg1.gif");
            theStage.setBackground(bg);

            Sprite theSprite = new Sprite();
            theSprite.addGIFSequence(getDocumentBase(),"images/T", ".gif", 17, this);
            //theSprite.addImage(getImage(getDocumentBase(),"f0.gif"));

            PathMover thePath = new PathMover();
            thePath.addPointRange(0, 0, 150, 300, 50);
            thePath.addPointRange(150, 300, 300, 0, 40);
            thePath.setLoop(true);

            theSprite.setMover(thePath);

            theStage.addSprite(theSprite);

            theSprite = new Sprite();
            theSprite.addImage(getImage(getDocumentBase(),"f1.gif"));
            //theSprite.addImage(getImage(getDocumentBase(),"f2.gif"));
            //theSprite.addImage(getImage(getDocumentBase(),"f3.gif"));

            thePath = new PathMover();
            thePath.addPointRange(0, 100, 300, 100, 100);
            thePath.setLoop(true);

            theSprite.setMover(thePath);

            theStage.addSprite(theSprite);

            theStage.setLoop(true);
    }

    public void start() {
        theStage.start();
```

```java
    }

    public void stop() {
        theStage.stop();
    }

}

class Sprite {

    Vector frames = new Vector();
    int startFrame = 0;
    int endFrame = 100;
    int curFrame;
    Mover theMover;
    Point thePoint = new Point(0, 0);
    StageCanvas theCanvas;

    Sprite () {
    }

    Sprite (int startFrame, int endFrame) {
        this.startFrame = startFrame;
        this.endFrame = endFrame;
    }

    public void addImage(Image theImage) {
        addImage(theImage, 1);
    }

    public void addImage(Image theImage, int num_frames) {
        for (int i =1; i <= num_frames; i++)
            frames.addElement(theImage);
    }
```

```java
public void addGIFSequence(URL base,
                    String name,
                    String suffix,
                    int img_count,
                    Applet theApplet) {
    for (int i = 1; i <= img_count; i++) {
        Image img = theApplet.getImage(base, name + i + suffix);
        frames.addElement(img);
    }
}


public void setMover(Mover theMover) {
    this.theMover = theMover;
}


public void setStartFrame(int startFrame) {
    this.startFrame = startFrame;
}


public void setEndFrame(int endFrame) {
    this.endFrame = endFrame;
}


public void goToFrame(int frame) {
    curFrame = frame;
    if ((curFrame >= startFrame) & (curFrame <= endFrame)) {
        if (theMover != null)
            thePoint = theMover.pointAtFrame(curFrame -
                                        startFrame);
    }
}


public Image getImage(int frame_num) {
    if (frames.size() > 0) {
```

```
            int whichImage = frame_num % frames.size();
            return (Image)frames.elementAt(whichImage);
        }
        else return null;
    }


    public void draw(Graphics g, int frame_num) {
        Image curImage = getImage(frame_num);
        if ((curImage != null) & (thePoint != null))
            g.drawImage(curImage,
                    thePoint.x,
                    thePoint.y,
                    theCanvas);
    }

}


class Mover {

    Mover () {
    }


    public Point pointAtFrame(int frame) {
        return null;
    }

}


class PathMover extends Mover {

    Vector points = new Vector();
    boolean loop;

    PathMover () {
```

```
    }

    PathMover (boolean loop) {
        setLoop(loop);
    }

    public void addPoint(int x, int y) {
        addPoint(x, y, 1);
    }

    public void addPoint(int x, int y, int frames) {
        for (int i =1; i <= frames; i++)
            points.addElement(new Point(x, y));
    }

    public void addPointRange(int x1, int y1,
                              int x2, int y2,
                              int frames) {
        int x_step = (x2 - x1) / frames;
        int y_step = (y2 - y1) / frames;
        int x = x1;
        int y = y1;
        points.addElement(new Point(x, y));
        for (int i =1; i <= frames; i++) {
            x += x_step;
            y += y_step;
            points.addElement(new Point(x, y));
        }
    }

    public void setLoop(boolean loop) {
        this.loop = loop;
    }

    public Point pointAtFrame(int frame) {
```

```
        if (points.size() > 0) {
            if (loop)
                frame = frame % points.size();
            if (frame >= points.size())
                return null;
            return (Point)points.elementAt(frame);
        }
        else return null;
    }


}


class StageCanvas extends Canvas implements Runnable{

    Vector sprites = new Vector();
    boolean prepared = false;
    boolean prepareError = false;
    Thread timer;
    Thread preparer;
    int framecount = 100;
    int framedelay = 100;
    int curFrame = 0;
    boolean loop;
    MediaTracker theTracker;
    Image stageBuffer;
    Graphics stageGraphics;
    Applet theApplet;
    boolean show_frames = false;
    Image stageBackground;
    boolean erase_stage = true;

    StageCanvas(Applet theApplet) {
        this.theApplet = theApplet;
        theTracker = new MediaTracker(this);
        setFrameCount(100);
```

```
        setFrameRate(10);
    }

    StageCanvas(Applet theApplet, int framecount) {
        this.theApplet = theApplet;
        theTracker = new MediaTracker(this);
        setFrameCount(framecount);
        setFrameRate(10);
    }

    StageCanvas(Applet theApplet, int framecount, int framerate) {
        this.theApplet = theApplet;
        theTracker = new MediaTracker(this);
        setFrameCount(framecount);
        setFrameRate(framerate);
    }

    public void addSprite(Sprite theSprite) {
        sprites.addElement(theSprite);
        theSprite.theCanvas = this;
    }

    public void setFrameCount(int framecount) {
        this.framecount = framecount;
    }

    public void setFrameRate(int framerate) {
        framedelay = 1000 / framerate;
    }

    public void setLoop(boolean loop) {
        this.loop = loop;
    }

    public void showFrameCount() {
```

```java
        show_frames = true;
    }

    public void hideFrameCount() {
        show_frames = false;
    }

    public void setBackground(Image theBackground) {
        stageBackground = theBackground;
    }

    public void setEraseStage(boolean erase) {
        erase_stage = erase;
    }

    public void start() {
        if (!prepared) prepare();
        timer = new Thread(this);
        timer.start();
    }

    public void stop() {
        timer.stop();
        timer = null;
    }

    public void rewind() {
        curFrame = 0;
    }

    public void prepare() {
        prepared = false;
        preparer = new StagePreparer(this);
        preparer.start();
```

```
        }

    public void run() {
        while(preparer != null) {
            Thread.yield();
        }

        if (prepareError) {
            theApplet.showStatus("Error preparing stage");
            return;
        }

        if (prepared) {
            theApplet.showStatus("Animation started");

            curFrame = 0;

            while(timer != null) {

                handleSprites(curFrame);

                repaint();

                try {
                    Thread.sleep(framedelay);
                } catch (InterruptedException e) {
                    break;
                }

                curFrame++;

                if (curFrame > framecount) {
                if (loop) curFrame = 0;
                else return;
```

```
            }

        if (show_frames)
            theApplet.showStatus("Frame:" + curFrame);
        }
        theApplet.showStatus("Animation finished");
    }
}


public void handleSprites(int frame) {
    if (erase_stage) {
        stageGraphics.setColor(getBackground());
        stageGraphics.fillRect(0, 0,
                                size().width, size().height);
        stageGraphics.setColor(getForeground());
    }

    if (stageBackground != null)
        stageGraphics.drawImage(stageBackground, 0, 0, this);

    for (Enumeration e = sprites.elements();
         e.hasMoreElements();) {
        Sprite theSprite = (Sprite)e.nextElement();
        theSprite.goToFrame(frame);
        theSprite.draw(stageGraphics, frame);
    }

}


public void paint(Graphics g) {
    if (stageBuffer != null)
        g.drawImage(stageBuffer, 0, 0, this);
}


public void update(Graphics g) {
```

```
        paint(g);
    }
}


class StagePreparer extends Thread {

    StageCanvas theCanvas;

    StagePreparer(StageCanvas theCanvas) {
        this.theCanvas = theCanvas;
    }

    public void run() {
        MediaTracker theTracker = theCanvas.theTracker;

        theCanvas.prepared = false;
        theCanvas.prepareError = false;

        theCanvas.theApplet.showStatus("Collecting sprites");

        for (Enumeration e = theCanvas.sprites.elements();
             e.hasMoreElements();) {
          Sprite theSprite = (Sprite)e.nextElement();
          for (Enumeration e2 = theSprite.frames.elements();
               e2.hasMoreElements();) {
            Image theImage = (Image)e2.nextElement();
            theTracker.addImage(theImage, 0);
          }
        }

        if (theCanvas.stageBackground != null) {
            theTracker.addImage(theCanvas.stageBackground, 0);
```

```
        }


        theCanvas.theApplet.showStatus("Loading sprites");

        try {
            theCanvas.theTracker.waitForAll();
        } catch (InterruptedException e) {
            theCanvas.prepareError = true;
            theCanvas.preparer = null;
            return;
        }



        if (theCanvas.theTracker.isErrorAny()) {
            theCanvas.prepareError = true;
            theCanvas.preparer = null;
            return;
        }

        theCanvas.theApplet.showStatus("Creating buffers");

        int w = theCanvas.size().width;
        int h = theCanvas.size().height;
        Image offImage = theCanvas.createImage(w, h);
        theCanvas.stageBuffer =   offImage;
        theCanvas.stageGraphics = offImage.getGraphics();

        theCanvas.preparer = null;
        theCanvas.prepared = true;
    }
}
```

This chapter provided you with some useful code for creating your own multimedia applets. While these examples are far from the last word on multimedia programming, they do provide a good starting point for building multimedia-enriched Web pages, and they demonstrate the basics of creating objects with graphical representations. The techniques for drawing and moving sprites are conceptually very similar to those for dragging and sizing graphics in a draw program, or in any other programs which deal with graphical objects.

We've used a number of different types of programs and applets to demonstrate various aspects of Java programming. Hopefully, we've given you a pretty good sense of how Java and the API classes work and have presented a variety of code sample that can be drawn from when you create your own programs.

As you continue with Java, we recommend that you make use of the resources that we've mentioned along the way. The Sub Java Web site should be your starting point. In our appendixes, we include references to some of the Java APIs; however, on the Sun site, you will find the complete API reference, as well as additional platform-specific documentation. Finally, the Wiley Web site will have companion materials and applets for this book and other Wiley Java titles online at www.wiley.com.

Good luck!

PART 4

PACKAGE

JAVA.APPLET

*T*he following appendixes provide you with an alternative source of reference material for the applet, awt, and image packages. These packets are included because they are essential for applet creation, and due to the fact that they have been extensively updated in recent Java releases, the Sun supplied reference documentation had not yet caught up with the changes. Sun's complete Java API reference is available on the Sun Java Web site and should be considered the last word on the usage of the API class packages.

The java.applet package contains the classes and interfaces necessary for Java applets to interact with web browsers.

- AppletContext
- AppletStub
- AudioClip
- Applet

Class java.applet.Applet

java.applet.Applet → java.awt.Panel → java.awt.Container → java.awt.Component
→ java.lang.Object

```
public class Applet
extends Panel
```

Applet base class, parent class for all applets.

Constructors

• Applet

```
public Applet()
```

Methods

• destroy

```
public void destroy()
```

Called by the browser to stop applet and to release any held resources.

• getAppletContext

```
public AppletContext getAppletContext()
```

Return reference to the applet context (i.e., browser or application that contains applet).

• getAppletInfo

```
public String getAppletInfo()
```

Return string containing applet author, version, and copyright info.

• getAudioClip

```
public AudioClip getAudioClip(URL url)
```

Returns an audio clip object.

• getAudioClip

```
public AudioClip getAudioClip(URL url,
                              String name)
```

Returns an audio clip object by base URL and file name.

- getCodeBase

  ```
  public URL getCodeBase()
  ```

  Returns the URL of the applet.

- getDocumentBase

  ```
  public URL getDocumentBase()
  ```

  Returns the URL of the document that contains the applet.

- getImage

  ```
  public Image getImage(URL url)
  ```

  Returns an Image object given a URL.

- getImage

  ```
  public Image getImage(URL url,
                             String name)
  ```

  Returns an Image object given a URL and file name.

- getParameter

  ```
  public String getParameter(String name)
  ```

  Returns specified applet parameter.

- getParameterInfo

  ```
  public String[][] getParameterInfo()
  ```

  Returns a two-dimensional array of strings representing the parameters that are understood by this applet. Each parameter accessed by the first dimension of the array contains an array of three strings representing the name, type, and description.

- init

  ```
  public void init()
  ```

  Called by the browser to initialize the applet.

- isActive

  ```
  public boolean isActive()
  ```

  Returns true if the applet is active.

- play

  ```
  public void play(URL url)
  ```

  Plays an audio clip if the audio clip referred to by the URL is found.

- play

  ```
  public void play(URL url,
                      String name)
  ```

  Plays an audio clip if the audio clip referred to by the URL is found.

- setStub

  ```
  public final void setStub(AppletStub stub)
  ```

  Called by the browser/viewer to set the applet stub.

- showStatus

  ```
  public void showStatus(String msg)
  ```

  Shows a status message in the applet's context (usually status line of the browser).

- start

  ```
  public void start()
  ```

  Called by the browser to start the applet.

- stop

  ```
  public void stop()
  ```

  Called by the browser to stop the applet; is always called before destroy() is called.

Interface
java.applet.AppletContext

```
public interface AppletContext
```

Applet context. Used by the applet to communicate with the browser or controlling application.

Methods

- getApplet

  ```
  public abstract Applet getApplet(String name)
  ```

  Gets an applet by name (specified in the <APPLET> tag).

- getApplets

  ```
  public abstract Enumeration getApplets()
  ```

  Returns an Enumeration of all the applets in this context.

- getAudioClip

  ```
  public abstract AudioClip getAudioClip(URL url)
  ```

  Returns an audio clip given a URL.

- getImage

  ```
  public abstract Image getImage(URL url)
  ```

  Gets an image over the Net or from the cache if it has been previously loaded.

- showDocument

  ```
  public abstract void showDocument(URL url)
  ```

  Tells the browser to show a new document. Not guaranteed that the browser will actually show the document.

- showStatus

  ```
  public abstract void showStatus(String status)
  ```

  Show a status string in the browser status bar.

Interface java.applet.AppletStub

```
public interface AppletStub
```

Applet stub class used by applet viewer type applications.

Methods

- getAppletContext

  ```
  public abstract AppletContext getAppletContext()
  ```

  Returns a reference to the applet's context.

- getCodeBase

  ```
  public abstract URL getCodeBase()
  ```

  Returns the base URL.

- getDocumentBase

  ```
  public abstract URL getDocumentBase()
  ```

  Returns the document URL.

- getParameter

  ```
  public abstract String getParameter(String name)
  ```

  Returns the specified applet parameter.

- isActive

  ```
  public abstract boolean isActive()
  ```

  Returns true if the applet is active.

Interface java.applet.AudioClip

```
public interface AudioClip
```

A platform-independent interface for playing back audio clips.

Methods

- loop

  ```
  public abstract void loop()
  ```

  Play the clip in a continuous loop.

- play

  ```
  public abstract void play()
  ```

  Start playing the clip from its beginning.

- stop

  ```
  public abstract void stop()
  ```

  Stop the clip if it is currently playing.

PACKAGE JAVA.AWT

The java.awt package contains the classes and interfaces necessary for constructing user interfaces and on-screen graphics.

- AWTError
- AWTException
- BorderLayout
- Button
- Canvas
- CardLayout
- Checkbox
- CheckboxGroup
- CheckboxMenuItem
- Choice
- Color
- Component
- Container

- Dialog
- Dimension
- Event
- FileDialog
- FlowLayout
- Font
- FontMetrics
- Frame
- Graphics
- GridLayout
- Image
- Insets
- Label
- LayoutManager
- List
- MediaTracker
- Menu
- MenuBar
- MenuComponent
- MenuContainer
- MenuItem
- Panel
- Point
- Polygon
- Rectangle
- Scrollbar
- TextArea
- TextComponent
- TextField
- Toolkit
- Window

Class java.awt.AWTError

java.awt.AWTError → java.lang.Error → java.lang.Throwable → java.lang.Object

```
public class AWTError
extends Error
```

A generic AWT error. See java.lang.Error for a description of error methods.

Class java.awt.AWTException

java.awt.AWTException → java.lang.Exception → java.lang.Throwable →
java.lang.Object

```
public class AWTException
extends Exception
```

Thrown by the AWT to signal an exception. See java.lang.Exception for a description of exception methods.

Class java.awt.BorderLayout

java.awt.BorderLayout → java.lang.Object

```
public class BorderLayout
extends Object
implements LayoutManager
```

Lays out components by their compass position using the strings "North," "South," "East," "West," and "Center." See LayoutManager interface in this package for a description of implemented methods.

Constructors

- BorderLayout

```
public BorderLayout()
```

Default constructor.

- BorderLayout

```
public BorderLayout(int hgap,
                    int vgap)
```

Construct new BorderLayout using specified horizontal and vertical gap values.

Methods

- Methods implemented from interface

    addLayoutComponent(), layoutContainer(), minimumLayoutSize(),
    preferredLayoutSize(), removeLayoutComponent(), toString()

Class java.awt.Button

java.awt.Button → java.awt.Component → java.lang.Object

    public class Button
    extends Component

AWT Button component. Buttons take on appearance of native button control.

Constructors

- Button

    public Button()

Default constructor for button with no label.

- Button

    public Button(String label)

Constructs button with specified label string.

Methods

- getLabel

    public String getLabel()

Returns the button label.

- setLabel

    public void setLabel(String label)

Sets the button label.

- Methods overriden from superclass

    addNotify(), paramString()

Class java.awt.Canvas

java.awt.Canvas → java.awt.Component → java.lang.Object

```
public class Canvas

extends Component
```

Canvas component is subclassed for creating drawing areas and custom controls. Subclass Canvas instead of component for creating your own component classes.

Constructors

- Canvas

```
public Canvas()
```

Default Constructor

Methods

- paint

```
public void paint(Graphics g)
```

Paints the canvas with the default background color. The canvas should have already been cleared to the background color by the update() method, so you shouldn't need to do this if you override this method.

- Methods overridden from superclass

```
addNotify()
```

Class java.awt.CardLayout

java.awt.CardLayout → java.lang.Object

```
public class CardLayout

extends Object

implements LayoutManager
```

A layout manager for creating a HyperCard-style set of cards. Each component is a different "card." Usually each component is a container such as Panel. See LayoutManager interface in this package for a description of implemented methods.

Methods

- first

```
public void first(Container parent)
```

Display first "card."

- last

```
public void last(Container parent)
```

Display last "card."

- next

```
public void next(Container parent)
```

Display "next" card.

- previous

```
public void previous(Container parent)
```

Display "previous" card.

- show

```
public void show(Container parent,
                    String name)
```

Display named "card."

- Methods overriden from superclass

```
addLayoutComponent(), layoutContainer(), minimumLayoutSize(),
preferredLayoutSize(), removeLayoutComponent(),toString()
```

Class java.awt.Checkbox

java.awt.Checkbox → java.awt.Component → java.lang.Object

```
public class Checkbox
extends Component
```

AWT Checkbox component for creating on/off checkboxes. On-screen representation will vary across platforms, but will usually look something like a square with a check or an x within it to indicate that it has been checked.

Constructors

- Checkbox

  ```
  public Checkbox()
  ```

  Default constructor. Checkbox will have no label and no Checkbox group. Newly created checkbox will be checked off (false state).

- Checkbox

  ```
  public Checkbox(String label)
  ```

  Checkbox will have specified label and no Checkbox group. Newly created checkbox will be checked off (false state).

- Checkbox

  ```
  public Checkbox(String label,
                  CheckboxGroup group,
                  boolean state)
  ```

  Checkbox will have specified label and specified Checkbox group. Newly created checkbox will be checked to specified state.

Methods

- getCheckboxGroup

  ```
  public CheckboxGroup getCheckboxGroup()
  ```

  Returns this Checkbox object's associated CheckboxGroup or null if none.

- getLabel

  ```
  public String getLabel()
  ```

  Gets the Checkbox object's label.

- getState

  ```
  public boolean getState()
  ```

  Returns Checkbox state using true for on and false for off.

- setCheckboxGroup

  ```
  public void setCheckboxGroup(CheckboxGroup g)
  ```

  Associates this Checkbox object with the specified CheckboxGroup.

- setLabel

  ```
  public void setLabel(String label)
  ```

  Sets the Checkbox object's label.

- setState

  ```
  public void setState(boolean state)
  ```

  Sets the Checkbox on/off state to the specifed boolean.

- Methods overridden from superclass

  ```
  addNotify(), paramString()
  ```

Class java.awt.CheckboxGroup

java.awt.CheckboxGroup → java.lang.Object

```
public class CheckboxGroup
extends Object
```

Used to manage radio-button style groups of Checkbox objects. Only one of the Checkbox objects associated with the CheckboxGroup can be checked on at a time.

Constructors

- CheckboxGroup

  ```
  public CheckboxGroup()
  ```

  Default constructor.

Methods

- getCurrent

  ```
  public Checkbox getCurrent()
  ```

  Gets the current checked Checkbox.

- setCurrent

  ```
  public synchronized void setCurrent(Checkbox t)
  ```

  Called by setState() in CheckBox. Sets the specifed Checkbox to be current choice. Checks off previously on Checkbox object.

- Methods overridden from superclass

  ```
  toString()
  ```

Class
java.awt.CheckboxMenuItem

java.awt.CheckboxMenuItem → java.awt.MenuItem → java.awt.MenuComponent →
java.lang.Object

```
public class CheckboxMenuItem

extends MenuItem
```

Used to represent a menu item that can have a check next to it. Don't confuse this with other Checkbox classes such as Checkbox and Checkbox
group—it is used only in menus and, as a consequence, will seldom be used
by applets unless they construct external windows. Refer to the MenuItem
class for more information.

Methods

- getState

   ```
   public boolean getState()
   ```

   Returns true if this menu item is checked.

- setState

   ```
   public void setState(boolean t)
   ```

   Sets the state of the Checkbox MenuItem.

- Methods overriden from superclass

   ```
   addNotify(), paramString()
   ```

Class java.awt.Choice

java.awt.Choice → java.awt.Component → java.lang.Object

```
public class Choice

extends Component
```

Choice objects are represented on-screen as a pop-up menu with the current
choice used as title of the menu.

Constructors

- Choice

  ```
  public Choice()
  ```

  Default constructor.

Methods

- addItem

  ```
  public synchronized void addItem(String item)
  ```

  Adds the specified string as an item to this Choice object.

- countItems

  ```
  public int countItems()
  ```

  Returns the number of items.

- getItem

  ```
  public String getItem(int index)
  ```

  Returns String item of this Choice object at the given index (counting from 0 to countItems()-1).

- getSelectedIndex

  ```
  public int getSelectedIndex()
  ```

  Returns index of the currently selected item (counting from 0 to countItems()-1).

- getSelectedItem

  ```
  public String getSelectedItem()
  ```

  Returns String of the currently selected item.

- select

  ```
  public synchronized void select(int pos)
  ```

  Selects item at the specified position (counting from 0 to countItems()-1).

- select

  ```
  public void select(String str)
  ```

  Selects the item with the specified String.

- Methods overridden from superclass

  ```
  addNotify(), paramString()
  ```

Class java.awt.Color

java.awt.Color → java.lang.Object

```
public final class Color
extends Object
```

An RGB color.

Variables

- black

  ```
  public final static Color black
  ```

  The color black (R:0, G:0, B:0).

- blue

  ```
  public final static Color blue
  ```

  The color blue (R:0, G:0, B:255).

- cyan

  ```
  public final static Color cyan
  ```

  The color cyan (R:0, G:255, B:255).

- darkGray

  ```
  public final static Color darkGray
  ```

  The color dark gray (R:64, G:64, B:64).

- gray

  ```
  public final static Color gray
  ```

  The color gray (R:128, G:128, B:128).

- green

  ```
  public final static Color green
  ```

  The color green (R:0, G:255, B:0).

- lightGray

  ```
  public final static Color lightGray
  ```

  The color light gray (R:192, G:192, B:192). Although this is the color that many browsers use as their background color, don't hard code your backgrounds to this color because many factors can change the browser background color.

- magenta

  ```
  public final static Color magenta
  ```

  The color magenta (R:255, G:0, B:255).

- orange

  ```
  public final static Color orange
  ```

  The color orange (R:255, G:200, B:0).

- pink

  ```
  public final static Color pink
  ```

  The color pink (R:255, G:175, B:175).

- red

  ```
  public final static Color red
  ```

  The color red (R:255, G:0, B:0).

- white

  ```
  public final static Color white
  ```

  The color white (R:255, G:255, B:255).

- yellow

  ```
  public final static Color yellow
  ```

  The color yellow (R:255, G:255, B:0).

Constructors

- Color

  ```
  public Color(int r,
               int g,
               int b)
  ```

  Constructs a 24-bit color with the specified red, green, and blue values. RGB values must be in the range (0 - 255).

- Color

  ```
  public Color(int rgb)
  ```

  Constructs a color from a 24-bit color value (0x00rrggbb).

- Color

```
public Color(float r,

              float g,

              float b)
```

Constructs a 24-bit color with the specified red, green, and blue values. RGB values must be in the range (0.0 - 1.0). Floats are converted within the constructor to values in the range (0-255).

Methods

- brighter

```
public Color brighter()
```

Constructs and returns new Color object with a brighter version of this color.

- darker

```
public Color darker()
```

Constructs and returns a new Color object with a darker version of this color.

- equals

```
public boolean equals(Object obj)
```

Correctly compares this Color object against specified object if it is also an instance of Color.

- getBlue

```
public int getBlue()
```

Gets the blue component of this Color object. Value is between 0 and 255.

- getGreen

```
public int getGreen()
```

Gets the green component of this Color object. Value is between 0 and 255.

- getHSBColor

```
public static Color getHSBColor(float h,

                                 float s,

                                 float b)
```

Creates a new Color object from HSB values.

- getRed

  ```
  public int getRed()
  ```

  Gets the red component of this Color object. Value is between 0 and 255.

- getRGB

  ```
  public int getRGB()
  ```

  Gets the RGB value representing the color in the default RGB ColorModel. (bits 24-31 are 0xff, 16-23 are red, 8-15 are green, 0-7 are blue).

- HSBtoRGB

  ```
  public static int HSBtoRGB(float hue,

                             float saturation,

                             float brightness)
  ```

  Returns an RGB value corresponding to the specified HSB color components.

- RGBtoHSB

  ```
  public static float[] RGBtoHSB(int r,

                                 int g,

                                 int b,

                                 float hsbvals[])
  ```

  Returns an array of three values representing the H, S, and B values corresponding to the specified R, G, and B values. If an array is passed to hold the values, it is used; otherwise, a new array is allocated.

- Methods overridden from superclass

  ```
  hashCode(), toString()
  ```

Class java.awt.Component

java.awt.Component → java.lang.Object

```
public class Component
extends Object
implements ImageObserver
```

Abstract base class of all on-screen AWT components. If you are creating your own components or need to instantiate a generic component, use the Canvas class instead.

Methods

- action

```
public boolean action(Event evt,
                      Object what)
```

Called by HandleEvent if action occurs in the Component. Returns true if the component handles the action. Override this method to handle actions in this component or (when this component is a container) any of its child components.

- addNotify

```
public void addNotify()
```

Used internally. Notifies the Component to create a peer.

- bounds

```
public Rectangle bounds()
```

Returns the component bounds.

- createImage

```
public Image createImage(ImageProducer producer)
```

Creates an image using the specified image producer.

- createImage

```
public Image createImage(int width,
                         int height)
```

Creates an off-screen drawable Image. Usually used for double buffering by drawing into the image and then drawing the image to the screen in the component's paint() method.

- deliverEvent

```
public void deliverEvent(Event e)
```

Called by the browser/viewer to deliver an event to this component or one of its subcomponents. The event travels down the component tree until it reaches the bottom-most child component, which accepts ownership of the event. The event is then posted up the component tree via postEvent until it hits a parent component, which indicates that it has handled the event.

- disable

  ```
  public synchronized void disable()
  ```

  Disables a component so that it does not respond to user events.

- enable

  ```
  public synchronized void enable()
  ```

  Enables a component so that it responds to user events.

- enable

  ```
  public void enable(boolean cond)
  ```

  Sets the components enables state to the specified condition.

- getBackground

  ```
  public Color getBackground()
  ```

  Returns the background color of the component, or the background color of its parent if the component does not have its own background color.

- getColorModel

  ```
  public synchronized ColorModel getColorModel()
  ```

  Gets the ColorModel object used by this component.

- getFont

  ```
  public Font getFont()
  ```

  Returns the font of the component or the font of its parent, if the component does not have its own font.

- getFontMetrics

  ```
  public FontMetrics getFontMetrics(Font font)
  ```

  Returns the font metrics for displaying the given font within this component, or returns null if the component is not on the screen.

- getForeground

  ```
  public Color getForeground()
  ```

  Returns the foreground color of the component or the foreground color of its parent if the component does not have its own foreground color.

- getGraphics

  ```
  public Graphics getGraphics()
  ```

  Returns a Graphics context for this component or null if the component is not on-screen.

- getParent

  ```
  public Container getParent()
  ```

Returns the component's parent container (or null for top-most components).

- getPeer

  ```
  public ComponentPeer getPeer()
  ```

Used internally. Gets the peer of the component.

- getToolkit

  ```
  public Toolkit getToolkit()
  ```

Used internally. Gets the toolkit of the component, which is used to create the component's peer.

- gotFocus

  ```
  public void gotFocus()
  ```

Called by the browser when this component has received the input focus. Override if you want to perform some action when the component gets the focus.

- handleEvent

  ```
  public boolean handleEvent(Event evt)
  ```

Called by postEvent to handle the event. The default behavior is to determine whether this is a mouse event, key event, or action event using the contents of evt.id, and call mouseEnter(), mouseExit(), mouseMove(), mouseDown(), mouseDrag(), or mouseUp() to handle the mouse event, keyDown() to handle key events, or action() to handle action events. The method is expected to return true if the event is handled and false if the event is not handled. Unhandled events are passed to the parent container of this component via postEvent so that they can have a chance to handle the event. If you override this method, remember to return true if you handle the event, and call super.handleEvent(evt) if you want the default event handling to be invoked.

- hide

  ```
  public synchronized void hide()
  ```

Hides this component.

- imageUpdate

  ```
  public boolean imageUpdate(Image img,
                             int flags,
  ```

```
                                     int x,
                                     int y,
                                     int w,
                                     int h)
```

Because this object implements the ImageObserver interface, this method must be present. The default behavior is to repaint the component, based on the assumption that the component needs to draw an image that has just finished asynchronously loaded.

- inside

```
public synchronized boolean inside(int x,
                                         int y)
```

Called by locate to determine whether a specified x,y location is inside the bounding box of this component. Used to determine which mouse events are inside a component and should be handled by it.

- invalidate

```
public void invalidate()
```

Invalidates a component. Invalidating a component indicates that it must be laid out using its parent's layout manager and should not be confused with a similar term used by some window managers (such as the Macintosh window manager) to indicate that an area needs to be repainted.

- isEnabled

```
public boolean isEnabled()
```

Returns true if this component is enabled.

- isShowing

```
public boolean isShowing()
```

Returns true if the component is visible and in a visible on-screen container.

- isValid

```
public boolean isValid()
```

Returns true if this component is valid (i.e., laid out).

- isVisible

```
public boolean isVisible()
```

Returns true if this component is visible.

- keyDown

```
public boolean keyDown(Event evt,
                              int key)
```

Called if a character is typed and the component has the focus.

- keyUp

```
public boolean keyUp(Event evt,
                            int key)
```

Called if a character is typed and the component has the focus.

- layout

```
public void layout()
```

Called by the validate() method. Lays out the component.

- list

```
public void list()
```

Prints string representation of this component to System.out.

- list

```
public void list(PrintStream out)
```

Prints string representation of this component to the specified print out stream.

- list

```
public void list(PrintStream out,
                        int indent)
```

Prints indented string representation of this component to the specified print stream.

- locate

```
public Component locate(int x,
                              int y)
```

Called by the Container deliverEvent() method to locate the component or subcomponent that contains the x,y location.

- location

```
public Point location()
```

Returns the current location of this component in the parent container's coordinate space.

- lostFocus

```
public void lostFocus()
```

Indicates that this component has lost the input focus. Override when you want to be notified of this.

- minimumSize

```
public Dimension minimumSize()
```

Returns the minimum size that this component can be resized to by the parent container's layout manager.

- mouseDown

```
public boolean mouseDown(Event evt,
                              int x,
                              int y)
```

Called by handleEvent if the mouse is down. Override to handle mouse down events and return true if you handle the event.

- mouseDrag

```
public boolean mouseDrag(Event evt,
                              int x,
                              int y)
```

Called by handleEvent if the mouse is moved while the mouse button is down. Override to handle mouse drag events and return true if you handle the event.

- mouseEnter

```
public boolean mouseEnter(Event evt,
                              int x,
                              int y)
```

Called by handleEvent if the mouse enters the component. Override to handle mouse enter events and return true if you handle the event.

- mouseExit

```
public boolean mouseExit(Event evt,
                              int x,
                              int y)
```

Called by handleEvent if the mouse exits the component. Override to handle mouse exit events and return true if you handle the event.

- mouseMove

```
public boolean mouseMove(Event evt,
                                int x,
                                int y)
```

Called by handleEvent if the mouse moves while the mouse button is up. Override to handle mouse move events and return true if you handle the event.

- mouseUp

```
public boolean mouseUp(Event evt,
                               int x,
                               int y)
```

Called by handleEvent if the mouse is up. Override to handle mouse up events and return true if you handle the event.

- move

```
public void move(int x,
                        int y)
```

Moves the component to a new x, y location in the parent container's coordinate space.

- nextFocus

```
public void nextFocus()
```

Moves the focus to the next component (i.e., the tab key is hit).

- paint

```
public void paint(Graphics g)
```

Paints the component. Override to implement display code in your component (Canvas) subclasses.

- paintAll

```
public void paintAll(Graphics g)
```

Paints the component and, if it is a container, its subcomponents.

- paramString

```
protected String paramString()
```

Called by toString() to construct and return the parameter string of this component for debugging purposes. The parameter string is a string containing information about the component's position, size, and state information. Although we don't indicate it in each subclass of component, many of the component subclasses override this method to add information about any additional properties that they implement. If you subclass component (via Canvas) you may wish to override this method to add more information.

- postEvent

```
public void postEvent(Event e)
```

Posts an event to this component. The default behavior is to call handleEvent to process the event. If handleEvent indicates that it did not handle the event by returning false, the event is sent up to the parent container of this component.

- preferredSize

```
public Dimension preferredSize()
```

Returns the preferred size of this component. Usually called by the layout manager of the parent container when laying out the component.

- print

```
public void print(Graphics g)
```

Called when the browser prints the page on which this component resides. The default behavior is to call paint(), but you may choose to override this in order to implement special printing behavior, such as dealing with better resolution.

- printAll

```
public void printAll(Graphics g)
```

Prints this component and, if it is a container, its subcomponents.

- removeNotify

```
public synchronized void removeNotify()
```

Used internally to notify the component to destroy its peer.

- repaint

```
public void repaint()
```

Requests that the browser/viewer update this component as soon as possible.

- repaint

```
public void repaint(long tm)
```

Requests that the browser/viewer update this component within the specified number of milliseconds or as soon as possible after that.

- repaint

```
public void repaint(int x,
                    int y,
                    int width,
                    int height)
```

Requests that the browser/viewer update the specified area of this component as soon as possible.

- repaint

```
public void repaint(long tm,
                    int x,
                    int y,
                    int width,
                    int height)
```

Requests that the browser/viewer update the specified area of this component within the specified number of milliseconds or as soon as possible after that.

- requestFocus

```
public void requestFocus()
```

Request the input focus so that the component can receive keyboard events.

- reshape

```
public synchronized void reshape(int x,
                                 int y,
                                 int width,
                                 int height)
```

Move the component to the specified location and resize it to the specified dimensions. If you don't get the results you expect from this call, the parent container's layout manager is likely to be interfering.

- resize

```
public void resize(int width,
                   int height)
```

Resizes the component to the specified width and height. If you don't get the results you expect from this call, the parent container's layout manager is likely to be interfering.

- resize

  ```
  public void resize(Dimension d)
  ```

  Resizes the component to the width and height of the specified dimension. If you don't get the results you expect from this call, the parent container's layout manager is likely to be interfering.

- setBackground

  ```
  public synchronized void setBackground(Color c)
  ```

  Sets the background color for the component. Some AWT subclasses of this (such as button) may not use this color.

- setFont

  ```
  public synchronized void setFont(Font f)
  ```

  Sets the specified font of the component.

- setForeground

  ```
  public synchronized void setForeground(Color c)
  ```

  Sets the foreground color for the component. Some AWT subclasses of this (such as button) may not use this color.

- show

  ```
  public synchronized void show()
  ```

  Shows the component.

- show

  ```
  public void show(boolean cond)
  ```

  Sets the components show/hide state to the boolean condition (true = show, false = hide).

- size

  ```
  public Dimension size()
  ```

  Returns the current width and height of this component as a dimension.

- toString

  ```
  public String toString()
  ```

  Returns the string representation of this component's values. Useful for debugging. Call the list() method to have the results of toString() printed to System.out.

- update

  ```
  public void update(Graphics g)
  ```

  Called by the Screen Updater thread to update the component in response to a repaint request. The background at this point has not been cleared, so when double-buffering, override this method to draw an image buffer to the screen.

- validate

  ```
  public void validate()
  ```

  Validates a component, meaning that has been laid out by its parent container's layout manager.

Class java.awt.Container

java.awt.Container → java.awt.Component → java.lang.Object

```
public class Container
extends Component
```

Container is a subclass of Component that is used to contain other AWT components. Use the Panel class as your parent class when creating your own container subclasses. The java.applet.Applet class is a subclass of Container via the Panel class. Every container has a layout associated with it.

Methods

- add

  ```
  public synchronized Component add(Component comp)
  ```

  Adds the specified component to this container, using the current layout manager to position and size the component.

- add

  ```
  public synchronized Component add(String name,
                                    Component comp)
  ```

  Adds the specified component to this container. Calls the addLayoutComponent() method of the current layout manager with the name string and component as arguments. The name string is used by some layout managers such as BorderLayout to indicate that special rules need to be used in positioning and sizing the new component.

- countComponents

  ```
  public int countComponents()
  ```

  Returns the number of components in this container.

- deliverEvent

  ```
  public void deliverEvent(Event e)
  ```

  Overrides deliverEvent() method in Component. Delivers an event to the appropriate subcomponent or to this container if none of the subcomponents are appropriate.

- getComponent

  ```
  public synchronized Component getComponent(int n)
  ```

  Gets the component at the specified index, which is in the range of 0 to countComponents() - 1.

- getComponents

  ```
  public synchronized Component[] getComponents()
  ```

  Returns an array of the subcomponents in this container.

- getLayout

  ```
  public LayoutManager getLayout()
  ```

  Returns the layout manager of this container.

- insets

  ```
  public Insets insets()
  ```

  Returns the insets of the container's border.

- layout

  ```
  public synchronized void layout()
  ```

  Uses this component's layout manager to lay out its components.

- remove

  ```
  public synchronized void remove(Component comp)
  ```

  Removes the specified subcomponent from this container.

- removeAll

  ```
  public synchronized void removeAll()
  ```

  Removes all the subcomponents from this container.

- setLayout

  ```
  public void setLayout(LayoutManager mgr)
  ```

  Sets the container's layout manager.

- Methods overridden from superclass

  ```
  addNotify(), list(), locate(), minimumSize(),
  paintComponents(),paramString(), preferredSize(),
  printComponents(), removeNotify(), validate()
  ```

Class java.awt.Dialog

java.awt.Dialog → java.awt.Window → java.awt.Container →
java.awt.Component → java.lang.Object

```
public class Dialog
extends Window
```

A standard dialog box window class that takes input from the user. The
default layout for a dialog is BorderLayout. Modal dialogs must be dis-
missed before other windows can become active.

Constructors

- Dialog

  ```
  public Dialog(Frame parent,
                boolean modal)
  ```

  Constructs a Dialog object to be displayed in the specified Frame parent. If
  specified, the dialog will be modal. Dialogs are initially invisible and must
  be shown with Show().

- Dialog

  ```
  public Dialog(Frame parent,
                String title,
                boolean modal)
  ```

  Constructs a titled Dialog object to be displayed in the specified Frame parent. If specified, the dialog will be modal. Dialogs are initially invisible and
  must be shown with Show().

Methods

- getTitle

  ```
  public String getTitle()
  ```

  Returns the title string of the Dialog box.

- isModal

  ```
  public boolean isModal()
  ```

  Returns true if the Dialog is modal.

- isResizable

  ```
  public boolean isResizable()
  ```

  Returns true if the user can resize the frame containing the dialog.

- setResizable

  ```
  public void setResizable(boolean resizable)
  ```

  Allows or disallows the frame containing the dialog to be resized.

- setTitle

  ```
  public void setTitle(String title)
  ```

  Sets the title string of the dialog.

- Methods overridden from superclass

  ```
  addNotify(), paramString()
  ```

Class java.awt.Dimension

java.awt.Dimension → java.lang.Object

```
public class Dimension
extends Object
```

The Dimension class is used to contain a width and height value.

Variables

- height

  ```
  public int height
  ```

  Height value.

- width

  ```
  public int width
  ```

  Width value.

Constructors

- Dimension

  ```
  public Dimension()
  ```

  Default constructor sets width and height to 0.

- Dimension

  ```
  public Dimension(Dimension d)
  ```

  Constructs a dimension using the width and height of the specified dimension.

- Dimension

  ```
  public Dimension(int width,
                         int height)
  ```

  Constructs a dimension with the specified width and height.

- Methods overridden from superclass

  ```
  toString()
  ```

Class java.awt.Event

java.awt.Event → java.lang.Object

```
public class Event
extends Object
```

Used to pass information to event handling methods.

Variables

- ACTION_EVENT

  ```
  public final static int ACTION_EVENT
  ```

  Event ID for action events.

- arg

  ```
  public Object arg
  ```

  An argument passed with action events. Typically you will call its toString() method to get the label string of the component where the event occurred.

- CTRL_MASK

  ```
  public final static int CTRL_MASK
  ```

  Control key modifier constant.

- DOWN

  ```
  public final static int DOWN
  ```

  Key code for Down arrow key.

- END

  ```
  public final static int END
  ```

  Key code for End key.

- evt

  ```
  public Event evt
  ```

  A reference to the next event when stored in a linked list.

- HOME

  ```
  public final static int HOME
  ```

  Key code for Home key.

- id

  ```
  public int id
  ```

  Event ID for event type. Use the final static int values provided as part of this class to identify the event by comparing them to this value.

- key

  ```
  public int key
  ```

  The key that was pressed in a keyboard event.

- KEY_ACTION

  ```
  public final static int KEY_ACTION
  ```

  Event ID for key action keyboard event.

- KEY_PRESS

  ```
  public final static int KEY_PRESS
  ```

  Event ID for key press keyboard event.

- KEY_RELEASE

  ```
  public final static int KEY_RELEASE
  ```

  Event ID for key release keyboard event.

- LEFT

  ```
  public final static int LEFT
  ```

  Key code for left arrow key.

- LIST_DESELECT

  ```
  public final static int LIST_DESELECT
  ```

  Event ID for list deselection.

- LIST_EVENT

  ```
  public final static int LIST_EVENT
  ```

  Event ID for list event.

- LIST_SELECT

  ```
  public final static int LIST_SELECT
  ```

  Event ID for list selection.

- LOAD_FILE

  ```
  public final static int LOAD_FILE
  ```

  Event ID for file loading event.

- META_MASK

  ```
  public final static int META_MASK
  ```

  The meta modifier constant.

- modifiers

  ```
  public int modifiers
  ```

  The state of the modifier keys.

- MOUSE_DOWN

  ```
  public final static int MOUSE_DOWN
  ```

  Event ID for mouse down event.

- MOUSE_DRAG

  ```
  public final static int MOUSE_DRAG
  ```

  Event ID for mouse drag event.

- MOUSE_ENTER

  ```
  public final static int MOUSE_ENTER
  ```

  Event ID for mouse enter event.

- MOUSE_EXIT

  ```
  public final static int MOUSE_EXIT
  ```

  Event ID for mouse exit event.

- MOUSE_MOVE

  ```
  public final static int MOUSE_MOVE
  ```

  Event ID for mouse move event.

- MOUSE_UP

  ```
  public final static int MOUSE_UP
  ```

  Event ID for mouse up event.

- PGDN

  ```
  public final static int PGDN
  ```

  Key code for page down key.

- PGUP

  ```
  public final static int PGUP
  ```

  Key code for page up key.

- RIGHT

  ```
  public final static int RIGHT
  ```

  Key code for right arrow key.

- SAVE_FILE

  ```
  public final static int SAVE_FILE
  ```

  Event ID for file saving event.

- SCROLL_ABSOLUTE

  ```
  public final static int SCROLL_ABSOLUTE
  ```

  Event ID for absolute scroll event.

- SCROLL_LINE_DOWN

    ```
    public final static int SCROLL_LINE_DOWN
    ```

    Event ID for line down scroll event.

- SCROLL_LINE_UP

    ```
    public final static int SCROLL_LINE_UP
    ```

    Event ID for line up scroll event.

- SCROLL_PAGE_DOWN

    ```
    public final static int SCROLL_PAGE_DOWN
    ```

    Event ID for page down scroll event.

- SCROLL_PAGE_UP

    ```
    public final static int SCROLL_PAGE_UP
    ```

    Event ID for page up scroll event.

- SHIFT_MASK

    ```
    public final static int SHIFT_MASK
    ```

    The shift modifier constant.

- target

    ```
    public Object target
    ```

    The component where this event occurred.

- UP

    ```
    public final static int UP
    ```

    Key code for up arrow key.

- when

    ```
    public long when
    ```

    The time stamp of when this event occurred.

- WINDOW_DEICONIFY

    ```
    public final static int WINDOW_DEICONIFY
    ```

    Event ID for de-iconify window event.

- WINDOW_DESTROY

    ```
    public final static int WINDOW_DESTROY
    ```

    Event ID for destroy window event.

- WINDOW_EXPOSE

  ```
  public final static int WINDOW_EXPOSE
  ```

  Event ID for expose window event.

- WINDOW_ICONIFY

  ```
  public final static int WINDOW_ICONIFY
  ```

  Event ID for iconify window event.

- WINDOW_MOVED

  ```
  public final static int WINDOW_MOVED
  ```

  Event ID for move window event.

- x

  ```
  public int x
  ```

  The x coordinate of the event (i.e., the mouse x position).

- y

  ```
  public int y
  ```

  The y coordinate of the event (i.e., the mouse y position).

Constructors

- Event

  ```
  public Event(Object target,
               long when,
               int id,
               int x,
               int y,
               int key,
               int modifiers,
               Object arg)
  ```

  Constructs event with the specified target component, time stamp, event type, x and y coordinates, keyboard key, state of the modifier keys, and argument.

- Event

  ```
  public Event(Object target,
               long when,
               int id,
  ```

```
                     int x,

                     int y,

                     int key,

                     int modifiers)
```

Constructs event with the specified target component, time stamp, event type, x and y coordinates, keyboard key, state of the modifier keys, and null argument.

- Event

```
    public Event(Object target,

                 int id,

                 Object arg)
```

Constructs event with the specified target component, event type, and argument.

Methods

- controlDown

```
    public boolean controlDown()
```

Returns true if the control key is down.

- metaDown

```
    public boolean metaDown()
```

Returns true if the meta key is down.

- shiftDown

```
    public boolean shiftDown()
```

Returns true if the shift key is down.

- translate

```
    public void translate(int x,

                          int y)
```

Translates an event by adding the specified x and y values to those contained within the event.

- Methods overridden from superclass

```
    paramString(), toString()
```

Class java.awt.FileDialog

java.awt.FileDialog → java.awt.Dialog → java.awt.Window → java.awt.Container →
java.awt.Component → java.lang.Object

```
public class FileDialog
extends Dialog
```

Used for creating a modal standard file dialog.

Variables

- LOAD

```
public final static int LOAD
```

Mode ID for file load.

- SAVE

```
public final static int SAVE
```

Mode ID for file save.

Constructors

- FileDialog

```
public FileDialog(Frame parent,
                  String title)
```

Creates a file dialog for loading a file using the specified Frame and title.

- FileDialog

```
public FileDialog(Frame parent,
                  String title,
                  int mode)
```

Creates a file dialog using the specified Frame, title, and mode.

Methods

- getDirectory

```
public String getDirectory()
```

Gets the directory path of the dialog.

- getFile

```
public String getFile()
```

Gets the file name of the dialog.

- getFilenameFilter

  ```
  public FilenameFilter getFilenameFilter()
  ```

  Gets the FilenameFilter.

- getMode

  ```
  public int getMode()
  ```

  Gets the mode ID (SAVE, LOAD) of the file dialog.

- setDirectory

  ```
  public void setDirectory(String dir)
  ```

  Set the directory path of the dialog to the specified directory.

- setFile

  ```
  public void setFile(String file)
  ```

  Sets the file name for this dialog to the specified file name string. Sets this before the dialog is shown in order to make it the default name.

- setFilenameFilter

  ```
  public void setFilenameFilter(FilenameFilter filter)
  ```

  Sets the filter for this dialog to the specified FilenameFilter.

- Methods overridden from superclass

  ```
  addNotify(), paramString()
  ```

Class java.awt.FlowLayout

java.awt.FlowLayout → java.lang.Object

```
public class FlowLayout
extends Object
implements LayoutManager
```

Flow layout is used to lay out components from left to right until no more components fit on the same line. By default, each line is centered, but this behavior can be set either as a parameter to the constructor or via method call. See LayoutManager interface in this package for a description of implemented methods.

Variables

- CENTER

  ```
  public final static int CENTER
  ```

  Alignment ID for center alignment.

- LEFT

  ```
  public final static int LEFT
  ```

  Alignment ID for left alignment.

- RIGHT

  ```
  public final static int RIGHT
  ```

  Alignment ID for right alignment.

Constructors

- FlowLayout

  ```
  public FlowLayout()
  ```

  Default constructor. New FlowLayout object will use centered alignment.

- FlowLayout

  ```
  public FlowLayout(int align)
  ```

  Constructs new FlowLayout object using the specified alignment ID.

- FlowLayout

  ```
  public FlowLayout(int align,
                    int hgap,
                    int vgap)
  ```

  Constructs new FlowLayout object using the specified alignment ID and gap values.

Methods

- Methods implemented from interface

  ```
  addLayoutComponent(), layoutContainer(), minimumLayoutSize(),
  preferredLayoutSize(), removeLayoutComponent(), toString()
  ```

Class java.awt.FontMetrics

java.awt.FontMetrics → java.lang.Object

```
public class FontMetrics
extends Object
```

An object for obtaining metric information about a font.

Variables

- font

```
protected Font font
```

A reference to the Font object.

Constructors

- FontMetrics

```
protected FontMetrics(Font font)
```

Constructs new FontMetrics object with the specified font.

Methods

- bytesWidth

```
public int bytesWidth(byte data[],
                      int off,
                      int len)
```

Returns width in device units of the specified array of bytes using this font.

- charsWidth

```
public int charsWidth(char data[],
                      int off,
                      int len)
```

Returns width in device units of the specified character array using this font.

- charWidth

  ```
  public int charWidth(int ch)
  ```

  Calculates and returns the width in device units of the specified character using this font.

- charWidth

  ```
  public int charWidth(char ch)
  ```

  Calculates and returns the width in device units of the specified character using this font.

- getAscent

  ```
  public int getAscent()
  ```

  Calculates and returns the average font ascent.

- getDescent

  ```
  public int getDescent()
  ```

  Calculates and returns the average font descent.

- getFont

  ```
  public Font getFont()
  ```

  Returns the font to which this FontMetrics instance refers.

- getHeight

  ```
  public int getHeight()
  ```

  Calculates and returns the total height of the font.

- getLeading

  ```
  public int getLeading()
  ```

  Calculates and returns the standard leading, or line spacing, for the font.

- getMaxAdvance

  ```
  public int getMaxAdvance()
  ```

  Calculates and returns the maximum advance width of any character in this font.

- getMaxAscent

  ```
  public int getMaxAscent()
  ```

  Calculates and returns the maximum ascent of all characters in this font.

- getMaxDecent

  ```
  public int getMaxDecent()
  ```

  Calculates and returns the maximum descent of all characters in this font.

- getWidths

  ```
  public int[] getWidths()
  ```

  Returns an array of the widths of the first 256 characters in the font.

- stringWidth

  ```
  public int stringWidth(String str)
  ```

  Returns the width of the specified string in this font.

- Methods implemented from interface

  ```
  toString()
  ```

Class java.awt.Font

java.awt.Font → java.lang.Object

```
public class Font
extends Object
```

Font objects contain font and style information for use with methods that need to use fonts. Style information is constructed by combining style constants with the or (|) operator (for example, BOLD | ITALIC). The following are valid font names:

```
Dialog
Helvetica
TimesRoman
Courier
Symbol
```

Variables

- BOLD

  ```
  public final static int BOLD
  ```

  Bold character style constant.

- ITALIC

```
public final static int ITALIC
```

Italicized style constant.

- name

```
protected String name
```

The font name.

- PLAIN

```
public final static int PLAIN
```

Plain character style constant.

- size

```
protected int size
```

Font point size.

- style

```
protected int style
```

Font style.

Constructors

- Font

```
public Font(String name,
               int style,
               int size)
```

Creates a new font object using the specified name, style, and point size.

Methods

- equals

```
public boolean equals(Object obj)
```

Correctly compares this font to the specified object if it is an instance of the font class.

- getFamily

```
public String getFamily()
```

Returns platform-specific font family name.

- getFont

  ```
  public static Font getFont(String nm)
  ```

  Returns a font object from the system properties list.

- getFont

  ```
  public static Font getFont(String nm,
                               Font font)
  ```

  Gets the specified font from the system properties list.

- getName

  ```
  public String getName()
  ```

  Gets the logical name of the font.

- getSize

  ```
  public int getSize()
  ```

  Returns the point size of the font.

- getStyle

  ```
  public int getStyle()
  ```

  Returns the style code of the font.

- isBold

  ```
  public boolean isBold()
  ```

  Returns true if the font is bold.

- isItalic

  ```
  public boolean isItalic()
  ```

  Returns true if the font is italic.

- isPlain

  ```
  public boolean isPlain()
  ```

  Returns true if the font is plain.

- Methods overridden from superclass

  ```
  toString()
  ```

Class java.awt.Frame

java.awt.Frame → java.awt.Window → java.awt.Container → java.awt.Component → java.lang.Object

```
public class Frame

extends Window

implements MenuContainer
```

Frames are stand-alone windows. When you create a frame, a new native window is created, even if the frame is created from an applet running in a browser. Frames are created to be invisible, so they must be shown, and the default layout for a new frame is BorderLayout.

Constructors

- Frame

```
public Frame()
```

Default constructor.

- Frame

```
public Frame(String title)
```

Construct frame with specified title.

Methods

- getIconImage

```
public Image getIconImage()
```

Returns the icon image for this frame for use when it's iconized on systems that support iconized or minimized windows.

- getMenuBar

```
public MenuBar getMenuBar()
```

Returns the menu bar associated with this frame.

- getTitle

```
public String getTitle()
```

Returns the title of the frame.

- isResizable

```
public boolean isResizable()
```

Returns true if the frame is user resizable.

- remove

      public synchronized void remove(MenuComponent m)

  Removes the specified menu bar from this frame if it's used by this frame.

- setCursor

      public void setCursor(Image img)

  Set the cursor image. Results will vary depending on the system.

- setIconImage

      public void setIconImage(Image image)

  Sets the image to display when this frame is iconized when used on platforms that allow windows to be iconized.

- setMenuBar

      public synchronized void setMenuBar(MenuBar mb)

  Sets the frame's menubar.

- setResizable

      public void setResizable(boolean resizable)

  Sets the resizable flag so that users can resize the frame.

- setTitle

      public void setTitle(String title)

  Sets the frame's title.

- Methods overridden from superclass

      addNotify(), paramString()

Class java.awt.Graphics

java.awt.Graphics → java.lang.Object

      public class Graphics
      extends Object

Provides a device-independent graphics interface. All drawing operations use the current foreground and background colors unless otherwise specified. Drawing and filling geometric shapes use the current color. Text is drawn using the currently set font.

Constructors

- Graphics

```
protected Graphics()
```

Called by AWT methods to create a Graphics object. You cannot instantiate an object class yourself.

Methods

- clearRect

```
public abstract void clearRect(int x,
                               int y,
                               int width,
                               int height)
```

Clears the specified area to the background color of the display surface. Use the fillRect() method and set the color to the color you want to erase with instead of calling this method.

- clipRect

```
public abstract void clipRect(int x,
                              int y,
                              int width,
                              int height)
```

Sets the clipping area to the intersection of the current clipping area and the specified area.

- copyArea

```
public abstract void copyArea(int x,
                              int y,
                              int width,
                              int height,
                              int dx,
                              int dy)
```

Copies an area of the screen to a new location.

- create

```
public abstract Graphics create()
```

Creates and returns a copy of the current Graphics object. The new Graphics object will draw to the same surface (i.e., screen, pixmap, printer buffer) as the original Graphics object.

- create

```
public Graphics create(int x,

                       int y,

                       int width,

                       int height)
```

Creates and returns a copy of the current Graphics object. The new Graphics object will draw to the same surface (i.e., screen, pixmap, printer buffer) as the original Graphics object. The x,y coordinate is translated to the origin (0,0) of the new Graphics object and the clipping area of the new Graphics object is set to (0, 0, width, height).

- dispose

```
public abstract void dispose()
```

Disposes of this graphics context and any held resources. After calling this method, you can no longer use this Graphics object.

- draw3DRect

```
public void draw3DRect(int x,

                       int y,

                       int width,

                       int height,

                       boolean raised)
```

Draws a highlighted 3-D rectangle.

- drawArc

```
public abstract void drawArc(int x,

                             int y,

                             int width,

                             int height,

                             int startAngle,

                             int arcAngle)
```

Frames the arc specified with the given bounds from startAngle to endAngle.

- drawBytes

```
public void drawBytes(byte data[],
                          int offset,
                          int length,
                          int x,
                          int y)
```

Draws the specified array of bytes as characters using the current font and color settings.

- drawChars

```
public void drawChars(char data[],
                          int offset,
                          int length,
                          int x,
                          int y)
```

Draws the specified array of characters using the current font and color settings.

- drawImage

```
public abstract boolean drawImage(Image img,
                                      int x,
                                      int y,
                                      ImageObserver observer)
```

Draws the specified image object at the specified x, y coordinate. Returns true if image was ready to be drawn. Because images may be loaded asynchronously over the net, the image data might not be available at the time drawImage() is called. By providing a reference to an instance of a class that implements the ImageObserver interface, you can have the imageUpdate() method of the object passed as observer called when the image is loaded and ready to be drawn. The Component class implements ImageObserver, so in most cases, when calling this method from within any class that is a subclass of component, you can simply pass the variable "this" as the observer.

- drawImage

```
public abstract boolean drawImage(Image img,
                                  int x,
                                  int y,
                                  int width,
                                  int height,
                                  ImageObserver observer)
```

Same as the previous method, but allows image scaling via the width and height parameters.

- drawLine

```
public abstract void drawLine(int x1,
                              int y1,
                              int x2,
                              int y2)
```

Draws a line from x1,y1 to x2,y2.

- drawOval

```
public abstract void drawOval(int x,
                              int y,
                              int width,
                              int height)
```

Frames the oval specified by the given bounds.

- drawPolygon

```
public abstract void drawPolygon(int xPoints[],
                                 int yPoints[],
                                 int nPoints)
```

Frames the polygon specified by the arrays of x points, the array of y points, and the number of polygon points.

- drawPolygon

```
public void drawPolygon(Polygon p)
```

Frames the specified polygon object.

- drawRect

```
public void drawRect(int x,
                        int y,
                        int width,
                        int height)
```

Frames the specified rectangle.

- drawRoundRect

```
public abstract void drawRoundRect(int x,
                                      int y,
                                      int width,
                                      int height,
                                      int arcWidth,
                                      int arcHeight)
```

Frames the specified rounded corner rectangle.

- drawString

```
public abstract void drawString(String str,
                                   int x,
                                   int y)
```

Draws the specified string starting at the baseline specified at the x and y coordinate.

- fill3DRect

```
public void fill3DRect(int x,
                          int y,
                          int width,
                          int height,
                          boolean raised)
```

Fills a highlighted 3-D rectangle using the current color.

- fillArc

```
public abstract void fillArc(int x,
                                int y,
                                int width,
                                int height,
                                int startAngle,
                                int arcAngle)
```

Fills the arc specified with the given bounds from startAngle to endAngle.

- fillOval

```
public abstract void fillOval(int x,
                              int y,
                              int width,
                              int height)
```

Fills the oval specified by the given bounds.

- fillPolygon

```
public abstract void fillPolygon(int xPoints[],
                                 int yPoints[],
                                 int nPoints)
```

Fills the polygon specified by the arrays of x points, the array of y points, and the number of polygon points.

- fillPolygon

```
public void fillPolygon(Polygon p)
```

Fills the specified polygon object.

- fillRect

```
public abstract void fillRect(int x,
                              int y,
                              int width,
                              int height)
```

Fills the specified rectangle.

- fillRoundRect

```
public abstract void fillRoundRect(int x,
                                   int y,
                                   int width,
                                   int height,
                                   int arcWidth,
                                   int arcHeight)
```

Fills the specified rounded corner rectangle.

- getClipRect

```
public abstract Rectangle getClipRect()
```

Returns current clipping area.

- getColor

```
public abstract Color getColor()
```

Returns current color.

- getFont

```
public abstract Font getFont()
```

Returns current font.

- getFontMetrics

```
public FontMetrics getFontMetrics()
```

Returns current font metrics.

- getFontMetrics

```
public abstract FontMetrics getFontMetrics(Font f)
```

Returns the font metrics for the specified font.

- scale

```
public abstract void scale(float sx,
                                float sy)
```

Set horizontal and vertical scale factors for subsequent operations. Note that this does not affect the pen size, just the distance between points.

- setColor

```
public abstract void setColor(Color c)
```

Sets the current color for subsequent operations.

- setFont

```
public abstract void setFont(Font font)
```

Sets the font for subsequent text operations.

- setPaintMode

```
public abstract void setPaintMode()
```

Sets the transfer mode to paint mode, which replaces current colors (pixels) with new colors (pixels). This is the default mode.

- setXORMode

```
public abstract void setXORMode(Color c1)
```

Sets the transfer mode. XORMode performs an XOR operation between the current colors (pixels) and the new colors (pixels).

- translate

```
public abstract void translate(int x,
                               int y)
```

Sets the new origin of the graphics context to the specified coordinates.

- Methods overridden from superclass

```
toString()
```

Class java.awt.GridLayout

java.awt.GridLayout → java.lang.Object

```
public class GridLayout
extends Object
implements LayoutManager
```

GridLayout lays components out in a grid using a specified number of rows and columns. See LayoutManager interface in this package for a description of implemented methods.

Constructors

- GridLayout

```
public GridLayout(int rows,
                  int cols)
```

Constructs grid layout with the specified rows and specified columns.

- GridLayout

```
public GridLayout(int rows,
                  int cols,
                  int hgap,
                  int vgap)
```

Constructs grid layout with the specified rows, columns, horizontal gap, and vertical gap.

Methods

- Methods implemented from interface

  ```
  addLayoutComponent(), layoutContainer(), minimumLayoutSize(),
  preferredLayoutSize(), removeLayoutComponent(), toString()
  ```

Class java.awt.Image

java.awt.Image → java.lang.Object

```
public class Image
extends Object
```

Image objects are returned to you by methods that either create them or load them over the net. You never instantiate an Image yourself. The Image class itself is an abstract class. When you are returned an Image object, you are actually being returned an instance of a subclass of Image. This subclass is platform-specific for dealing with pixel maps on the platform the program is running on.

To deal with situations when the image is not yet ready because it is still loading from the net, or the image is still being constructed, many Image methods take an instance of a class that implements java.awt.image.ImageObserver as a parameter. These methods will return immediately with a value of -1, if they return numeric results, or null, if they return object reference. The ImageObserver object that you pass the method will have its imageUpdate() method called when the image is ready. The imageUpdate method will then be able to get the information it needs from the Image. Remember that the AWT component class implements the ImageObserver interface, so that you can usually pass "this" as the ImageObserver.

Variables

- UndefinedProperty

  ```
  public final static Object UndefinedProperty
  ```

Returned whenever a property that was not defined for a particular image is retrieved by getProperty().

Constructors

- Image

  ```
  public Image()
  ```

Never instantiate this class.

Methods

- getGraphics

  ```
  public abstract Graphics getGraphics()
  ```

  When used with off-screen images, this will return a Graphics object that can be used to draw onto the Image. Will throw a ClassCastException if used with an Image object that was not created with createImage().

- getHeight

  ```
  public abstract int getHeight(ImageObserver observer)
  ```

  Returns the height of the image, or -1 if the image is not yet ready (i.e., it is still loading over the net).

- getProperty

  ```
  public abstract Object getProperty(String name,
                                     ImageObserver observer)
  ```

  Returns an image property given the property's name or UndefinedProperty object if the property is not defined in this image. If the image is not yet ready, getProperty() will return null.

- getSource

  ```
  public abstract ImageProducer getSource()
  ```

  Returns the ImageProducer source object.

- getWidth

  ```
  public abstract int getWidth(ImageObserver observer)
  ```

  Returns the width of the image, or -1 if the image is not yet ready (i.e., it is still loading over the net).

Class java.awt.Insets

java.awt.Insets → java.lang.Object

```
public class Insets
extends Object
```

Container insets. Used to specify a border within the container in which components should not be laid out.

Variables

- bottom

    ```
    public int bottom
    ```

    Bottom inset.

- left

    ```
    public int left
    ```

    Left inset.

- right

    ```
    public int right
    ```

    Right inset.

- top

    ```
    public int top
    ```

    Top inset.

Constructors

- Insets

    ```
    public Insets(int top,
                  int left,
                  int bottom,
                  int right)
    ```

    Constructs inset using the specified top, bottom, left, and right.

Methods

- Methods overridden from superclass

    ```
    toString()
    ```

Class java.awt.Label

java.awt.Label → java.awt.Component → java.lang.Object

```
public class Label
extends Component
```

A static text component.

Variables

- CENTER

  ```
  public final static int CENTER
  ```

  Alignment ID for center alignment.

- LEFT

  ```
  public final static int LEFT
  ```

  Alignment ID for left alignment.

- RIGHT

  ```
  public final static int RIGHT
  ```

  Alignment ID for right alignment.

Constructors

- Label

  ```
  public Label()
  ```

  Constructs label component with empty label text.

- Label

  ```
  public Label(String label)
  ```

  Constructs label component with specified label text.

- Label

  ```
  public Label(String label,
               int alignment)
  ```

  Constructs Label component with specified label text and alignment ID.

Methods

- getAlignment

  ```
  public int getAlignment()
  ```

  Returns the label text alignment.

- getText

  ```
  public String getText()
  ```

  Returns the label text.

- setAlignment

  ```
  public void setAlignment(int alignment)
  ```

  Sets the label text alignment.

- setText

  ```
  public void setText(String label)
  ```

  Sets the label text.

- Methods overridden from superclass

  ```
  addNotify(), paramString()
  ```

Interface java.awt.LayoutManager

```
public interface LayoutManager
```

LayoutManager is implemented by classes that are used by containers to lay out their components.

Methods

- addLayoutComponent

  ```
  public abstract void addLayoutComponent(String name,
                                          Component comp)
  ```

  Called by a container to add the specified component to the layout using the specified name. Some classes (such as BorderLayout) use the name string to indicate where the component should be placed.

- layoutContainer

  ```
  public abstract void layoutContainer(Container parent)
  ```

  Called by a container to lay out its components.

- minimumLayoutSize

  ```
  public abstract Dimension minimumLayoutSize(Container parent)
  ```

  Called by a container to calculate and return the dimensions of the minimum size for the specified container in order for it to fit the container's components.

- preferredLayoutSize

  ```
  public abstract Dimension preferredLayoutSize(Container parent)
  ```

Called by a container to calculate and return the dimensions of the preferred size for the specified container in order for it to fit the container's components.

- removeLayoutComponent

```
public abstract void removeLayoutComponent(Component comp)
```

Called by a container to remove the specified component from the layout.

Class java.awt.List

java.awt.List → java.awt.Component → java.lang.Object

```
public class List
extends Component
```

A scrolling text list component. Using list with a visible row count of 0 will produce best results when used as the center item of a container that uses the BorderLayout. In this case, it will size to the dimension of its container, which is useful when you want to create a TextArea that fills an applet's display area, regardless of the size of the applet. Some layout managers, such as FlowLayout, may produce unsatisfactory results when attempting to lay out lists with visible rows counts of 0.

Constructors

- List

```
public List()
```

Default constructor for empty list with 0 visible rows, which means use the size of the container.

- List

```
public List(int rows,
            boolean multipleSelections)
```

Constructs new scrolling list with the specified number of visible rows and with multiple selections enabled to the specified state.

Methods

- addItem

```
public synchronized void addItem(String item)
```

Adds the specified item to the end of the list.

- allowsMultipleSelections

  ```
  public boolean allowsMultipleSelections()
  ```

  Returns true if multiple selections are enabled.

- clear

  ```
  public synchronized void clear()
  ```

  Clears the list of items.

- countItems

  ```
  public int countItems()
  ```

  Returns the number of list items.

- delItem

  ```
  public synchronized void delItem(int position)
  ```

  Deletes item at specified position from the list.

- delItems

  ```
  public synchronized void delItems(int start,
                                    int end)
  ```

  Deletes items from specified start and end positions from the list.

- deselect

  ```
  public synchronized void deselect(int index)
  ```

  Deselects item at specified list index.

- getItem

  ```
  public String getItem(int index)
  ```

  Returns item at specified list index.

- getRows

  ```
  public int getRows()
  ```

  Returns number of visible rows in this list. This is not the same as the number of items in the list.

- getSelectedIndex

  ```
  public synchronized int getSelectedIndex()
  ```

  Returns the index of the selected item on the list or -1 for no selection or multiple selections.

- getSelectedIndexes

  ```
  public synchronized int[] getSelectedIndexes()
  ```

  Returns an array containing the indexes of the selected list items.

- getSelectedItem

  ```
  public synchronized String getSelectedItem()
  ```

  Returns the item string of the selected item or null for no selection or if there are multiple selections.

- getSelectedItems

  ```
  public synchronized String[] getSelectedItems()
  ```

  Returns an array containing the item strings of the selected list items.

- getVisibleIndex

  ```
  public int getVisibleIndex()
  ```

  Returns the index of the last item made visible by makeVisible().

- isSelected

  ```
  public synchronized boolean isSelected(int index)
  ```

  Returns true if the list item at the specified index has been selected.

- makeVisible

  ```
  public void makeVisible(int index)
  ```

  Makes the item at the specified index visible, scrolling the list if necessary.

- minimumSize

  ```
  public Dimension minimumSize(int rows)
  ```

  Returns the minimum size needed to display the specified number of rows.

- minimumSize

  ```
  public Dimension minimumSize()
  ```

  Returns the minimum size needed for the list.

- preferredSize

  ```
  public Dimension preferredSize(int rows)
  ```

  Returns the preferred size needed to display the specified number of rows.

- preferredSize

```
public Dimension preferredSize()
```

Returns the preferred size needed for the list.

- select

```
public synchronized void select(int index)
```

Selects item at the specified index.

- setMultipleSelections

```
public void setMultipleSelections(boolean v)
```

Enables or disables multiple selections.

- Methods overridden from superclass

```
addNotify(), paramString()
```

Class java.awt.MediaTracker

java.awt.MediaTracker → java.lang.Object

- public class MediaTracker

  extends Object

  The MediaTracker simplifies the usage of asynchronously loaded media objects such as images. A MediaTracker object is created and attached to a component that wants to make use of images (or other supported media objects). Images that the component is going to want to use are assigned (by you) an ID number and added to the MediaTracker, which provides several methods for obtaining information about the image. More than one image can be assigned the same ID number, in which case the images form an image group, all of which must be loaded for some action to proceed.

  The most important functions that the MediaTracker method provides are the checkID() and waitForID() methods. The checkID() method provides a simple true or false answer to the question whether all the images in a given group are ready. The waitForID() method is perhaps the most important method in the class, and also the one that must be used with the most care. This method will block the current thread until the images associated with the specified ID are loaded. For this reason, this method must be called only from a thread that you create, and not from within your init() or start() methods, and especially not within your paint() method. This method can take a very long time to return, for example, in the case of large images being loaded over slow net connections.

Constructors

- MediaTracker

```
public MediaTracker(Component comp)
```

Creates a MediaTracker to track images for a given component.

Methods

- addImage

```
public void addImage(Image image,
                     int id)
```

Adds the specified image to the image group indicated by the specified ID. The ID code indicates the order in which images will be loaded; lower IDs are loaded before higher ones. You can assign the same ID to several images, in which case they will all need to be loaded for the image group to be considered fully loaded.

- addImage

```
public synchronized void addImage(Image image,
                                  int id,
                                  int w,
                                  int h)
```

Performs the same operation as the previous method, but is used to load a scaled version of the image. Each scaled version of an image is considered a different image by the MediaTracker (as well as by drawImage()). If, when you later go to draw an image, you do so at a different scale than you specified when calling this method, the image may have to be reloaded, thus losing any benefits of using the MediaTracker. Remember to call addImage() for all scaled versions of an image that you intend to use.

- checkAll

```
public boolean checkAll()
```

Checks to see if all images that have been added to the MediaTracker either have been loaded or have encountered errors that halted the image-loading process. This method does not initiate any image loading that is not already in progress.

- checkAll

```
public synchronized boolean checkAll(boolean load)
```

The same as the previous method, but allows you to pass a boolean value which, if true, initiates image loading if necessary. This method will not wait for images to complete loading before returning.

- checkID

```
public boolean checkID(int id)
```

Checks to see if images that have been added to the MediaTracker with the specified ID code either have been loaded or have encountered errors that halted the image-loading process. This method does not initiate any image loading that is not already in progress.

- checkID

```
public synchronized boolean checkID(int id,

                                    boolean load)
```

The same as the previous method, but allows you to also pass a boolean value that, if true, initiates asynchronous image loading if necessary. This method will not wait for images to complete loading before returning.

- isErrorAny

```
public synchronized boolean isErrorAny()
```

Returns true if an error was encountered while loading any of the images that have been added to the MediaTracker.

- isErrorID

```
public synchronized boolean isErrorID(int id)
```

Returns true if an error was encountered while loading any of the images that have been added to the MediaTracker with the specified ID code.

- waitForAll

```
public synchronized void waitForAll() throws InterruptedException
```

Blocks the currently executing thread until all images that have been added to the MediaTracker either have been loaded or have encountered errors that halted the image-loading process. Do not call this method from a paint() method or other system-called method or you risk blocking a system thread such as the Screen Updater.

- waitForID

```
public synchronized void waitForID(int id) throws InterruptedException
```

Blocks the currently executing thread until all images that have been added to the MediaTracker with the specified ID code either have been loaded or have encountered errors that halted the image loading process. Do not call this method from a paint() method or other system-called method or you risk blocking a system thread such as the Screen Updater.

Class java.awt.Menu

java.awt.Menu → java.awt.MenuItem → java.awt.MenuComponent →
java.lang.Object

```
public class Menu
extends MenuItem
implements MenuContainer
```

Menu are collections of MenuItems and are contained in MenuBars. Menus can be specified to be able to be torn off, if the platform supports tear-off menus, which means that the menu becomes a windoid that remains on-screen until an item is selected from it. The default for new menus is for them not to be able to be torn off.

Constructors

- Menu

```
public Menu(String label)
```

Constructs menu with the specified label.

- Menu

```
public Menu(String label,
            boolean tearOff)
```

Constructs a new menu with the specified label. If specified, the menu will be able to be torn off.

Methods

- add

    ```
    public synchronized MenuItem add(MenuItem mi)
    ```

    Adds MenuItem to this menu.

- add

    ```
    public void add(String label)
    ```

    Creates a new MenuItem with the specified label and adds it to this menu.

- addSeparator

    ```
    public void addSeparator()
    ```

    Adds a separator line to the end of the menu.

- countItems

    ```
    public int countItems()
    ```

    Returns the number of MenuItems in this menu.

- getItem

    ```
    public MenuItem getItem(int index)
    ```

    Returns the MenuItem at the specified index.

- isTearOff

    ```
    public boolean isTearOff()
    ```

    Returns true if this menu can be torn off.

- remove

    ```
    public synchronized void remove(int index)
    ```

    Deletes the MenuItem at the specified index.

- remove

    ```
    public synchronized void remove(MenuComponent item)
    ```

    Deletes the specified MenuItem (MenuComponent subclass).

- Methods overridden from superclass

    ```
    addNotify(), paramString(), removeNotify()
    ```

Class java.awt.MenuBar

java.awt.MenuBar → java.awt.MenuComponent → java.lang.Object

```
public class MenuBar
extends MenuComponent
implements MenuContainer
```

MenuBars are attached to frames. A MenuBar object will reference a number of Menu objects, each of which will reference a number of MenuItem objects.

Constructors

- MenuBar

```
public MenuBar()
```

Default constructor.

Methods

- add

```
public synchronized Menu add(Menu m)
```

Adds specified menu to this menu bar. Returns the same menu that it is passed.

- countMenus

```
public int countMenus()
```

Returns the number of menus on the menu bar.

- getHelpMenu

```
public Menu getHelpMenu()
```

Returns the menu bar's help menu.

- getMenu

```
public Menu getMenu(int i)
```

Returns the menu at the specified index.

- remove

    ```
    public synchronized void remove(int index)
    ```

    Removes the menu at the specified index.

- remove

    ```
    public synchronized void remove(MenuComponent m)
    ```

    Removes the specified menu.

- setHelpMenu

    ```
    public synchronized void setHelpMenu(Menu m)
    ```

    Makes the specified menu the menu bar help menu.

- Methods overridden from superclass

    ```
    addNotify(), removeNotify()
    ```

Class java.awt.MenuComponent

java.awt.MenuComponent → java.lang.Object

```
public class MenuComponent
extends Object
```

MenuComponent is the base class for all the Menu classes (MenuBar, Menu, MenuItem). MenuComponent is not a subclass of component, so it duplicates some of the methods present in the component class.

Constructors

- MenuComponent

    ```
    public MenuComponent()
    ```

    Default constructor.

Methods

- getFont

    ```
    public Font getFont()
    ```

    Returns the MenuComponent font.

- getParent

    ```
    public MenuContainer getParent()
    ```

    Returns the MenuContainer containing this MenuComponent.

- postEvent

  ```
  public void postEvent(Event evt)
  ```

  Posts the specified event to the MenuComponent. This is not an override of the postEvent method in component since the MenuComponent and component are unrelated.

- setFont

  ```
  public void setFont(Font f)
  ```

  Sets the MenuComponent font.

- Methods overridden from superclass

  ```
  getPeer(), paramString(), removeNotify(), toString()
  ```

Interface java.awt.MenuContainer

```
public interface MenuContainer
```

Interface implemented by menu container classes.

Methods

- getFont

  ```
  public abstract Font getFont()
  ```

- postEvent

  ```
  public abstract void postEvent(Event evt)
  ```

- remove

  ```
  public abstract void remove(MenuComponent comp)
  ```

Class java.awt.MenuItem

java.awt.MenuItem → java.awt.MenuComponent → java.lang.Object

```
public class MenuItem
extends MenuComponent
```

MenuItem represents a single string item in a menu.

Constructors

- MenuItem

  ```
  public MenuItem(String label)
  ```

  Constructs MenuItem using the specified string label.

Methods

- disable

  ```
  public void disable()
  ```

  Disables this menu item choice. Item will be grayed out.

- enable

  ```
  public void enable()
  ```

  Enables this menu item choice.

- enable

  ```
  public void enable(boolean cond)
  ```

  Sets the MenuItems enable state to the specified boolean value.

- getLabel

  ```
  public String getLabel()
  ```

  Returns the menu item label.

- isEnabled

  ```
  public boolean isEnabled()
  ```

  Returns true if menu item is enabled.

- setLabel

  ```
  public void setLabel(String label)
  ```

  Sets the menu item label.

- Methods overridden from superclass

  ```
  addNotify(), paramString()
  ```

Class java.awt.Panel

java.awt.Panel → java.awt.Container → java.awt.Component → java.lang.Object

```
public class Panel
    extends Container
```

The Panel class is a subclass of Container that can either be instantiated directly or subclassed in your programs and should be used instead of Container. Newly created panels default to using the FlowLayout.

Constructors

- Panel

```
public Panel()
```

Default constructor.

Methods

- Methods overridden from superclass

```
addNotify()
```

Class java.awt.Point

java.awt.Point → java.lang.Object

```
public class Point
extends Object
```

Used to contain an x, y coordinate.

Variables

- x

```
public int x
```

The x coordinate.

- y

```
public int y
```

The y coordinate.

Constructors

- Point

```
public Point(int x,
             int y)
```

Constructs a point using the specified x and y coordinates.

Methods

- equals

    ```
    public boolean equals(Object obj)
    ```

    Correctly compares this point to the specified object if it is an instance of point.

- move

    ```
    public void move(int x,
                     int y)
    ```

    Sets the point's x and y coordinates to the specified values.

- translate

    ```
    public void translate(int x,
                          int y)
    ```

    Translate the point by adding the x and y values to the current point coordinates.

- Methods overridden from superclass

    ```
    hashCode(), toString()
    ```

Class java.awt.Polygon

java.awt.Polygon → java.lang.Object

```
public class Polygon
extends Object
```

The Polygon class encapsulates two arrays of coordinates—one for the x values of the polygon, and one for the y values.

Variables

- npoints

    ```
    public int npoints
    ```

    The number of points in the polygon.

- xpoints

    ```
    public int xpoints[]
    ```

    An array of x coordinates.

- ypoints

  ```
  public int ypoints[]
  ```

  An array of y coordinates.

Constructors

- Polygon

  ```
  public Polygon()
  ```

  Default constructor for empty polygon.

- Polygon

  ```
  public Polygon(int xpoints[],
                 int ypoints[],
                 int npoints)
  ```

  Constructs a polygon using the array of x coordinates, y coordinates, and number of points.

Methods

- addPoint

  ```
  public void addPoint(int x,
                       int y)
  ```

  Adds a point to the polygon.

Class java.awt.Rectangle

java.awt.Rectangle → java.lang.Object

```
public class Rectangle
extends Object
```

The Rectangle class encapsulates the values to represent a rectangle as well as providing a number of methods for operations that can be performed on rectangles.

Variables

- height

  ```
  public int height
  ```

  Rectangle height.

- width

    ```
    public int width
    ```

    Rectangle width.

- x

    ```
    public int x
    ```

    Rectangle x position.

- y

    ```
    public int y
    ```

    Rectangle y position.

Constructors

- Rectangle

    ```
    public Rectangle()
    ```

    Default constructor for empty rectangle.

- Rectangle

    ```
    public Rectangle(int x,
                     int y,
                     int width,
                     int height)
    ```

    Constructs a rectangle using the specified parameters.

- Rectangle

    ```
    public Rectangle(int width,
                     int height)
    ```

    Constructs a rectangle at 0,0 using the specified width and height.

- Rectangle

    ```
    public Rectangle(Point p,
                     Dimension d)
    ```

    Constructs a rectangle from the specified point and dimension.

- Rectangle

    ```
    public Rectangle(Point p)
    ```

    Constructs a rectangle from the specified point and a height and width of 0.

- Rectangle

  ```
  public Rectangle(Dimension d)
  ```

  Constructs a rectangle at 0,0 using the specified dimension for width and height.

Methods

- add

  ```
  public void add(int x,
                      int y)
  ```

  Expands the rectangle to contain the given x, y coordinate.

- add

  ```
  public void add(Point pt)
  ```

  Expands the rectangle to contain the given point.

- add

  ```
  public void add(Rectangle r)
  ```

  Expands the rectangle to contain the given rectangle.

- equals

  ```
  public boolean equals(Object obj)
  ```

  Correctly compares this rectangle object against another instance of rectangle.

- grow

  ```
  public void grow(int h,
                      int v)
  ```

  Expands the rectangle in the given horizontal and vertical directions.

- inside

  ```
  public boolean inside(int x,
                          int y)
  ```

  Returns true if the specified point lies inside a rectangle.

- intersection

  ```
  public Rectangle intersection(Rectangle r)
  ```

  Returns a new rectangle that is the intersection of this rectangle and the specified rectangle.

- intersects

  ```
  public boolean intersects(Rectangle r)
  ```

  Returns true if this rectangle and the specified rectangle intersect.

- isEmpty

  ```
  public boolean isEmpty()
  ```

  Returns true if the rectangle is empty.

- move

  ```
  public void move(int x,

                   int y)
  ```

  Moves the rectangle to the specified location.

- reshape

  ```
  public void reshape(int x,

                      int y,

                      int width,

                      int height)
  ```

  Reshapes the rectangle to the specified values.

- resize

  ```
  public void resize(int width,

                     int height)
  ```

Sets the width and height of the rectangle.

- translate

  ```
  public void translate(int x,

                        int y)
  ```

  Translates the rectangle by adding the specified values to the current location.

- Union

  ```
  public Rectangle union(Rectangle r)
  ```

  Returns new rectangle that is the union of this rectangle and the specified rectangles.

- Methods overridden from superclass

  ```
  hashCode(), toString()
  ```

Class java.awt.Scrollbar

java.awt.Scrollbar → java.awt.Component → java.lang.Object

```
public class Scrollbar
extends Component
```

A Scrollbar component.

Variables

- HORIZONTAL

  ```
  public final static int HORIZONTAL
  ```

  Orientation ID for horizontal scrollbar.

- VERTICAL

  ```
  public final static int VERTICAL
  ```

  Orientation ID for vertical scrollbar.

Constructors

- Scrollbar

  ```
  public Scrollbar()
  ```

  Default constructor for vertical scrollbar.

- Scrollbar

  ```
  public Scrollbar(int orientation)
  ```

  Constructs new scrollbar with the given orientation ID.

- Scrollbar

  ```
  public Scrollbar(int orientation,
                   int value,
                   int visible,
                   int minimum,
                   int maximum)
  ```

  Constructs new scrollbar with the given orientation ID, current value, visibility per page, and minimum and maximum values.

Methods

- getMaximum

  ```
  public int getMaximum()
  ```

  Returns the maximum scroll value.

- getMinimum

  ```
  public int getMinimum()
  ```

  Returns the minimum scroll value.

- getOrientation

  ```
  public int getOrientation()
  ```

  Returns the orientation ID.

- getValue

  ```
  public int getValue()
  ```

  Returns the current value.

- getVisible

  ```
  public int getVisible()
  ```

  Returns the visible amount of the Scrollbar (amount to increment/decrement by when clicking in the page up/page down area).

- setValue

  ```
  public void setValue(int value)
  ```

  Sets the current value of the Scrollbar.

- setValues

  ```
  public void setValues(int value,
                        int visible,
                        int minimum,
                        int maximum)
  ```

  Sets the Scrollbar to the specified values.

- Methods overridden from superclass

  ```
  addNotify(), paramString()
  ```

Class java.awt.TextArea

java.awt.TextArea → java.awt.TextComponent → java.awt.Component →
java.lang.Object

```
public class TextArea
extends TextComponent
```

A multiline editable text area. Using TextArea with visible rows and
columns of 0 will produce best results when used as the center item of a
container that uses the BorderLayout. In this case, it will size to the dimension of its container, which is useful when you want to create a TextArea
that fills an applet's display area, regardless of the size of the applet. Some
layout managers, such as FlowLayout, may produce unsatisfactory results
when attempting to layout text areas with rows and columns of 0.

Constructors

- TextArea

```
public TextArea()
```

Default constructor for a new empty TextArea. When this constructor is
used, the visible rows and columns are set to 0, which means use the size of
the container.

- TextArea

```
public TextArea(int rows,
                int cols)
```

Constructs new TextArea using the specified rows and columns.

- TextArea

```
public TextArea(String text)
```

Constructs new TextArea and sets initial contents to the specified text.
When this constructor is used, the visible rows and columns are set to 0,
which means use the size of the container.

- TextArea

```
public TextArea(String text,
                int rows,
                int cols)
```

Constructs new TextArea using the specified rows and columns and specified initial text.

Methods

- getColumns

```
public int getColumns()
```

Returns number of columns.

- getRows

```
public int getRows()
```

Returns number of rows.

- insertText

```
public void insertText(String str,
                          int pos)
```

Inserts specified text at the given position.

- minimumSize

```
public Dimension minimumSize(int rows,
                               int cols)
```

Calculates and returns the minimum size of a TextArea given the specified rows and columns.

- minimumSize

```
public Dimension minimumSize()
```

Calculates and returns the minimum size of the TextArea.

- preferredSize

```
public Dimension preferredSize(int rows,
                                 int cols)
```

Calculates and returns the preferred size of a TextArea given the specified rows and columns.

- preferredSize

```
public Dimension preferredSize()
```

Calculates and returns the preferred size of the TextArea.

- replaceText

```
public void replaceText(String str,
                        int start,
                        int end)
```

Replaces text range indicated by start and end position with the given text string.

- Methods overridden from superclass

```
addNotify(), paramString()
```

Class java.awt.TextComponent

java.awt.TextComponent → java.awt.Component → java.lang.Object

```
public class TextComponent
extends Component
```

An editable text component. Use TextArea or TextField instead of this component.

Methods

- getSelectedText

```
public String getSelectedText()
```

Returns the selected text.

- getSelectionEnd

```
public int getSelectionEnd()
```

Returns the end position of the text selection.

- getSelectionStart

```
public int getSelectionStart()
```

Returns the start position of the text selection.

- getText

```
public String getText()
```

Returns the TextComponent text.

- isEditable

      public boolean isEditable()

  Returns true if TextComponent is editable.

- select

      public void select(int selStart,
                                int selEnd)

  Sets the selection to the given start and end positions.

- selectAll

      public void selectAll()

  Selects all the text.

- setEditable

      public void setEditable(boolean t)

  Enables or disables text editing.

- setText

      public void setText(String t)

  Sets the text of the TextComponent.

- Methods overridden from superclass

      paramString(),removeNotify()

Class java.awt.TextField

java.awt.TextField → java.awt.TextComponent → java.awt.Component →
java.lang.Object

      public class TextField
      extends TextComponent

An editable line of text. If created without specifying a column width, the
text field will attempt to size to the width of its container.

Constructors

- TextField

      public TextField()

  Default constructor for text field with a column count of 0, meaning that it
  will attempt to size to the width of its container.

- TextField

  ```
  public TextField(int cols)
  ```

Constructs new TextField with the specified columns.

- TextField

  ```
  public TextField(String text)
  ```

Constructs new TextField and sets initial contents to the specified text. The text field will have a column count of 0, meaning that it will attempt to size to the width of its container.

- TextField

  ```
  public TextField(String text,
                        int cols)
  ```

Constructs new TextField with the specified columns and sets initial contents to the specified text.

Methods

- echoCharIsSet

  ```
  public boolean echoCharIsSet()
  ```

Returns true if this TextField has a character set for echoing. Typically used for entering passwords.

- getColumns

  ```
  public int getColumns()
  ```

Returns the number of columns.

- getEchoChar

  ```
  public char getEchoChar()
  ```

Returns the character to be used for echoing.

- minimumSize

  ```
  public Dimension minimumSize(int cols)
  ```

Calculates and returns the minimum size of a TextField given the specified columns.

- minimumSize

  ```
  public Dimension minimumSize()
  ```

Calculates and returns the minimum size of this TextField.

- preferredSize

    ```
    public Dimension preferredSize(int cols)
    ```

    Calculates and returns the preferred size of a TextField given the specified columns.

- preferredSize

    ```
    public Dimension preferredSize()
    ```

    Calculates and returns the preferred size of this TextField.

- setEchoCharacter

    ```
    public void setEchoCharacter(char c)
    ```

    Sets the echo character for this TextField for entering characters such as passwords that shouldn't be visible on-screen. Call with a value of 0 to clear the echo character.

- Methods overridden from superclass

    ```
    addNotify(), paramString()
    ```

Class java.awt.Toolkit

java.awt.Toolkit → java.lang.Object

```
public class Toolkit
extends Object
```

The AWT toolkit is the core of the system that the AWT uses to talk with native windowing systems. The class contains a number of methods for creating "peers," which we don't include in this abridged version of the class reference. If you need to get a reference to the Toolkit object, call the Toolkit static method getDefaultToolkit() and call the methods in that object. The main reasons to use this class are to get a list of the available fonts, find the screen dimensions, or determine the screen resolution.

Constructors

- Toolkit

    ```
    public Toolkit()
    ```

    Never instantiate this class yourself.

Methods

- createImage

  ```
  public abstract Image createImage(ImageProducer producer)
  ```

  Returns a new Image object that uses the specified producer.

- getDefaultToolkit

  ```
  public static synchronized Toolkit getDefaultToolkit()
  ```

  Returns the default toolkit for dealing with this platform.

- getFontList

  ```
  public abstract String[] getFontList()
  ```

  Returns an array containing the names of the available fonts.

- getScreenResolution

  ```
  public abstract int getScreenResolution()
  ```

  Returns the screen resolution as dots-per-inch.

- getScreenSize

  ```
  public abstract Dimension getScreenSize()
  ```

  Gets the screen bounds.

- sync

  ```
  public abstract void sync()
  ```

  Syncs the graphics state, which is useful when doing animation.

- Methods for creating component peers

  ```
  createButton(), createCanvas(), createCheckbox(),
  createCheckboxMenuItem(), createChoice(), createDialog(),
  createFileDialog(), createFrame(), createLabel(), createList(),
  createMenu(), createMenuBar(), createMenuItem(), createPanel(),
  createScrollbar(), createTextArea(), createTextField(), createWindow()
  ```

  Called by AWT classes—do not call directly yourself.

Class java.awt.Window

java.awt.Window → java.awt.Container → java.awt.Component →
java.lang.Object

```
public class Window
extends Container
```

A Window is a top-level window with no borders and no menu bar. It could be used to implement a pop-up menu. Windows are modal and block events to other components when they are visible. New Windows are initially invisible and have their default layout set to BorderLayout.

Constructors

- Window

```
public Window(Frame parent)
```

Constructs a new Window.

Methods

- dispose

```
public synchronized void dispose()
```

Releases any held resources that are used for the window. These may be system resources held by the window's peer that are outside the control of the garbage collector.

- getToolkit

```
public Toolkit getToolkit()
```

```
Returns the toolkit of this window.
```

- pack

```
public synchronized void pack()
```

Packs the components of the Window by attempting to resize the window and its subcomponents to their preferred size and laying them out.

- show

```
public synchronized void show()
```

Shows the Window and brings it to the front.

- toBack

```
public void toBack()
```

Sends the window to the back.

- toFront

```
public void toFront()
```

Brings the window to the front.

- Methods overridden from superclass

```
addNotify()
```

PACKAGE

JAVA.AWT.IMAGE

The java.awt.image package contains the classes and interfaces for the manipulation of pixel images. Most of these classes will be used only in image processing applications, but we've found enough occasions to use them that we feel they merit being documented in their own appendix.

- ColorModel
- CropImageFilter
- DirectColorModel
- FilteredImageSource
- ImageConsumer
- ImageFilter
- ImageObserver
- ImageProducer
- IndexColorModel
- MemoryImageSource
- RGBImageFilter

Class java.awt.image.ColorModel

- java.awt.image.ColorModel → java.lang.Object

  ```
  public class ColorModel
  extends Object
  ```

  An abstract base class used to translate a device-dependent pixel value to its component channel values (alpha, red, green, blue) or into a device-independent pixel value. The device-independent pixel value is represented as a 32-bit int value formatted as 0xAARRGGBB. One byte each is for the alpha, red, green, and blue channels.

Variables

- pixel_bits

  ```
  protected int pixel_bits
  ```

  Bits per pixel.

Constructors

- ColorModel

  ```
  public ColorModel(int bits)
  ```

  Constructs ColorModel for the specified bits per pixel.

Methods

- getAlpha

  ```
  public abstract int getAlpha(int pixel)
  ```

  Abstract method that returns the alpha channel value of the given pixel.

- getBlue

  ```
  public abstract int getBlue(int pixel)
  ```

  Abstract method that returns the blue channel value of the given pixel.

- getGreen

  ```
  public abstract int getGreen(int pixel)
  ```

  Abstract method that returns the green channel value of the given pixel.

- getPixelSize

  ```
  public int getPixelSize()
  ```

  Returns the bits per pixel of this ColorModel.

- getRed

  ```
  public abstract int getRed(int pixel)
  ```

  Abstract method that returns the red channel value of the given pixel.

- getRGB

  ```
  public int getRGB(int pixel)
  ```

  Returns the 32-bit device-independent pixel value (0xAARRGGBB) of the pixel in the default RGB color model.

- getRGBdefault

  ```
  public static ColorModel getRGBdefault()
  ```

  Returns the default ColorModel for integer RGB values.

Class java.awt. image.CropImageFilter

- java.awt.image.CropImageFilter → java.awt.image.ImageFilter → java.lang.Object

  ```
  public class CropImageFilter

  extends ImageFilter
  ```

  Subclass of ImageFilter for use with a FilteredImageSource object to extract a given rectangular region from the output of an ImageProducer. A common use of this filter and FilteredImageSource is to create a series of animation frames from a large GIF image. This is often done because it is faster to pull one large image over the net than a number of small ones.

  CropImageFilter adds a property called "croprect" that is stored as an instance of java.awt.Rectangle. You can retrieve this property from an Image object by calling its getProperty() method with the string "croprect."

  See ImageFilter class and ImageConsumer interface in this package for a description of implemented methods.

Constructors

- CropImageFilter

  ```
  public CropImageFilter(int x,
                         int y,
                         int w,
                         int h)
  ```

Uses the specified rectangle to construct an image source (ImageProducer) from an existing image.

Methods

- Methods overridden from superclass

  setDimensions(), setPixels(), setProperties()

Class java.awt. image.DirectColorModel

- java.awt.image.DirectColorModel → java.awt.image.ColorModel → java.lang.Object

  ```
  public class DirectColorModel
  extends ColorModel
  ```

The DirectColorModel class is used to translate a device-dependent pixel value to its component channel values (alpha, red, green, blue) or into a device-independent pixel value. The device-dependent value will have the color values encoded within the pixel value and is usually a 16-, 24-, or 32-bit value. The device independent pixel value is represented as a 32-bit int value formatted as 0xAARRGGBB. One byte each is for the alpha, red, green, and blue channels. See ColorModel class in this package for a description of available methods.

When instantiating DirectColorModel, you must specify the bit mask for each color component within the pixel value.

Constructors

- DirectColorModel

  ```
  public DirectColorModel(int bits,

                          int rmask,
                          int gmask,
                          int bmask)
  ```

  Constructs a DirectColorModel using the specified bits per pixel, and the contiguous bit masks for each color channel component of the pixel value. When this version of the constructor is used, the alpha channel is ignored.

- DirectColorModel

  ```
  public DirectColorModel(int bits,

                          int rmask,
  ```

```
int gmask,
int bmask,
int amask)
```

Constructs a DirectColorModel using the specified bits per pixel, and the contiguous bit masks for each color channel component of the pixel value.

Methods

• getAlphaMask

```
public int getAlphaMask()
```

Returns the mask indicating which bits in a pixel contain the alpha transparency component.

• getBlueMask

```
public int getBlueMask()
```

Returns the mask indicating which bits in a pixel contain the blue color component.

• getGreenMask

```
public int getGreenMask()
```

Returns the mask indicating which bits in a pixel contain the green color component.

• getRedMask

```
public int getRedMask()
```

Returns the mask indicating which bits in a pixel contain the red color component.

• Methods overriden from super class

```
getAlpha(), getBlue(), getGreen(), getRed()
```

Class java.awt.image. FilteredImageSource

• java.awt.FilteredImageSource → java.lang.Object

```
public class FilteredImageSource
extends Object
implements ImageProducer
```

FilteredImageSource takes the output of an existing ImageProducer and filters it using a specified ImageFilter. Refer to ImageFilter classes such as CropImageFilter and RGBImageFilter for ready-made image processing filters, and refer to their source for more details on creating your own filters.

Constructors

- FilteredImageSource

```
public FilteredImageSource(ImageProducer orig,
                                  ImageFilter imgf)
```

Filters the specified ImageProducer image source with the given ImageFilter.

Methods

- Methods implemented from interface

```
addConsumer(), isConsumer(), removeConsumer(),
requestTopDownLeftRightResend(), startProduction()
```

Interface java.awt.
image.ImageConsumer

```
public interface ImageConsumer
```

Objects that implement ImageConsumer can request that an image source (ImageProducer) object deliver the pixels for an image to them. The ImageFilter classes are the main examples of classes that implement ImageConsumer. Usually you will subclass one of those rather than creating your own class that implements the ImageConsumer interface.

Variables

- COMPLETESCANLINES

```
public final static int COMPLETESCANLINES
```

Hint flag (sent by producer to consumer via setHints()) to indicate that pixels will be delivered in the form of complete scan lines.

- IMAGEERROR

```
public final static int IMAGEERROR
```

Status code (sent by producer to consumer via imageComplete()) that indicates that error occurred in the producer.

- RANDOMPIXELORDER

  ```
  public final static int RANDOMPIXELORDER
  ```

  Hint flag (sent by producer to consumer via setHints()) to indicate that pixels will be delivered in a random order. This is the default unless otherwise indicated.

- SINGLEFRAME

  ```
  public final static int SINGLEFRAME
  ```

  Hint flag (sent by producer to consumer via setHints()) to indicate that the image contains a single static image. After the image is delivered, STATICIMAGEDONE will be sent to imageComplete() and no more pixels will be delivered.

- SINGLEFRAMEDONE

  ```
  public final static int SINGLEFRAMEDONE
  ```

  Status code (sent by producer to consumer via imageComplete()) that a single frame of a multiple frame image sequence has been delivered. More frames will be delivered.

- SINGLEPASS

  ```
  public final static int SINGLEPASS
  ```

  Hint flag (sent by producer to consumer via setHints()) to indicate that pixels will be delivered only once via the setPixels call. If this flag is not set, it is possible that the same pixel (or scanline of pixels) could be sent several times. In future releases, interlaced images and progressive JPEGs will be supported, and checking for the SINGLEPASS flag will become more important.

- STATICIMAGEDONE

  ```
  public final static int STATICIMAGEDONE
  ```

  Status code (sent by producer to consumer via imageComplete()) that the current image has finished being delivered and no more frames are on the way.

- TOPDOWNLEFTRIGHT

  ```
  public final static int TOPDOWNLEFTRIGHT
  ```

  Hint flag (sent by producer to consumer via setHints()) to indicate that pixels are delivered starting from the top-left corner of the image and continuing across the image until each scanline row is completed, then moving down to the next scanline row, until all pixels have been delivered.

Methods

- imageComplete

  ```
  public abstract void imageComplete(int status)
  ```

  Called by producer to indicate that the current image is complete. The status code will indicate whether an image occurred during delivery, if this is the last frame, or if there are more frames on the way. The ImageConsumer needs to remove itself from the producer with a call to the producer's removeConsumer() method; otherwise, the image might be resent.

- setColorModel

  ```
  public abstract void setColorModel(ColorModel model)
  ```

  Called by producer to indicate the default ColorModel object for the pixels delivered via the setPixels() method. A different ColorModel may be sent to the setPixels() method than the one indicated here.

- setDimensions

  ```
  public abstract void setDimensions(int width,
                                     int height)
  ```

  Called by the producer with the size of the source image.

- setHints

  ```
  public abstract void setHints(int hintflags)
  ```

  Called by the producer before it calls setPixels to deliver information in the form of hint flags relevant to the subsequently delivered pixel information. The hint flags are sent as a value constructed by combining flags with the | (or) operator such as COMPLETESCANLINES | SINGLEFRAME.

- setPixels

  ```
  public abstract void setPixels(int x,
                                 int y,
                                 int w,
                                 int h,
                                 ColorModel model,
                                 byte pixels[],
                                 int off,
                                 int scansize)
  ```

  Called by the producer to deliver pixel bytes (8-bit values—usually index colors) to the consumer. The x and y coordinates specify the position of the delivered pixels within the image. The w and h parameters represent the width and height of the delivered pixels. The pixels byte array contains the delivered pixels and the offset index indicates the first byte of the delivered pixels within the array. The scansize indicates the number of bytes per scan-line (i.e., the number of bytes to skip when parsing through the pixel array to get to the same horizontal position in the next vertical line). This method is called repeatedly until all the pixels for an image have been delivered.

- setPixels

  ```
  public abstract void setPixels(int x,
                                 int y,
                                 int w,
                                 int h,
                                 ColorModel model,
                                 int pixels[],
                                 int off,
                                 int scansize)
  ```

  Called by the producer to deliver pixel values (32-bit ints) to the consumer. The x and y coordinates specify the position of the delivered pixels within the image. The w and h parameters represent the width and height of the delivered pixels. The pixels int array contains the delivered pixels and the offset index indicates the first int of the delivered pixels within the array. The scansize indicates the number of ints per scanline (i.e., the number of ints to skip when parsing through the pixel array to get to the same horizontal position in the next vertical line). This method is called repeatedly until all the pixels for an image have been delivered.

- setProperties

  ```
  public abstract void setProperties(Hashtable props)
  ```

  Called by the producer to allow the consumer to add properties to the properties hashtable and to allow the consumer to look at any already set properties.

Class java.awt.image.ImageFilter

- java.awt.image.ImageFilter → java.lang.Object

  ```
  public class ImageFilter
  extends Object
  implements ImageConsumer
  ```

Base filter class for use with the FilteredImageSource producer in order to process the pixels from an image producer. This class implements the methods from the ImageConsumer interface; you should look at the description of that interface for more information regarding the methods such as imageComplete() or setPixels() that are implemented from it.

Variables

* consumer

```
protected ImageConsumer consumer
```

Set by getFilterInstance with the consumer that will receive the pixels filtered by the instance of this class.

Constructors

* ImageFilter

```
public ImageFilter()
```

Methods

* getFilterInstance

```
public ImageFilter getFilterInstance(ImageConsumer ic)
```

Returns a unique instance of this class assigned to perform the filtering operation for the specified consumer.

* Methods implemented from interface

```
imageComplete(), setColorModel(), setDimensions(), setHints(),
setPixels(), setProperties()
```

Interface java.awt. image.ImageObserver

```
public interface ImageObserver
```

The ImageObserver class is implemented by classes that want to be informed of the status on images that are being asynchronously loaded or are otherwise not yet ready to be displayed. Many of the AWT class methods, such as the Graphics method drawImage, that take an Image object as a parameter also take as a second parameter an object that implements ImageObserver, so that if the image is not yet ready at the time the method is called, the ImageObserver can be notified when the image is ready and the method can be called again to perform the operation. The interface specifies a single method that must be implemented by these classes called imageUpdate() as well as constants for the flags that are sent to it to indicate the status of the observed image. The Component class implements ImageObserver, so often you will just need to override that class's imageUpdate method rather than create your own class that implements ImageObserver.

Variables

- ALLBITS

    ```
    public final static int ALLBITS
    ```

    Info flag (sent to observer via imageUpdate()) to indicate that the specified image is ready to be drawn or the last frame in a sequence has been delivered. The dimension and position parameters sent to imageUpdate() are undefined at this point, and the action image dimensions (i.e., obtained via getWidth()) should instead be used.

- ERROR

    ```
    public final static int ERROR
    ```

    Info flag (sent to observer via imageUpdate()) to indicate that the image construction and/or loading process has failed and the image is unusable.

- FRAMEBITS

    ```
    public final static int FRAMEBITS
    ```

    Info flag (sent to observer via imageUpdate()) to indicate that the image object contains the complete frame of a frame sequence and is ready to be drawn. The dimension and position parameters sent to imageUpdate() are undefined at this point, and the action image dimensions (i.e., obtained via getWidth()) should instead be used.

- HEIGHT

    ```
    public final static int HEIGHT
    ```

    Info flag (sent to observer via imageUpdate()) to indicate that the height of the image is available in the height parameter to the imageUpdate() method.

- PROPERTIES

    ```
    public final static int PROPERTIES
    ```

    Info flag (sent to observer via imageUpdate()) to indicate that the properties of the image are available by calling the getProperty() method of the specified image object.

- SOMEBITS

  ```
  public final static int SOMEBITS
  ```

  Info flag (sent to observer via imageUpdate()) to indicate that enough pixels are available to draw a partial or scaled representation of the specified image using the given position and dimensions as the parameters to drawImage().

- WIDTH

  ```
  public final static int WIDTH
  ```

  Info flag (sent to observer via imageUpdate()) to indicate that the height of the image is available in the height parameter to the imageUpdate() method.

Methods

- imageUpdate

  ```
  public abstract boolean imageUpdate(Image img,
                                      int infoflags,
                                      int x,
                                      int y,
                                      int width,
                                      int height)
  ```

  Called by the AWT to notify the observer that additional information about an image has become available. The method is called with a reference to the image that the supplied information pertains to and an information flags value constructed by combining flags with the | (or) operator such as WIDTH | HEIGHT. Depending on the specified flags, the value passed in the position and dimension parameters can be used to obtain specific information about an image or to draw a partial representation of the image. If no more information is required about the image, this method should return false; otherwise, it will continue to be called until no more information about the image is available (i.e., all the bits of the image have been delivered or an error occurs).

Interface java.awt. image.ImageProducer

```
public interface ImageProducer
```

ImageProducer is implemented by objects that can deliver pixel data to an ImageConsumer. The AWT image classes use the naming convention

ImageSource to refer to classes that implement ImageProducer, but there is no abstract ImageSource class that implements ImageProducer in the same way that there is an abstract ImageFilter class that implements ImageConsumer. This is important to know because the Sun documentation often refers to image sources when it means objects that implement ImageProducer, and you might be led to believe that there is an ImageSource class. An ImageProducer can be obtained from an existing Image object using the Image's getSource() method.

Methods

- addConsumer

  ```
  public abstract void addConsumer(ImageConsumer ic)
  ```

  Registers the specified consumer as interested in receiving pixel data from the producer. Pixel data is delivered to the consumer using the consumer's SetPixels() method. Some producers, such as the MemoryImageSource, may send the consumer the pixel data immediately, while others will wait for a subsequent call to startProduction. Consumers should be sure to call the producer's removeConsumer() method after the pixels have been delivered; otherwise, a second set of pixels might be delivered in response to the startProduction() call.

- isConsumer

  ```
  public abstract boolean isConsumer(ImageConsumer ic)
  ```

  Returns true if the specifed consumer is registered with this producer.

- removeConsumer

  ```
  public abstract void removeConsumer(ImageConsumer ic)
  ```

  If the specified consumer is a target of this producer, this method removes the consumer from the internal consumer list maintained by this producer and discontinues pixel delivery as soon as possible.

- requestTopDownLeftRightResend

  ```
  public abstract void requestTopDownLeftRightResend(ImageConsumer ic)
  ```

  Requests that the pixels be delivered in TOPDOWNLEFTRIGHT order if possible. Ignored by the consumer if this format is unsupported or, as in the case of the MemoryImageSource, the data is always delivered in this format.

- startProduction

```
public abstract void startProduction(ImageConsumer ic)
```

Adds the consumer if not already added, and attempts to deliver the pixel data as soon as possible. Refer to the description of addConsumer() for information on the delivery of pixels, etc.

Class java.awt. image.IndexColorModel

- java.awt.image.indexColorModel → java.awt.image.ColorModel → java.lang.Object

```
public class IndexColorModel
extends ColorModel
```

The IndexColorModel is used to implement color lookup tables of up to 256 colors so that pixel values can be mapped to actual color values. Each pixel in an image that uses the IndexColorModel is an index value. IndexColorModels are typically used to store 8-bit color palettes that hold 256 colors. In addition to alpha channels, you can specify an index value for the transparency color.

Constructors

- IndexColorModel

```
public IndexColorModel(int bits,
                       int size,
                       byte r[],
                       byte g[],
                       byte b[])
```

Constructs an IndexColorModel using the given bits per pixel and arrays of red, green, and blue values, each of which has at least the number of entries specified in the size parameter.

- IndexColorModel

```
public IndexColorModel(int bits,
                       int size,
                       byte r[],
                       byte g[],
```

```
                        byte b[],

                        int trans)
```

Constructs an IndexColorModel using the given bits per pixel and arrays of red, green, and blue values, each of which has at least the number of entries specified in the size parameter. The value specified in the transparency parameter is used to indicate the index value used for the transparent color.

- IndexColorModel

```
    public IndexColorModel(int bits,

                           int size,

                           byte r[],

                           byte g[],

                           byte b[],

                           byte a[])
```

Constructs an IndexColorModel using the given bits per pixel and arrays of red, green, blue, and alpha values, each of which has at least the number of entries specified in the size parameter. The value specified in the transparency parameter is used to indicate the index value used for the transparent color.

- IndexColorModel

```
    public IndexColorModel(int bits,

                           int size,

                           byte cmap[],

                           int start,

                           boolean hasalpha)
```

Constructs an IndexColorModel using the given bits per pixel and an array of color values. This array is stored as red, green, and blue values or red, green, blue, and alpha values. The first byte in the array is at the array index specified as start, and the next size * 3 (in the case of no alpha channel) or size * 4 (if the alpha channel is included) bytes represent the entries in the color tables of red, green, and blue values, each of which has at least the number of entries specified in the size parameter. The value specified in the transparency parameter is used to indicate the index value used for the transparent color.

- IndexColorModel

```
    public IndexColorModel(int bits,

                           int size,
```

```
                              byte cmap[],

                              int start,

                              boolean hasalpha,

                              int trans)
```

Constructs an IndexColorModel from a single array of packed red, green,
blue, and optional alpha components. The specified transparent index represents a pixel that will be considered entirely transparent regardless of any
alpha value specified for it. The array must have enough values in it to fill
all of the needed component arrays of the specified size.

Methods

- getAlphas

  ```
  public void getAlphas(byte a[])
  ```

  Copies the array of alpha transparency values into the given array. Only the
  initial entries of the array as specified by getMapSize() will be written.

- getBlues

  ```
  public void getBlues(byte b[])
  ```

  Copies the array of blue color components into the given array. Only the
  initial entries of the array as specified by getMapSize() will be written.

- getGreens

  ```
  public void getGreens(byte g[])
  ```

  Copies the array of green color components into the given array. Only the
  initial entries of the array as specified by getMapSize() will be written.

- getMapSize

  ```
  public int getMapSize()
  ```

  Returns the size of the color component arrays in this IndexColorModel.

- getReds

  ```
  public void getReds(byte r[])
  ```

  Copies the array of red color components into the given array. Only the initial entries of the array as specified by getMapSize() will be written.

- getTransparentPixel

  ```
  public int getTransparentPixel()
  ```

  Returns the index of the transparent pixel in this IndexColorModel or -1 if
  there is no transparent pixel.

- setTransparentPixel

  ```
  public void setTransparentPixel(int trans)
  ```

  Sets the index of the pixel to be used to represent transparency

- Methods overridden from superclass

  ```
  getAlpha(), getBlue(), getGreen(), getRed(), getRGB()
  ```

Class java.awt.image. MemoryImageSource

- java.awt.image MemoryImageSource → java.lang.Object

  ```
  public class MemoryImageSource
  extends Object
  implements ImageProducer
  ```

  This class allows you to construct an Image from an array of pixel values. These values can be of any color model. While memory image sources afford a great degree of flexibility in image processing, they can have an adverse impact on memory usage.

  MemoryImageSources are constructed from an array of bytes, for indexed colors, or an arrays of ints, for direct colors. Constructors are passed a width and height of the image contained within the array. An offset index indicates the first array element of the image pixels within the array, and the scansize indicates the number of pixels per scanline (i.e., the number of elements to skip when parsing through the pixel array to get to the same horizontal position in the next vertical line).

- MemoryImageSource

  ```
  public MemoryImageSource(int w,
                           int h,
                           ColorModel cm,
                           byte pix[],
                           int off,
                           int scan)
  ```

  Constructs the image producer using the given width, height, color model, pixel byte array, offset, and scansize.

- MemoryImageSource

```
public MemoryImageSource(int w,

                              int h,

                              ColorModel cm,

                              byte pix[],

                              int off,

                              int scan,

                              Hashtable props)
```

Constructs the image producer using the given width, height, color model, pixel byte array, offset, scansize, and hashtable of image properties.

- MemoryImageSource

```
public MemoryImageSource(int w,

                              int h,

                              ColorModel cm,

                              int pix[],

                              int off,

                              int scan)
```

Constructs the image producer using the given width, height, color model, pixel int array, offset, and scansize.

- MemoryImageSource

```
public MemoryImageSource(int w,

                              int h,

                              ColorModel cm,

                              int pix[],

                              int off,

                              int scan,

                              Hashtable props)
```

Constructs the image producer using the given width, height, color model, pixel int array, offset, scansize, and hashtable of properties.

- MemoryImageSource

```
public MemoryImageSource(int w,

                              int h,
```

```
                                        int pix[],
                                        int off,
                                        int scan)
```

Constructs the image producer using the given width, height, pixel int
array, offset, and scansize. The producer is constructed using the
RGBColorModel.

- MemoryImageSource

```
        public MemoryImageSource(int w,
                                        int h,
                                        int pix[],
                                        int off,
                                        int scan,
                                        Hashtable props)
```

Constructs the image producer using the given width, height, color model,
pixel int array, offset, scansize, and hashtable of properties. The producer is
constructed using the RGBColorModel.

Methods

- Methods implemented from interface

```
        addConsumer(), isConsumer(), removeConsumer(),
        requestTopDownLeftRightResend(), startProduction()
```

Class
java.awt.image.RGBImageFilter

- java.awt.image.RGBImageFilter → java.awt.image.ImageFilter →
  java.lang.Object

```
        public abstract class RGBImageFilter
        extends ImageFilter
```

Subclass of ImageFilter for use with a FilteredImageSource object to filter
the pixels from an image producer by converting them to RGB values and
passing these values to the filterRGB() method. By subclassing this class and
overriding filterRGB(), you can perform whatever operation you choose on
the RGB values.

Variables

- canFilterIndexColorModel

  ```
  protected boolean canFilterIndexColorModel
  ```

  Sets this to true if your subclass can work with values from index color tables.

- newmodel

  ```
  protected ColorModel newmodel
  ```

- origmodel

  ```
  protected ColorModel origmodel
  ```

Constructors

- RGBImageFilter

  ```
  public RGBImageFilter()
  ```

Methods

- filterIndexColorModel

  ```
  public IndexColorModel filterIndexColorModel(IndexColorModel icm)
  ```

  Filters the color table contained within the given IndexColorModel and returns a new IndexColorModel with the filtered colors.

- filterRGB

  ```
  public abstract int filterRGB(int x,

                                int y,

                                int rgb)
  ```

  Called to filter the given RGB value, which is located at the specified coordinates of the source image. If the x and y coordinates are equal to -1, the RGB value came from a color lookup table.

- filterRGBPixels

  ```
  public void filterRGBPixels(int x,

                              int y,

                              int w,

                              int h,

                              int pixels[],

                              int off,

                              int scansize)
  ```

Filters an array of pixel ints. The x and y coordinates specify the position of the delivered pixels within the image. The w and h parameters represent the width and height of the delivered pixels. The pixel int array contains the delivered pixels and the offset index indicates the first array element of the delivered pixels within the array. The scansize indicates the number of array elements per scanline (i.e., the number of elements to skip when parsing through the pixel array to get to the same horizontal position in the next vertical line).

- setColorModel

```
public void setColorModel(ColorModel model)
```

If the ColorModel is an IndexColorModel, and the subclass has set the canFilterIndexColorModel flag to true, then we substitute a filtered version of the color model here and whenever we see that original ColorModel object in the setPixels methods; otherwise, we override the default ColorModel used by the ImageProducer and specify the default RGB ColorModel instead.

- substituteColorModel

```
public void substituteColorModel(ColorModel oldcm,

                                 ColorModel newcm)
```

Registers two ColorModel objects for substitution. If the oldcm is encountered during any of the setPixels methods, then the newcm will be substituted for it and the pixels will be passed through untouched (but with the new ColorModel object).

- Methods overridden from superclass

```
setPixels()
```

I N D E X